teach yourself ®

**the second
world war**

teach yourself®

the second world war
alan farmer

For over 60 years, more than 40 million people have learnt over 750 subjects the **teach yourself** way, with impressive results.

be where you want to be
with **teach yourself**

For UK order enquiries: please contact Bookpoint Ltd, 130 Milton Park, Abingdon, Oxon OX14 4SB. Telephone: +44 (0) 1235 827720. Fax: +44 (0) 1235 400454. Lines are open 09.00–18.00, Monday to Saturday, with a 24-hour message answering service. Details about our titles and how to order are available at www.teachyourself.co.uk

For USA order enquiries: please contact McGraw-Hill Customer Services, PO Box 545, Blacklick, OH 43004-0545, USA. Telephone: 1-800-722-4726. Fax: 1-614-755-5645.

For Canada order enquiries: please contact McGraw-Hill Ryerson Ltd, 300 Water St, Whitby, Ontario L1N 9B6, Canada. Telephone: 905 430 5000. Fax: 905 430 5020.

Long renowned as the authoritative source for self-guided learning – with more than 40 million copies sold worldwide – the **teach yourself** series includes over 300 titles in the fields of languages, crafts, hobbies, business, computing and education.

British Library Cataloguing in Publication Data: a catalogue record for this title is available from the British Library.

Library of Congress Catalog Card Number: on file.

First published in UK 2004 by Hodder Arnold, 338 Euston Road, London, NW1 3BH.

First published in US 2004 by Contemporary Books, a Division of the McGraw-Hill Companies, 1 Prudential Plaza, 130 East Randolph Street, Chicago, IL 60601 USA.

This edition published 2004.

The **teach yourself** name is a registered trade mark of Hodder Headline Ltd.

Copyright © 2004 Alan Farmer

Typeset by Transet Limited, Coventry, England.
Printed in Great Britain for Hodder Arnold, a division of Hodder Headline, 338 Euston Road, London NW1 3BH, by Cox & Wyman Ltd, Reading, Berkshire.

Hodder Headline's policy is to use papers that are natural, renewable and recyclable products and made from wood grown in sustainable forests. The logging and manufacturing processes are expected to conform to the environmental regulations of the country of origin.

Impression number 10 9 8 7 6 5 4 3 2 1
Year   2010 2009 2008 2007 2006 2005 2004

contents

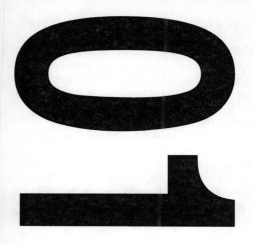

01

the origins

This chapter will cover:
- the Versailles Settlement
- European diplomacy between the wars
- the coming of war 1937–9.

At 8.00 p.m. on 31 August 1939 a unit of German soldiers disguised as Poles 'attacked' a German customs building on the Polish–German border and briefly occupied a German radio station. The 'Poles' then retreated, leaving behind a number of dead bodies as proof that a fight had taken place. The bodies, dressed in German uniforms, were concentration camp victims. This scheme, devised by SS Security Service Chief Reinhard Heydrich, gave Adolf Hitler a perfect excuse for launching an attack on Poland. That attack began at 4.45 a.m. on Friday 1 September. Two days later Britain and France, honouring pledges to Poland, declared war on Germany. Most Britons still regard 1939 as the date of the start of the Second World War. Arguably the war did not become a real 'world' war until 1941 when Germany attacked Russia and Japan attacked the USA. However, Germany's invasion of Poland was certainly the spark that lit the fuse to world war.

For years after 1945, most historians blamed Hitler for the outbreak of the Second World War. Yet in 1961 historian A. J. P. Taylor argued that Hitler should not shoulder sole, or even major, responsibility. Taylor focused attention on German expansionist ambitions which the First World War failed to satisfy – or crush. The Versailles Treaty, which left Germany embittered but potentially strong, was a major problem. A second war was 'implicit', thought Taylor, since the moment the First World War ended. Was the Second World War simply the second military phase of a European civil war to determine the mastery of Europe? Were the Versailles peacemakers to blame? Or was the Second World War essentially 'Hitler's War'?

The Versailles Settlement

The US President Woodrow Wilson, the British Prime Minister Lloyd George, and the French Premier Clemenceau were the men most responsible for the Treaty of Versailles. Each had a different solution to the main question: how to provide security for the future. Clemenceau was determined on a punitive peace. Twice in his lifetime France had been invaded by Germany. He wanted German power reduced so that all prospect of a future military threat was eliminated. Wilson, by contrast, came to the peace conference affirming general principles and hoping to establish an equitable system of international relations. In particular, he wanted to set up a League of Nations and favoured the principle of self-determination. Lloyd George

	Lost by Germany 1919		Austria–Hungary until 1918
	Saar: League of Nations control		Plebiscite areas
	Demilitarized Rhineland		Former territory of imperial Russia

0   200 km (125 miles)

figure 1 the Versailles Settlement

wished to preserve Britain's naval supremacy and enlarge the British Empire. Although he talked 'hard' for home consumption, he thought it unwise to persecute Germany's new democratic leaders for the sins of the Kaiser. Conscious of the danger of leaving an embittered Germany, he was inclined to leniency.

By the terms of the Versailles Treaty (signed on 28 June 1919), Germany lost all her colonies. In Europe, Alsace-Lorraine was returned to France. Though the Rhineland was not divorced from Germany (as Clemenceau had hoped), it was to be occupied by Allied troops for 15 years and was then to remain demilitarized. In the East, Germany lost land to Poland. To provide Poland access to the sea, Danzig was made a Free City under the League of Nations, and the Polish Corridor separated East Prussia from the rest of Germany. Despite the principle of self-determination, Germany was forbidden to unite with Austria. The German army was limited to 100,000 men. Its armed forces were not allowed tanks, planes, battleships or submarines. Article 231 of the treaty blamed Germany for starting the war. This war guilt clause provided a moral basis for the Allied demands for Germany to pay reparations for 'all damage done to the civilian population of the Allies'. In 1921, the reparations sum was fixed at £6,600 million.

Germans of all political persuasions claimed they had been treated harshly and unfairly. Most French, by contrast, considered the treaty far too soft. After a long and costly war, for which she was largely responsible, Germany remained potentially the strongest state in Europe. The German population was twice that of France and her heavy industry was four times greater. To make matters worse, a patchwork quilt of small states – economically weak and politically unstable – had been established throughout east-central Europe in place of the old Austro–Hungarian and Russian Empires. These new units, many of which contained large minorities of Germans, were unlikely to pose much of a threat if and when Germany recovered her power.

It is often claimed that Versailles was the worst of all worlds – too severe to be acceptable to most Germans and too lenient to constrain Germany for long. All Germans meant to shake off some or all of the treaty as soon as possible. The main difference among Germans was about the timing and the methods they should use. A. J. P. Taylor claimed that the treaty laid the foundations of the Second World War. This is a harsh verdict on the peacemakers. Given the problems they faced – the background of revolution, economic chaos, the collapse of empires and the problem of nationalism – it is perhaps amazing that they came up with a treaty at all. Even with hindsight, it is difficult to suggest a solution to the 'German problem'. The Germans would probably have resented any treaty if only because it represented a defeat which most were not willing to acknowledge. The peacemakers were not unaware of the treaty's deficiencies. This was why the League of Nations was created. Lloyd George said that it would 'be there as a Court of Appeal to readjust crudities, irregularities, injustices'. This was perhaps putting too much faith in an organization that lacked enforcement powers and the USA. The US Senate refused to ratify the Treaty of Versailles, and thus the USA did not become a member of the League.

The Versailles Treaty and the wider Versailles Settlement, encompassing the Treaties of St Germain (with Austria), Trianon (with Hungary), Neuilly (with Bulgaria) and Sevres (with the Ottoman Empire) left many countries, not only Germany, with grievances. Italy, despite being among the victors, had left Versailles almost empty-handed or thought she had. Italian disappointment helped Mussolini, Europe's first fascist dictator, to come to power in 1922. Fascism, in many ways a socialist heresy, put its faith in the nation rather than in class. Mussolini's dreams of forging a dynamic Italy were not translated into reality. Italy did not become a first-rate power. It was German, not Italian, grievances which caused most of the crises between 1919 and 1939.

Versailles by itself did not draw the geopolitical map of interwar Europe. The Bolshevik Revolution (1917) and the Treaty of Brest Litovsk (1918) also had a huge impact. Finland and the Baltic States won their independence from Russia while Poland (as a result of a successful war with Russia in 1920) was able to establish its frontiers beyond those of the Treaty of Versailles. Russia, the Soviet Union after 1922, was very much an aggrieved power. Indeed, given that she was dedicated to the export of communist revolution, Russia remained an enemy to all other non-communist states.

Troubled peace 1919–33

Arguably the main defect of the peace settlement was not so much the terms but the lack of agreement on how the terms should be enforced. Given that the USA showed little inclination to uphold the settlement, the job fell mainly upon Britain and France. They did not always see eye to eye. France, fearing that a strong Germany would re-emerge, still felt insecure. Thus, as well as maintaining the largest military force in Europe, France also sought alliances, particularly with Britain. Britain, however, was not prepared to underwrite French security by a military alliance. Britain's main concerns were the survival of its empire and the recovery of trade. The first concern consumed most of what force it had, leaving little to spare for guaranteeing French security. The second concern depended upon a peaceful and prosperous Europe, including a peaceful and prosperous Germany. The French, initially, were determined to uphold every aspect of Versailles; British opinion, by contrast, was soon of the view that Germany had been treated unfairly in 1919. France's occupation of the Ruhr in 1923, in order to extract reparation payments, marked the end of its effort to enforce the letter of Versailles strictly.

Gustav Stresemann, a pragmatic nationalist who controlled German foreign policy for much of the 1920s, believed that co-operation with Britain and France was the best way of achieving his aim of overthrowing Versailles. Exploiting British guilt over Versailles (arising from the belief that Germany was not solely to blame for war in 1914), Stresemann helped to negotiate a series of agreements which undermined the treaty. Reparations were scaled back and Germany's position as a diplomatic equal was restored by the Locarno Treaty (1925) and by Germany's admission to the League of Nations (1926). By 1929, Britain and France had agreed to end their occupation of the Rhineland five years ahead of schedule. France, still distrusting German intentions, began to build the Maginot Line defences in 1929.

For most of the interwar years, the British placed their faith in the League of Nations. The League established itself in the 1920s as an international organization capable of resolving disputes between minor powers. Nevertheless, the most important issues of the day were settled not by the League but by the foreign ministers of Britain, France, Italy and Germany. However, in 1929 there seemed good reason for optimism. Germany and France were reasonably friendly. If Mussolini's oratory was sometimes warlike, his escapades were minor. Russia was an embarrassment rather than a serious problem.

The collapse of the world economy in the early 1930s had a major impact on international relations. While the Great

Depression made some countries less keen to spend money on armaments, in others it led to governments which favoured foreign conquest as a means of alleviating the economic situation coming to power. In 1931, Japanese troops seized Manchuria from China. The League's failure to act against Japan was a sign of things to come.

Adolf Hitler

In 1933, Adolf Hitler came to power in Germany. Created by both Versailles and the depression, he was determined to challenge the existing order. A huge amount has been written about Hitler and there is still no consensus about his aims and dynamics. A. J. P. Taylor claimed that he was a rather ordinary German statesman with a rather ordinary mission – that of increasing Germany's standing among the world's nations. In Taylor's view, Hitler took advantage of situations as they arose, rarely taking the initiative himself. More recently, a number of historians have claimed that Hitler had little control of anything in the Third Reich, insisting that the competing agencies over which he presided produced results that he went along with rather than willed. Far from being an efficient dictatorship, the Third Reich was a state of – and in – considerable administrative chaos. Nevertheless, the direction of German foreign policy was certainly a reflection of Hitler's wishes. Although there was certainly a large degree of opportunism in his policy, he also had a number of clear aims. These included overthrowing Versailles, creating a Greater Germany, and winning living space (*lebensraum*) in the East. Convinced of the necessity of armed struggle, he was willing to risk war to achieve his aims. While many 'ordinary' German statesmen would have been delighted to have accomplished what he had done by 1939, few would have used his methods or taken the risks he did.

Given Germany's military weakness, Hitler's first moves in foreign policy were cautious. Yet in October 1933, claiming that the other powers would not treat Germany as an equal, he withdrew from the League. Early hopes of friendship with Britain and Italy did not materialize. Attempts to achieve a formal agreement with Britain failed, while a state visit by Hitler to Italy in 1934 was a disaster. Events in Austria in July 1934 further worsened relations between Hitler and Mussolini. A Nazi-inspired putsch led to the death of Austrian Chancellor Dollfus. Mussolini regarded Austria as an Italian satellite and rushed troops to the Austrian border. Hitler did nothing and the Nazi putsch failed.

Hitler's first major gamble came in March 1935 when he publicly repudiated the disarmament clauses of Versailles. This was an overt challenge to Germany's former enemies. In April, Britain, France and Italy condemned Hitler's action and resolved to resist any attempt to change the existing treaty agreement by force. This so-called Stresa Front quickly collapsed. In June, Britain made a naval agreement with Germany by which Germany could build the equivalent of up to 35 per cent of Britain's capital ships and was allowed parity in submarines. Britain seemed to be condoning German rearmament despite the Stresa Front's condemnation.

France, by the mid-1930s, was left with a series of alliances with small states in eastern Europe (dating from the 1920s), a defence pact with Russia (1935) and the conviction that Britain must not be alienated. French reliance on British goodwill meant that Britain could take the lead in determining how to respond to Hitler. For centuries one of Britain's main strategic interests had been to prevent any single power from achieving hegemony on the Continent. In essence, this was why Britain had gone to war against Germany in 1914. The fact that 750,000 Britons had died in that war generated widespread revulsion against war as an instrument of policy.

Britain and France hoped that Mussolini might be a useful ally against Hitler. However, Mussolini had his own ambitions, not least to increase the Italian Empire. In October 1935, Italian forces invaded Abyssinia (Ethiopia). When Abyssinian Emperor Haile Selassie appealed to the League of Nations, Britain and France faced a dilemma. To take action against Italy might force Mussolini into the arms of Hitler. But serious principles were at stake – not least whether the Western powers would honour their obligations under the League's covenant. The British government, influenced by public opinion, condemned the invasion and supported League action. France did likewise. The result – economic sanctions against Italy – had little effect. Italian forces overran Abyssinia. Had Britain and France been willing to fight Italy, this might have deterred Hitler. As it was, the Abyssinian crisis was a death blow to the League which had again failed to halt an aggressor. Mussolini moved closer to Hitler who had supported his actions.

In March 1936, Hitler violated the Versailles Treaty by sending troops into the demilitarized Rhineland. He knew he was taking a gamble: Germany was still too weak to fight a long war. Yet his reading of the situation – that Britain and France would not

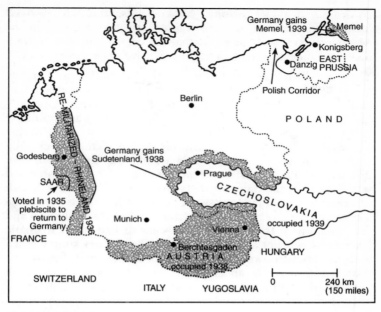

figure 2 German gains

oppose his action – proved accurate. France did nothing except pass the problem to Britain by asking if she would support French action. British opinion saw Hitler's move as regrettable in manner but not threatening in substance. Most Members of Parliament (MPs) agreed with Lord Lothian's remark that Germany had every right to walk into its own 'backyard'. Germany began building fortifications in the Rhineland, ensuring that from now on it would be more difficult for France to take action. In retrospect, the Rhineland was probably the last chance to stop Hitler without a major war.

In July 1936, the Spanish Civil War broke out. Germany benefited most. As well as giving Hitler an opportunity to test new weapons, the war also led to improved relations with Italy. In October 1936, Mussolini proclaimed the Rome–Berlin Axis, boasting that the two nations would dominate Europe, and that all the other states would revolve around this 'axis'. (In the Second World War, the term 'Axis' was used to describe all the powers fighting on Germany's side.) In November, Germany and Japan signed the Anti-Comintern Pact – an agreement to stop the spread of communism (Italy joined in 1937). It was not much of an alliance, if only because the signatories never co-ordinated their actions. Nevertheless, the Pact looked formidable. Germany was rearming; Italy was a threat in the Mediterranean; and Japan was strong in the Far East. Britain had little alternative but to begin extensive rearmament.

There is still an influential view that the Second World War was a war against fascism. The Anti-Comintern Pact suggests that there was an ideological dimension to the conflict. Certainly Italian fascism and German Nazism had much in common: the cult of a charismatic leader; an emphasis on action; extreme nationalism; paramilitary trappings; the state becoming synonymous with the party and leader. But there were also differences. The Nazis, for example, were far more obsessed with race than the Italian fascists were (Mussolini had a Jewish mistress). Imperial Japan was not fascist. While there were some similarities – a rejection of democracy, extreme nationalism and an adulation of the armed forces – Japan had no charismatic leader and was not a one-party state. The country simply allied with the fascist powers – in a fashion. Rather than fascist, the Axis was essentially an empathy between states which were authoritarian, militaristic, nationalistic, and anti-communist.

The coming of war 1937–9

In May 1937, Neville Chamberlain became British Prime Minister. His feeble appearance belied his confidence and strength of purpose. The word indissolubly linked to Chamberlain's name is appeasement – the name given to policies of giving in to threatening demands in order to avoid war. Appeasement has generally had a bad press. Those who supported it, not least Chamberlain, are often seen as 'guilty men', whose misguided policies helped to bring about war. Chamberlain's critics still insist that appeasement simply whetted Hitler's appetite and encouraged him to make fresh demands. However, appeasement can be viewed more positively. For hundreds of years, a cardinal principle of British policy had been that it was better to resolve disputes through negotiation and compromise than through war. Nor should appeasement be associated solely with Chamberlain; readiness to give way to German demands for revisions to Versailles was established British policy by the mid-1920s. France too was committed to appeasement. Traumatized by the loss of life in the First World War, and politically and socially divided, France feared conflict with Germany. For France, appeasement was essentially negative – a policy forced upon her by weakness. For Britain, there was a more positive side. While few people in Britain liked the Nazi regime, the view that Germany had real grievances, particularly over the position of Germans outside the German state, commanded considerable support. Once Hitler began to rearm and threaten, the desire to negotiate rather than confront took on more urgency. A sense that Hitler might have legitimate grievances, coupled with fears of another bloody struggle on the continent and of mass destruction of British cities by the rapidly expanding *Luftwaffe* (the German air force) combined to make appeasement appear the best course to follow.

Sympathetic to Hitler's desire to unite the German-speaking people of Austria, Poland and Czechoslovakia, Chamberlain hoped that this could be effected peacefully. Until Britain was adequately armed he accepted that, 'we must ... bear with patience and good humour actions which we would like to treat in a very different fashion'. He had little confidence in France or the USA, and even less in Russia. Nevertheless, he remained optimistic. He wrote in 1937 that, 'I believe the double policy of rearmament and better relations with Germany and Italy will carry us safely through the dangerous period'. Churchill, the most prominent anti-appeaser, was later to acquire the reputation of having been right about Hitler whereas Chamberlain had been wrong. In reality, Chamberlain probably had a shrewder appreciation of the situation – not least Britain's lack of strength – than Churchill.

In July 1937 Chinese–Japanese hostility escalated into full-scale war. Japanese forces took over much of China. In the late 1930s British attention was focused more on Europe than the Far East. However, fear of Japanese aggression was an important factor in understanding why Britain was keen to conciliate Italy and Germany.

In November 1937, at a meeting with some of his leading commanders, Hitler outlined his aims. He asserted that he was set on winning *lebensraum*, which could only be achieved by war. The first objective was the takeover of Czechoslovakia and Austria. The significance of this meeting – the so-called Hossbach Conference – has become the focus of controversy. Some think it proves that Hitler had a timetable for aggression. Others think that he was simply day-dreaming. Certainly, events did not unfold exactly as he anticipated. Nonetheless, the winter of 1937–8 marked the start of a new phase in German policy. Several leading conservatives were removed from influential positions and replaced by loyal Nazis. Ribbentrop, for example, became Foreign Minister.

Despite the fact that it was forbidden by Versailles, Hitler was determined to unite Austria and Germany. Many pro-Nazi Austrians held similar views. Since 1934, the Austrian government, which could no longer rely on Italian help, had struggled to keep its Nazis under control. In early 1938, Austrian police discovered plans for a Nazi uprising, the repression of which would provide the pretext for a German invasion. In February 1938, Austrian Chancellor Schuschnigg decided to visit Hitler, hoping to persuade him to restrain the Austrian Nazis. This was a mistake. Bullied and threatened, the Austrian leader agreed to Hitler's demands to include Nazis in his cabinet. Hitler planned to do little more at this stage. Ironically, Schuschnigg again precipitated events by announcing in early March that he intended to hold a plebiscite on whether Austria should join Germany. Hitler, fearing the vote might go against him, demanded the plebiscite's cancellation and threatened war. Schuschnigg resigned. Austrian Nazis now took power and invited Hitler to send troops into Austria to preserve order. Hitler returned in triumph to his homeland and declared that Austria was to be fully integrated into the Third Reich. The union (or *Anschluss*) was approved by a massive majority in a Nazi-run plebiscite. Britain and France had little warning of the Austrian crisis – not surprisingly because Hitler had only decided to act at the last minute. Chamberlain, recognizing there was little he could do, did nothing. France simply protested. It was hard to argue a great crime had occurred when so many Austrians expressed their joy at joining Germany

Czechoslovakia

The *Anschluss* immediately focused attention on Czechoslovakia, now surrounded by German territory. Only half the country's 15 million population were Czechs. It also contained Slovaks, Hungarians, Ruthenians, Poles and some three million Germans who lived in the Sudetenland. By 1938, the Sudeten German Party was demanding either home rule or union with Germany. It received support from Germany where the Nazi press launched bitter attacks on the Czechs (with some justification) for victimizing Sudeten Germans. Hitler hated the democratic Czech state. The fact that it had strong military forces meant it was also a potential threat. In March 1938, he instructed Sudeten leaders to demand virtual independence.

Benes, the Czech President, determined to stand firm against German pressure, confident that he would receive support from Britain and France. Most Western politicians had some sympathy with Czechoslovakia and a few, like Churchill, thought it worth fighting for. Chamberlain was not among that number. He was quite willing to see the Sudetenland handed over to Germany, provided this was done peacefully. Britain had no treaty obligation to defend Czechoslovakia, and was not able to offer military aid. Chamberlain's main concern was not so much Czechoslovakia but France. If Germany attacked Czechoslovakia, France might well go to its aid. Britain might then be forced to help France. In fact, French leader Daladier had no wish to be drawn into war. His strategic view was similar to Chamberlain's: Czechoslovakia could not be defended. He would be delighted if Britain gave him an excuse to avoid France's 1935 obligations.

In May 1938 after reports of German troop movements, which were in fact false, the Czechs mobilized their reserves and prepared for war. Britain and France warned Hitler against attacking Czechoslovakia. Hitler was outraged. The Western powers had won a diplomatic victory because he seemed to have stepped back from invasion – an invasion which he was not then planning! He now ordered his military leaders to prepare to attack Czechoslovakia in September. As the summer wore on, tension increased. By September, opinion in Britain and France was divided. Some thought the Western powers should support the Czechs; others thought that war must be averted at all cost. Hitler kept up the pressure. In September, he demanded self-determination for the Sudeten Germans, and threatened war. Benes responded by declaring martial law in the Sudetenland. Thousands of Sudeten Germans fled to Germany with tales of brutal repression. A Czech–German war seemed imminent.

In an effort to maintain peace, Chamberlain flew to meet Hitler on 15 September. He accepted Hitler's main demand that the Sudetenland should be handed over to Germany. In return, Hitler agreed to delay attacking Czechoslovakia to allow time for Chamberlain to consult with the French and the Czechs. Hitler, assuming the Czechs would refuse to cede the Sudetenland and that Britain would then wash its hands of them, was delighted. Chamberlain's cabinet and the French quickly accepted Hitler's demands. Benes had little option but to do the same. On 22 September, Chamberlain flew back to Germany to meet Hitler at Godesberg. To Chamberlain's consternation, Hitler now said the previous proposals were insufficient. (Czech concessions were not what he had wanted!) Polish and Hungarian claims to Czech territory had also to be met. In addition, to protect Germans from Czech brutality, Hitler demanded the right to occupy the Sudetenland immediately. While Chamberlain favoured accepting Hitler's new proposals, many of his cabinet colleagues rejected them. Daladier now declared that France would honour its commitments to Czechoslovakia. Britain and France began to prepare for war. On 27 September, Chamberlain broadcast to the British people, 'How horrible, fantastic, incredible, it is that we should be digging trenches and trying on gas masks here because of a quarrel in a far away country between people of whom we know nothing ... I would not hesitate to pay even a third visit to Germany, if I thought it would do any good'. The next day, Chamberlain received his opportunity. Hitler, aware that most Germans were not enthusiastic for war, accepted Mussolini's suggestion of a Four Power Conference to work out an agreement to the Sudetenland question.

On 29 September, Chamberlain, Daladier, Hitler and Mussolini met at Munich. The agreement reached was very similar to Hitler's Godesberg demands. Benes was forced to surrender the Sudetenland. Chamberlain persuaded Hitler to sign a joint declaration by which both men pledged to do all they could to preserve peace. Munich is often seen as a terrible failure for the Western powers. Arguably, they should have done the honourable thing and gone to war to save a friend. However, Chamberlain saw Munich as a victory. From a position of weakness he had achieved most of his aims. War had been avoided; Germany's legitimate grievances had been settled; and Czechoslovakia remained a sovereign state. Most British and French in 1938 also regarded Munich as a triumph. Both Chamberlain and Daladier were treated as heroes on their return home. Chamberlain announced to cheering crowds that he had brought back 'peace with honour'. Churchill, who described British policy as a 'total and unmitigated disaster', was in a minority. The possible outcome of a war over Czechoslovakia has intrigued historians ever since. Many have accepted Churchill's view that it would have been better for Britain and France to have fought Germany in 1938 than in 1939. Germany gained considerably from massive rearmament in 1938–9 and from the collapse of Czech power. Moreover, Russia, bound by treaty, might well have supported the Czechs. Yet neither Britain nor France was ready for war. French forces, deployed along the Maginot Line, could have done little to help Czechoslovakia. Nor is it certain that Russia would have come to the Czechs' rescue.

Chamberlain was not convinced that Munich made peace more secure, and he was more determined than ever that the pace of rearmament should not slacken. At least Munich gave him a breathing space. However, in early 1939, he received a number of (incorrect) intelligence reports predicting German moves against Poland, Holland, Czechoslovakia or Switzerland. In February, his cabinet agreed that a German attack on Holland or Switzerland would lead to a British declaration of war. In a radical change of policy, Chamberlain committed Britain to raising a large army which, if needs be, could fight on the Continent. French opinion also swung in favour of resisting Nazi expansion. Many French feared that if Germany gobbled up more territory in the East, she might ultimately prove too strong in the West.

After Munich, Czechoslovakia faced serious internal problems. Most Slovaks had little love for the Czech-dominated state and sought independence. By March 1939, the situation was so bad, internally and externally, that new President Hacha proclaimed martial law. This desperate attempt to preserve Czechoslovakia speeded its downfall. Hitler instructed Slovak leaders to appeal to Germany for protection and to declare independence. With his country falling apart, Hacha asked to meet Hitler in the hope that he might do something to help. Hitler, receiving Hacha on 15 March, told him that German troops intended to invade Czechoslovakia in a few hours' time: his only choice was war or a peaceable occupation. Hacha broke down under the threats and agreed to German occupation on the pretext that this would prevent civil war. A German protectorate of Bohemia and Moravia was established while Slovakia became nominally independent. Hitler claimed to have acted legally, merely complying with the requests of the Czechs and Slovaks. However, he had clearly dismembered a small neighbour. Nor could he claim that he was uniting Germans within one German state. Chamberlain was outraged. Hitler had sent out an unambiguous signal that he was bent on more than righting the wrongs of Versailles.

Poland

In mid-March, Hitler forced Lithuania to hand back Memel – lost by Germany in 1919. Again Britain and France took no action. It was inconceivable to think of going to war over Memel, a German city to which Hitler could lay reasonable claim. Poland, seemingly Hitler's next target, was another matter. There were some 800,000 Germans in Poland. Most lived in Danzig and the Polish Corridor. No German government – certainly not Hitler's – was likely to accept the Danzig situation or the separation of East Prussia as permanent. Poland was equally determined that things should remain as they were. German relations with Poland had been remarkably friendly since the signing of a 1934 non-aggression treaty. On a number of occasions, Germany had suggested to the Poles that this agreement might be turned into an alliance against Russia. But Poland, anxious not to become a German satellite, did not take up these suggestions. In January 1939, Hitler met Beck, the Polish Foreign Minister, and requested Danzig and a German-controlled road or rail link across the Polish Corridor. The Poles refused. German demands became more insistent. By late March, there were rumours that a German attack on Poland was imminent.

On 31 March, Britain took the unprecedented step of offering a guarantee to Poland: if she were the victim of an unprovoked attack, Britain would come to her aid. France offered a similar guarantee. The guarantees have been widely condemned. Of all the east European states, Poland was probably the one that the Western powers liked least. Indeed, until 1939 Poland had few friends – except Germany. Hitler's demands of Poland were more reasonable than his demands of Czechoslovakia in 1938. The guarantees can be seen as 'blank cheques' given to a country notorious for its reckless diplomacy. Moreover, in the last resort, the 'cheques' were worthless because there was little that Britain or France could do to help Poland. However, Britain and France felt they had to do something. The guarantees were meant as a warning: if Hitler continued to push for expansion, he would face war. The guarantees were not a total commitment to Poland. Danzig's future was still thought to be negotiable, and Chamberlain hoped that the right mix of diplomacy and strength might persuade Hitler to negotiate. More angered than deterred, Hitler ordered his army leaders to prepare for war with Poland by the end of August.

Determined not to be outdone by Hitler, Mussolini embarked on his own 'adventure'. In April 1939, Italian forces occupied Albania. Mussolini also announced that the Balkans should in future be regarded as within the Italian sphere of influence. Mussolini's aggressive words and actions seemed to pose a further threat to east European stability. Britain and France now issued guarantees to both Greece and Romania in the same terms as those given to Poland. In May, Mussolini and Hitler signed the Pact of Steel, an alliance requiring each power to help the other in the event of war. As the summer wore on, the Polish situation deteriorated. The Germans accused Poland of launching a reign of terror against Polish Germans.

In the event of a German attack, only Russia could offer Poland immediate military help. Accordingly, the only sensible course of action for Britain and France seemed to be to ally with Russia. In the late 1930s, neither France nor Russia had made any real efforts to strengthen their 1935 defence pact. Throughout the 1930s, Britain opposed any alliance with Russia, suspecting that the real aim of Soviet policy was to embroil Britain and France in a war against Germany. In Chamberlain's view, there were many good reasons for not allying with Stalin who was even nastier and more hostile in long-term intent than Hitler. British intelligence indicated that Soviet forces, after Stalin's purges, were of little military value. Yet under pressure from the press and from Parliament, Chamberlain agreed to the opening of negotiations with Russia. His main aim seems to have been to use the possibility of a Soviet alliance as a further warning to Hitler. Stalin's thinking still remains a matter of guesswork. On the surface his position was serious. Hitler was a sworn enemy of Bolshevism, and Japan was a threat in the East. However, Britain's and France's guarantees to Poland gave him some room for manoeuvre. He could press for favourable terms from the Western powers and also seek a deal with Germany.

The Anglo–French–Soviet discussions were complex and slow. The talks finally deadlocked when the Russians asked whether Poland would accept the entry of Russian troops before the event of a German attack. The Poles, deeply suspicious of Russian intentions, would not budge on this issue. Chamberlain sympathized with Poland. He did not see why the presence of Russian troops in Poland was necessary or desirable. Stalin maintained that this attitude convinced him that Britain and France were not in earnest in their negotiations. More likely, the Russians made a series of demands that they knew Britain and France could not accept because Stalin had no wish for an alliance with the West.

From 1933 Russia had occasionally made approaches to Germany suggesting the need for improved relations. Hitler had rebuffed each of these probes. The idea of a Nazi–Soviet agreement made no sense at all in ideological terms. Nevertheless, throughout the spring and summer of 1939, Russian and German diplomats had been hard at work, trying to reach accommodation. With Germany's planned attack of Poland less than a week away, Ribbentrop flew to Moscow and on 23 August signed the Nazi–Soviet non-aggression Pact. Secret clauses of the Pact divided Poland and eastern Europe into spheres of German and Russian influence. Hitler was delighted. He realized that Poland could not now be defended, and thought that Britain and France would realize the same. The way was thus open for the German attack on Poland, planned to start on 26 August. Much criticism has been levelled at Chamberlain for his failure to secure a Russian alliance. Certainly he had little enthusiasm for it. But such an alliance was probably out of reach of any Western leader. The only thing the West had to offer Stalin was the prospect of war. Hitler, by contrast, offered peace and territory. From Stalin's point of view, the Pact seemed to protect Soviet interests, at least in the short term.

Hitler was prepared to risk – but still did not expect or want – a war on two fronts. He thought the Western leaders would wriggle out of their guarantees to Poland. Surprised by their determination to stand by Poland, and shaken by Mussolini's announcement that Italy intended to remain neutral, Hitler postponed his invasion. There was some desperate last-minute diplomatic activity – to no effect. On 1 September, German troops invaded Poland. Chamberlain, wishing to keep in step with French leaders who were anxious to complete their mobilization plans before declaring war, did not immediately issue an ultimatum to Germany. To many British MPs it seemed as though he was trying to evade his commitments. On 2 September, the British House of Commons made it clear that war must be declared. Thus at 9.00 a.m. on 3 September, Britain delivered an ultimatum to Germany. Germany made no reply, and at 11.00 a.m. Britain declared war. France followed suit at 5.00 p.m.

Conclusion

In a broad sense, the war which began in 1939 was the second half of a Thirty Year War. The First World War was fought by Britain, France and Russia in order to contain Germany. Much the same reason was to dictate Britain and France's declaration of war in 1939. Both countries feared German domination of Europe. However, the Thirty Year War thesis is, in itself, not enough to explain the outbreak of war. In 1939, Britain and France feared Germany because they feared Hitler.

The years between 1919 and 1939 were punctuated by a series of crises concerning the provisions of the Versailles Settlement. Nonetheless, it seems odd to see Versailles as causing the Second World War when so much of the Settlement had been overturned without war. Somewhat ironically, Germany went to war over her last, and most reasonable, grievance – Danzig and the Polish Corridor.

While it is possible to see the interwar years dominated by competing political ideologies, this by itself does not explain the origins of the war. The path to war involved shifting associations between disparate ideological partners. Moreover, the foreign policies of the powers were determined by national interests as well as by ideology. It is hard to say whether national interests or ideologies predominated (Hitler's ideology gave pride of place to national interests!).

Britain and France's reactions to Hitler's demolition of Versailles did much to contribute to war. With hindsight, both countries should have intervened militarily before 1939. Chamberlain is often seen as the main guilty man. In fairness to Chamberlain though, the only alternative to working with Hitler was war. Firmer action in 1938 would have precipitated – not prevented – war. Indeed, perhaps Chamberlain should be blamed not so much for appeasement but for his failure to stand by it to the end. Britain had no moral obligation or self-evident interest to defend Poland. Conceivably, Chamberlain should have allowed – even encouraged – Hitler to go eastwards against Russia.

Hitler's ambitions and actions were largely responsible for the outbreak of war. As a result of his policies, Europe stumbled from crisis to crisis, and this built up an almost irresistible pressure for war. There was nothing accidental about his attack on Poland. He hoped the Western powers would not fight but he was prepared to take that risk. Chamberlain and Daladier believed they had little option but to fight. Indeed, British and French opinion generally supported war in 1939, though its terrors were acknowledged and even (as with bombing) exaggerated. For Britain and France, the issue was as much Hitler as Poland. Here was a man who could not be trusted: he thus had to be stopped.

02

blitzkrieg

This chapter will cover:
- the conquest of Poland
- the Scandinavian war
- German success in the West
- the reasons for German success/Allied defeat.

On 9 May 1940, German General Erwin Rommel, commander of the 7th Panzer Division, wrote a brief note to his wife:

Dearest Lu,

We're packing up at last. Let's hope not in vain. You'll get all the news for the next few days from the papers. Don't worry yourself. Everything will go all right.

From Rommel's point of view, everything did go 'all right'. Four days later, thanks to his bold leadership, his division broke through the French defences on the River Meuse. In the days that followed, his tanks – and a host of tanks from other panzer divisions – drove through northern France, heading for the English Channel. By June 1940, France had surrendered and German victory in the European war seemed certain. Why were the Germans so successful during 1939–40? Did the Allies lose a contest they should really have won?

The conquest of Poland

German victory during 1939–40 was by no means as certain as it subsequently appeared. Few things in Nazi Germany were as impressive as its propaganda suggested. This was true of its armed forces. In 1939 there was really no central headquarters in the German command structure charged with strategy or the co-ordination of the various services. In effect, only the idiosyncratic will of Hitler determined strategy. The three service chiefs General Brauchitsch (army), Herman Göring (*Luftwaffe*) and Admiral Raeder (navy) jealously guarded their own prerogatives. Brauchitsch provided Hitler with competent military advice. Göring, one of the Third Reich's most successful political barons, retained the outlook of the fighter pilot he had once been, and lacked the wider perspectives necessary for command. Raeder had few new ideas.

The German army (*Wehrmacht*) had been planning an attack on Poland since March 1939. With the bulk of its forces committed in the east, *Wehrmacht* leaders knew that Germany's western border was vulnerable to French attack. Consequently, German forces had to win quickly. The plan was to mount a series of large drives through Polish defences, encircling and destroying the main enemy forces. The German high command had not yet fully evolved the concept of blitzkrieg – lightning war. Direct support of the army, for example, was not at the top of the *Luftwaffe*'s priorities. The Germans assembled 54 divisions.

Six were tank (or panzer) divisions. Four were motorized infantry divisions. Most of the rest were conventional infantry divisions that marched to battle on foot. Army Group North mustered 630,000 men; Army Group South had 886,000.

The odds against Poland's survival were slim. The Polish army, over one million strong, was poorly equipped. Poland did not have the industry to produce large quantities of modern weapons. The Poles had 180 tanks (against the *Wehrmacht*'s 2,000) and 313 combat aircraft (against the *Luftwaffe*'s 2,085). Geographical factors weakened Poland's position. It had no natural borders and was surrounded by Germany on three sides. Hoping to protect their country's economically vital western areas, Polish leaders spread their forces thinly along the border regions from the Carpathians to the Baltic. There was no meat behind the thin crust. To add to these problems, Poland did not begin mobilizing until 29 August. Britain and France, fearing that Polish mobilization would give Hitler an excuse for aggression, had advised against it. Thus when war began, only one-third of Poland's troops was ready for battle.

German forces attacked on 1 September 1939. The Polish air force was soon swept from the skies. *Luftwaffe* strikes against the railway system disrupted Polish mobilization. Polish troops fought bravely but cavalry with lances proved no match for German tanks. Panzer divisions made deep incursions into Poland, dividing the Polish army into 'pockets'. Ordinary infantry divisions mopped up. By 10 September, most of northern and western Poland was under German control. To make matters worse for the Poles, on 17 September the Russians invaded from the east, as planned for in a secret protocol to the Nazi–Soviet Pact. Neither Britain nor France went to war with Russia. The British excuse was that the Anglo–Polish alliance applied only to aggression by Germany.

Soviet intervention only brought forward a foregone conclusion. By 17 September, German forces had encircled Warsaw. The heavily bombed city capitulated ten days later. By 5 October, Polish resistance had ended. Polish losses were 70,000 killed, 133,000 wounded and 700,000 taken prisoner. The *Wehrmacht* lost some 14,000 dead. A Polish government-in-exile was formed in France under General Sikorski, and an army-in-exile of 84,000 men was created. However, Poland had effectively disappeared. Germany annexed Danzig and the land between East Prussia and Silesia. She also created a new area – the General Government. Russia took over eastern Poland. From the Polish perspective there was little to choose between the savagery meted out by Germany and Russia. Both set about destroying the Polish ruling classes. The Russian massacre of 15,000 captured Polish officers at Katyn in 1940 was the most chilling example.

Britain and France did nothing while German forces were crushing Poland. A Franco–Polish pact of May 1939 gave the Poles the guarantee that France would mount a full-scale attack on Germany within 15 days of the start of war. This promise was not honoured. Although France had a three to one superiority on the Western Front in September, it had no intention of launching a major offensive. French leaders considered themselves secure behind the Maginot Line. They had a complementary respect for the (far from complete) German defences – the Siegfried Line.

The miniscule British army could do nothing. In any case, premier Neville Chamberlain had no wish for an immediate shooting war. He believed that time was on the Allied side: superior Allied economic resources, coupled with a naval blockade, would be enough to bring Germany to its knees. Unfortunately, the Nazi–Soviet Pact ensured that Hitler could count on Soviet supplies of raw materials. He could also use Italy and a host of other neutral countries to bypass the Allied blockade. Nevertheless, the German economy did undoubtedly suffer. The value of German imports fell by some 75 per cent between September 1939 and April 1940. German fuel reserves fell by one-third, hampering military preparations.

On 6 October, Hitler offered peace proposals to Britain and France. He had, he said, no claims against France and wanted friendship with Britain. All the two countries had to do was accept the new order in eastern Europe. It does seem that Hitler genuinely wanted peace with Britain and France so that he could concentrate on Russia. Few Allied leaders, however, were prepared to trust him. Moreover, they had not gone to war for Poland alone: they wanted to preserve the European balance of power. Peace with Hitler would mark their humiliation and defeat.

French premier Daladier created a Government of National Defence. In Britain, Chamberlain appointed Winston Churchill as First Lord of the Admiralty. Various ministries of the previous war were revived – shipping, information and food. Ships sailed in convoy. News was censored. Rationing was introduced. Unfortunately, Allied leaders failed to agree on a uniform command structure. Nor did they have much success with Belgium. Convinced that Germany's only viable strategy was to attack France via the Low Countries (as in 1914), they failed to reach agreement with Belgium. The Belgium government hoped that, if it were circumspect, Hitler would not attack. It thus refused to have proper staff talks with Britain and France on whom it would depend if Germany did attack.

The phoney war

There was so little military activity over the winter of 1939–40 that US journalists referred to the conflict as the 'phoney war'. Warehouses around London were filled with cardboard coffins ready for the thousands that were expected to be killed by bombs. City children were evacuated to the countryside. In the event, both sides shied away from bombing civilian targets, partly to escape the blame that would fall upon the first to bomb cities and partly for fear of retaliation. The British Royal Air Force (RAF) dropped leaflets rather than bombs on Germany in a forlorn attempt to get Germans to rise against Hitler. Only at sea was there a reminder that this was a real war. Although Germany did not yet have enough U-boats (submarines) to pose a serious challenge to Allied shipping, German surface raiders and U-boats achieved several major kills. The *Graf Spee*, a German pocket battleship, was less successful. Cornered off Uruguay by three British cruisers, its commander scuttled the ship in Montevideo harbour after the Battle of the River Plate (13 December 1939).

Hitler wanted a real, not 'phoney', war. Once the Allies had rejected his peace proposals, he prepared for a Western offensive. In October 1939, he issued Führer Directive No. 6.

> An offensive will be planned ... through Luxembourg, Belgium and Holland [and] must be launched at the earliest possible moment ... The purpose of this offensive will be to defeat as much as possible of the French army and of the forces of the Allies fighting on their side, and at the same time to win as much territory as possible in Holland, Belgium and northern France to serve as a base for the successful prosecution of the air and sea war against England ...

The German plan, code named Case Yellow, was to be worked out in detail by the army high command. Commander-in-Chief Brauchitsch and his Chief of Staff General Halder doubted that a successful attack could be quickly mounted. Given that the French army was much stronger than that of Poland, it seemed unlikely that blitzkrieg (a word coined by Western journalists to convey something of the speed and destructiveness of German operations in Poland) would succeed in the West. Hitler thought differently. He had little respect for France. The power he really feared was Britain. Aware that there were as yet few British troops in France, he wanted to strike early. In late October, he proposed that German forces should attack in the Ardennes where the French would least expect them. Hitler's generals argued that late autumn was the wrong time of year to undertake offensive operations. German forces would quickly get bogged down, assuming they broke through the French defences. Bad weather prevented the implementation of Case Yellow in November and December. It was postponed indefinitely in January. This gave German forces useful time to iron out flaws revealed in the Polish campaign.

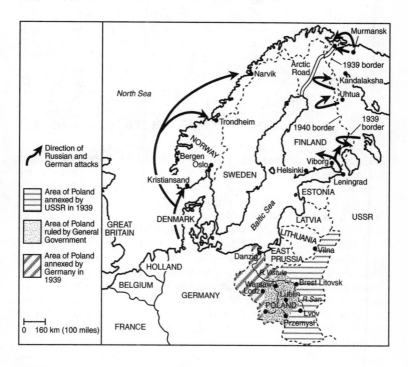

figure 3 Poland and Scandinavia 1939–40

The fact that neither Italy nor Japan tried to exploit the situation at this stage meant that the worst fears of British defence planners were not realized. However, Russia did act. In October, the Baltic States – Estonia, Latvia and Lithuania – were forced to accept Soviet garrisons. Stalin also demanded a large strip of Finnish territory. Finland refused. On 30 November, Russia invaded Finland. The 'Winter War' was a classic David and Goliath affair. The Finns, whose total strength never exceeded 175,000, fought with skill and bravery. Soviet troops were ill-prepared for a winter war or indeed for war at all. (This was partly due to Stalin's purge of his senior commanders in the late 1930s.) Along the entire front, the one-million-strong Red Army suffered humiliating defeat.

In December, Allied leaders resolved to aid Finland. 'The only charitable conclusion is to assume that the British and French governments had taken leave of their senses,' wrote A. J. P. Taylor. Daladier hoped that Norway and Sweden would allow Allied troops through their country and would assist Finland. Instead, both countries asserted their neutrality. Allied leaders determined that if they could not obtain Scandinavian co-operation, they would act without it. An elaborate plan to send 100,000 troops to Finland, via Norway and Sweden, was devised. In March 1940, just as the Allied force was about to move, the Winter War came to an end. Soviet forces broke through Finnish lines. Finland was forced to cede territory to Russia. Twenty-five thousand Finns and 200,000 Russians had died in the war.

Daladier was discredited. Having declared his intention to aid Finland, he had failed to do so. On 20 March he was replaced by Paul Reynaud. Reynaud's government was similar to Daladier's – a coalition of moderate right and left. Reynaud wanted some Scandinavian action. Swedish supplies of iron ore were seen as crucial to Germany's war effort. During the winter months, Swedish ore was shipped through the Norwegian port of Narvik and then down the Norwegian coast to Germany. Churchill supported seizing Narvik. The cabinet rejected this scheme. Instead it agreed to mine Norwegian waters, thus cutting off the iron-ore route. On 8 April, minelaying began. Admiral Raeder, anxious to acquire Norwegian bases, had long urged Hitler to intervene in Norway. Preoccupied by his plans for the forthcoming attack in the West, Hitler initially ignored Raeder's urging. However, he was outraged when, on 16 February, a British destroyer intercepted the *Altmark* in Norwegian waters, rescuing some 300 British prisoners on board. Convinced that

Britain would soon violate Norway's neutrality, Hitler instructed General Falkenhorst to prepare a plan for Norwegian invasion. Falkenhorst concluded that German forces should occupy Denmark as a 'land bridge' to Norway.

On 7 April, German transport ships carrying 10,000 soldiers set off to Norway. The venture was a huge gamble. The Germans had to seize Norwegian ports and airfields before the Royal Navy could intervene. British naval command's failure to realize what was afoot gave the Germans useful time. On 9 April, German forces struck. Denmark, quite unprepared for war and with no suspicion of Germany's hostile intent, simply surrendered and became a German protectorate for the rest of the war. Forewarned of German intentions, the Norwegian government dithered. Mobilization orders went out by post. On April 9, German troops quickly captured Oslo. Elsewhere, German sea and airborne forces met varying amounts of opposition.

The Germans suffered serious naval losses. The cruiser *Blucher* was sunk by a Norwegian coastal battery on 9 April. On 10 and 13 April, British naval forces sank ten German destroyers transporting German troops to Narvik. Later in the campaign, the German battleships *Scharnhorst* and *Gneisenau* were damaged by British torpedoes. Britain and France rushed troops to Norway. By late April, 25,000 Allied troops besieged 5,000 German infantry and sailors in Narvik; a further 12,000 men landed near Trondheim. However, the Allied campaign was badly planned and executed. Allied forces around Trondheim, without air cover and supplies, were soon forced to evacuate. Meanwhile, German forces doggedly defended Narvik. The town was not captured by the Allies until 28 May. Events in France led to its abandonment on 8 June.

Control of Norway provided Germany with useful naval and air bases from which to attack British shipping and Britain itself. The ease of German victory was certainly good for German morale. However, German gains were questionable. For the rest of the war, Norway tied down substantial German forces.

Between the 7 and 8 May, the Norwegian campaign was debated in the British House of Commons. Many MPs were angry at the way it had been conducted. Strangely their target was not Churchill, who had been largely responsible for the debacle, but Chamberlain. Criticism of the Prime Minister had been mounting: many felt that he failed to project vigour and vision. Some 100 Conservative MPs abstained or voted against the government. Chamberlain decided he must resign. On 10 May, Churchill became leader of a new coalition government. He said he had nothing to offer but 'blood, toil, tears and sweat'. His words were apt. The first weeks of his premiership coincided with a series of Allied military disasters.

The defeat of France

The postponement of Case Yellow in January granted the Germans time to change their plans. The change of plan is associated with Manstein, Chief of Staff of General Rundstedt. Manstein, one of the best military minds in the *Wehrmacht*, argued that a panzer force attacking through the Ardennes could smash through the Allied defences and win a knock-out victory. Halder was not impressed. Like most German generals, he was convinced that the hilly and wooded Ardennes was unsuitable terrain for panzers. In January, Hitler got wind of Manstein's plan. The two men met in mid-February. Hitler was quickly won over by Manstein's thinking which matched his own aspirations. The German high command had thus no option but to transform the elements of the Manstein-Hitler plan into a detailed order – code named Sickle Stroke. Army Group B was to invade Holland and Belgium, hoping to tempt Allied forces northwards. Army Group C was to engage the Maginot Line. Army Group A, led by Rundstedt, had the key role. Its 50 infantry and seven panzer divisions were to advance through the Ardennes, cross the River Meuse then drive along the line of the River Somme to the coast, trapping Allied forces in Belgium.

Sickle Stroke was a high-risk strategy. If the Germans were to achieve a decisive victory, the French would have to send large numbers of troops into Belgium, fail to defend the Ardennes and the Meuse, and have no reserves to deal with a German breakthrough. However, German forces possessed several advantages. Crucially, the *Luftwaffe* was superior in the quality of aircraft, in experience and in numbers – 3,200 aircraft as opposed to 1,800 Allied planes. Unlike its British and French equivalents, which had over-diversified in aircraft production, it had concentrated on procuring a large number of a few types of planes, each of which was well adapted to its specialized function. The Messerschmitt 109 was a fast, well-armed fighter. The Stuka was a formidable ground attack dive bomber. The Heinkel 111 was an effective bomber. Among the *Luftwaffe*'s senior officers were a number of first-rate men like Milch and Kesselring.

A further German advantage was their tank strategy. Model for model, German tanks were not notably superior to those of the Allies. Nevertheless, the tanks were organized into specific panzer divisions. Unencumbered by infantry, the panzer divisions were trained to maximize speed and independence of action. The French had more tanks than the Germans (3,000 to 2,400) but most were distributed haphazardly among the French armies. The French therefore had no real equivalent of the panzer divisions which would form the cutting edge of Army Group A.

Yet French leaders were confident. That confidence was founded on the belief in the strength of the Maginot Line. This hugely expensive defensive system protected the Franco–German frontier. France, however, had lacked the money to extend the Line along the 402-kilometre (250-mile) Franco–Belgium frontier. Ironically, the Maginot Line provided as much security for Germany as France. Given that the French had no intention of sallying forth from the Line to attack Germany, the Germans needed to take few defensive precautions. They had far fewer men opposite the Line than the French had in it.

French leaders knew that the Maginot Line was likely to act as a weir, diverting the German current through Belgium. In the event of a German attack, Gamelin, the French Commander-in-Chief, intended to rush his best troops, including the British Expeditionary Force (BEF), into Belgium. These troops would hold the Germans along the line of the River Dyle. Much weaker French troops would be left to defend the River Meuse opposite the Ardennes.

The BEF was of mixed quality. In 1918, the British army had been the most efficient fighting machine in the world. Years of defence cuts, however, had pared the army to the bone and also prompted military conservatism. Only five of its 13 divisions in France were regular troops; the rest were all Territorial Army (TA) reservists – high in enthusiasm but low in experience. In May 1940, Britain's only tank formation, the 1st Armoured Division, was still not ready for action. The 94 French divisions were a mixed bag, some good but many bad. The best troops were the ten 'active' conscript divisions and the seven divisions of the colonial army. Conscript reserve divisions were not so good. Divided by the extremism of French politics, and fearing a repetition of the blood sacrifice of 1914–18, many French troops were not committed to the cause. French General Ruby found that, 'every exercise was considered as a vexation, all work as a fatigue. After several months of stagnation, nobody believed in the war any more'.

Not having the benefit of the Polish campaign, Allied commanders did not recognize their weaknesses, much less correct them. Gamelin thought there was little to learn from Poland. This was not his only mistake. In allocating his troops, he had left himself with no reserves in the event of the war not going according to plan. French intelligence suggested that the Germans might attack via the Ardennes. Gamelin did not exclude this possibility. What he did not anticipate was the speed with which the Germans would move.

The Allied army's command arrangements gave the Germans another advantage. Operational authority rested with Gamelin but was exercised first through a Commander Land Forces (General Doumenc) and then by the commander for the north-east, General Georges. The BEF's commander, Lord Gort, answered operationally to Georges but tended to look ultimately to London for orders. Gamelin's headquarters was at Vincennes near Paris; that of Doumenc halfway to that of Georges in northern France; that of Gort separate from Georges, and those of both the British and French air forces separate again. Structural deficiencies were compounded by personal failings. Gort, a brave officer who had won the Victoria Cross, was not a brilliant strategist. More importantly, Gamelin had few military qualities.

In April 1940 Chamberlain claimed that Hitler 'had missed the bus'. Hitler had tanks and aircraft, not buses, and was ready to use them. 'Gentlemen,' Hitler told his staff on the eve of Case Yellow, 'you are about to witness the most famous victory in history!'

The German attack began at 4.30 a.m. on 10 May. The *Luftwaffe* bombed Dutch, Belgian and French airbases. Meanwhile, German ground forces crossed the Dutch and Belgian frontiers. Paratroops seized important targets. The most daring of the airborne attacks was against the Belgian fort of Eben Emael. Some 70 German glider-borne troops crash-landed on the fort's roof, penned the defenders inside and, using concrete-piercing charges, overwhelmed them within a few hours. The Dutch were taken by surprise by the German attack. They had taken no part in the First World War and wanted no

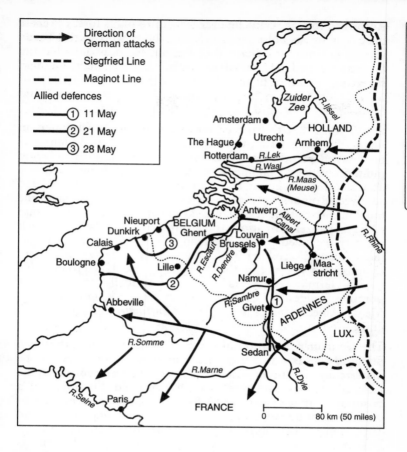

figure 4 the Battle of France 1940

part of the Second. They were a German enemy simply because parts of their territory offered an easy way round the Belgian water obstacles. The Dutch had minimal forces – ten army divisions and 125 aircraft. It seemed that their best hope of delaying defeat was to retreat inside 'Fortress Holland' – the waterlogged zone around Amsterdam and Rotterdam – and trust to the network of canals and rivers to delay the invader. German air power quickly overcame this strategy. The 22nd Airborne Division landed in the heart of 'Fortress Holland' on 10 May. Holland capitulated on 15 May.

According to plan, Gamelin ordered a third of his forces to cross into Belgium to bolster the Belgian troops who were already retreating before the German onslaught. He thus did what the Germans hoped. He failed to realize that the main German threat was about to be unleashed further south. From 10 to 14 May, seven German panzer divisions, deploying some 1,800 tanks, nudged forward nose to tail along the Ardennes defiles.

On 12 May, the 7th Panzer Division, led by Rommel, found an unguarded weir across the River Meuse, north of Sedan. The next day, Rommel sent forces across the river and began laying pontoon bridges, enabling his tanks to cross. A French counter-attack did not amount to much and the German bridgehead survived. Rommel's performance on the 13 May was one of the most inspired of the whole war. At the same time, Army Group A's main panzer formation struck further south at Sedan. French infantry defended poorly. German troops, by contrast, fought magnificently, crossing the Meuse (under heavy fire) and established a series of footholds. French tanks failed to dislodge them. German engineers worked frantically to construct pontoon bridges. By 14 May, panzers were pouring across the Meuse. Allied planes, savaged by the *Luftwaffe* and anti-aircraft guns, tried in vain to destroy the bridges.

The German penetration of the French line had occurred at a point so sensitive that any countermeasure would have to be massive and instantaneous. French generals were not up to the task. Efforts to move three French armoured divisions into a position to attack the German flanks collapsed in a muddle of conflicting orders. General Guderian, commanding the 2nd and 10th Panzer Divisions, exploited the situation by driving westwards. His tanks encountered little resistance. Thousands of French surrendered instead of fighting. By 17 May, Guderian had advanced more than 80 kilometres (50 miles) from Sedan. Further north, Rommel also broke through the French positions and pushed westwards. He noted:

> A chaos of guns, tanks and military vehicles of all kinds, inextricably entangled with horse-drawn refugee carts, covered the roads and verges ... The French troops were completely overcome by surprise at our sudden appearance, laid down their arms and marched off to the east beside our column. Nowhere was any resistance attempted.

In two days Rommel captured 10,000 soldiers and some 100 tanks.

The Allies' main concern was no longer how to defend Belgium but how to get out of it. Their only hope was to launch a major counter-stroke against the exposed flanks of the panzer corridor. *Luftwaffe* control of the skies made such attacks difficult to organize. Charles de Gaulle, commander of the French 4th Armoured Division, received orders to attack at Laon. An enthusiast for armoured warfare, de Gaulle eagerly accepted the challenge. His attack on 17 May was held up later as an example of what the French might have done if all their generals had been imbued with his offensive spirit. In fact, his attack was stopped by air attack before he really got to grips with the Germans.

On 15 May, Reynaud rang Churchill: 'We are beaten,' he said, 'We have lost the battle'. The next day Churchill flew to Paris to confer with French leaders. Gamelin admitted that he had no troops available to stem the German advance. Churchill returned to Britain promising to send ten additional squadrons of RAF fighters to join those already in France. Sir Hugh Dowding, head of Fighter Command, opposed Churchill's proposal, insisting that he needed 52 squadrons to ensure Britain's defence. He was down to 36 and could not afford to lose any more. Appealing to the War Cabinet, he convinced them that squadrons should operate over France from British bases. Dowding's action helped save Britain: within a few days the Germans had overrun most of the bases from which the RAF would have operated in France.

Philippe Petain, 84-year old hero of Verdun, now joined the French government as Reynaud's deputy. Seventy-three-year old Weygand, Chief of Staff to Foch in 1918, replaced Gamelin. Their heroic reputations suggested that something might yet be snatched from the jaws of defeat.

On 20 May, Guderian's panzer divisions reached Abbeville on the Channel coast, dividing the Allied armies into two. Weygand proposed that Allied forces north of the German break-in should co-ordinate attacks against the panzer corridor with French armies still operating to its south. His plan never really got off the ground. Many French troops were demoralized. On 21 May, a British force of infantry and 74 tanks crashed into the 7th Panzer Division at Arras. After some initial success, the attack stalled. By 22 May, the German spearhead was a firm defensive line, too strong to be broken. The Allied armies in the north were cut off. It seemed nothing could save them.

Hitler came to the Allies' rescue. While Brauchitsch urged that the panzers should press home their attacks, Hitler and Rundstedt were more cautious. Both feared that the coastal lowlands were unsuitable for tanks. Almost half of the panzers had already broken down and the rest were urgently in need of maintenance. Furthermore, Göring declared that the *Luftwaffe* could finish off the Allied forces in the north. Thus, on 24 May Hitler ordered his panzers to halt. They remained halted for two days – two days which, in retrospect, may have decided the war's outcome. Unbeknown to Hitler, the British government, responding to a warning from Gort, had decided on May 20 that the BEF might have to be evacuated at Dunkirk and had instructed the Admiralty to begin assembling a fleet for the job. Churchill still hoped that the BEF would be able to break through the panzer corridor to join the French armies south of the Somme. This hope was unrealistic. 'Nothing but a miracle can save the BEF now', wrote General Alan Brooke on 23 May. That same day, Gort ordered his forces to draw back towards Dunkirk. This decision saved the BEF.

Dunkirk

Hitler's 'stop order' allowed the BEF and a substantial portion of the French 1st Army to reach Dunkirk and construct a defensive perimeter around the town. When the 'stop order' was revoked, that part of the Allied army Hitler most wanted to destroy was – temporarily – safe. Evacuation from the Dunkirk beaches began on 26 May (Belgium surrendered on 27 May). French troops fought stubbornly to protect the evacuation. The *Luftwaffe* did its best to prevent it. Its best was not good enough. Although it sank eight destroyers in nine days of attack, it could not stop hundreds of ships reaching the shore. During the 26–27 May, only 8,000 men got off the Dunkirk beaches. On 28 May, as the fleet of naval ships and civilian craft – coastal steamers, pleasure boats and yachts – grew 19,000 were embarked. On 29 May, 47,000 were rescued; on May 31 68,000. By 4 June, when the last ship left Dunkirk, 338,000 Allied soldiers had escaped. The number included almost all of the BEF and 140,000 French soldiers, the majority of whom on arriving in England were transhipped and returned to French ports in Normandy and Brittany. Dunkirk is sometimes viewed as a success. Certainly the number of men who returned to Britain far exceeded the most optimistic forecasts at the start of the operation. Yet as Churchill admitted, 'Wars are not won by evacuations'. The evacuated troops had left behind all their heavy weapons and transport and were in a chaotic state. The evacuation also caused bitter feelings in France. It seemed that Britain had left the French in the lurch.

By early June, the French army consisted of 60 divisions, only three of which were armoured. Against them the Germans deployed 89 infantry divisions and 15 panzer and motorized divisions. The *Luftwaffe* had some 2,500 strike aircraft, France fewer than 1,000 planes. Weygand pinned his hopes on a new defensive line running from the Channel along the Rivers Somme and Aisne to join the Maginot Line. This 'Weygand Line' envisaged (rather than comprised) a series of 'hedgehogs'. The 'hedgehogs' – villages and woods – were to be filled with troops and to continue resistance even if bypassed by enemy spearheads. German panzers attacked the line on 5 June between Amiens and the coast. Some French troops fought hard but elsewhere the panzers quickly found a way into the French rear. On 9 June, Guderian's panzers attacked on the River Aisne. French resistance soon collapsed. One German force now swept through Normandy into Brittany. Another went through Champagne, taking the Maginot Line in the rear. A third headed south. On 10 June, Mussolini, anxious to declare war before its conclusion deprived him of a share of the glory and the spoils, joined the war on Germany's side. He did not win much glory. Four French divisions in southern France easily held their ground against 28 Italian divisions. The failure of the Italian forces cast into relief the *Wehrmacht*'s ability.

On 10 June, Reynaud evacuated Paris which was declared an 'open city' to spare its destruction. The first German soldiers arrived on 14 June and marched triumphantly down the Champs-Elysées. Churchill made several visits to France to encourage resistance but he had little to offer except words. On 16 June, Britain proposed an indissoluble union of Britain and France – to no avail. Late on 16 June, Reynaud resigned. Petain became French leader. 'It is with a heavy heart,' Petain told the French people, 'that I say we must end the fight'. On 21 June, at Rethondes near Compiegne, French emissaries alighted outside the railway coach in which German delegates had signed the armistice of November 1918. The German armistice terms did not allow for negotiations: Petain's government was to remain sovereign but northern and western France was to become a German occupation zone. Italy was to occupy parts of southern France. German 'occupation costs' were to be paid by France.

Two million French prisoners were to remain in German hands. France, in short, was to be emasculated and humiliated, as Hitler believed Germany had been in 1918. (The terms in truth were far more severe than those imposed on Germany.) On 22 June, the French delegates accepted the armistice terms.

Conclusion

Nazi Germany had triumphed. In 42 days the *Wehrmacht* had done what German troops had failed to achieve in four years of war from 1914–18. The campaign of 10 May to 22 June had cost the German army only 27,000 dead (France lost some 120,000). Guderian said that German success was 'almost a miracle'. Had the Allies or the Germans been most responsible for that 'miracle'? Many French still claim that Britain did not exert itself to the full and should not have fled from Dunkirk. The British, with more justification, tend to blame French leadership for the fall of France. Gamelin was by no means the only culprit. Scores of French generals who served between 1919 and 1940 failed to recognize that there were major problems with the doctrine and training of the French army. French miscalculation is one side of the coin. On the other, Germany waged war very successfully. In part, German success was the result of daring strategy. Hitler had gambled and won. This did not mean, as the future would demonstrate, that he was a military genius. He would gamble again and lose. In part, German success was the result of superior weaponry and tactics. Crack panzer divisions and the *Luftwaffe* made German victory possible. Even so, the struggle on the banks of the Meuse on 13 and 14 May was a close-run thing. Perhaps the ordinary German soldiers' superior skill, courage and morale were ultimately more important than superior leadership, technology or tactics. Superior skill may be explained by better training and preparation, not least the experience gained in Poland. Superior courage and morale are harder to explain. For whatever reason (ethnic pride? nationalism? propaganda?), most German troops believed they were fighting the good fight. Their willingness to absorb losses and keep going was vital to German victory.

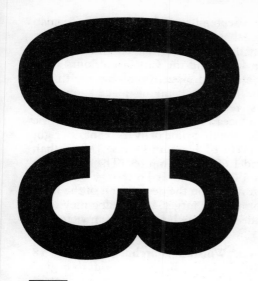

03

Britain alone

This chapter will cover:
- the Battle of Britain and the Blitz
- the search for allies
- the war in Africa 1940–1
- the war in the Balkans 1940–1.

Soon after 5.00 p.m. on 7 September 1940, over 300 German bombers, escorted by twice that number of fighters, attacked the East End of London. They bombed Woolwich Arsenal, a power station, a gas works, the docks and the City. Two hours later, another 200 bombers appeared. The bombing continued throughout the night, the last attack taking place soon after 4.00 a.m. German pilots, returning to their bases in France, spoke of London being an 'ocean of flames'. 'This is the historic hour when our air force for the first time delivers its blows right into the enemy's heart,' declared Herman Göring. More than 400 people were killed and 1,600 badly injured. The attack, the first mass bombing raid on Britain, marked a change of tactics. Rather than focusing their attack on the destruction of the RAF, the Germans had gone for a softer target. In so doing they were committing a major blunder that may have cost them victory in the Second World War.

'The Battle of France is over,' Winston Churchill declared on 18 June 1940, 'I expect that the Battle of Britain is about to begin.' Britain seemed to stand very little chance of winning this battle. If it was not quite alone – there was the support of the Dominions (Australia, Canada, South Africa, New Zealand, but not Eire) and other parts of the Empire – Britain's position seemed hopeless. By the summer of 1940, Nazi Germany dominated western and central Europe. Some states not taken over by Hitler were effectively German satellites (like Slovakia) or allies (like Hungary). Although Sweden and Switzerland remained democratic and neutral, they were tied to the German economic system. German military success during 1939–40 had been achieved at a trifling cost in men and materials. Most Germans assumed the war was effectively over. Final victory over Britain seemed just a matter of time. Yet Britain managed to survive. Why? What hope did it have during 1940–1?

The Battle of Britain

If the speed and scale of German victory left Britain stunned, it also left Hitler undecided as to how to use his triumph. He had never desired war with Britain. In early July, without much enthusiasm, he ordered plans to be made for an invasion of Britain. He hoped that the invasion – code named Operation Sealion – would not be necessary. In a speech on 19 July, Hitler offered peace terms to Britain. In return for recognition of Germany's hegemony in Europe, Britain would be allowed to maintain her empire and navy. He believed he had little to gain from Britain's defeat. In August he told his chief generals, 'Germany is not striving to smash Britain because the beneficiaries will not be Germany but Japan in the East, Russia in India, Italy in the Mediterranean and America in world trade'. Hitler's thoughts were already focused more on Russia than on Britain. Even while Sealion was being planned, German troops began to move eastwards.

Churchill's cabinet did not totally brush aside the possibility of peace. Churchill, himself, however, had no intention of 'parleying' with Hitler. Instead, he exhorted the British people to fight on. Many have stressed the importance of Churchill's oratory in strengthening British resolve. He was more modest, 'It was the nation and the race dwelling all round the globe that had the lion's heart. I had the luck to be called on to give the roar'. The 'Dunkirk spirit' was certainly not something that was conjured up by Churchill. Most Britons were determined to continue the war. Nevertheless, Churchill's 'roar' was important. Confidently citing history, he convinced his fellow countrymen that the war could be won.

Churchill was determined to preserve Britain's position as a great power. Yet he never really faced up to the mismatch between British resources and British commitments. Nor did he look far into the future. He seemed to think, like Hitler, that most problems could be overcome by will power. It is possible to question his judgement to fight on. If he had made peace in 1940, British power might have been left intact while Stalin and Hitler slugged it out in the East – to Britain's benefit. In many respects, Churchill's decision to continue the war was irrational. Britain by itself could not defeat Germany. Churchill's only hope was that Germany and Russia would fall out or that the USA would enter the war on Britain's side. Alliance with Russia would link Britain with a regime which was just as evil as that of Hitler's. Alliance with the USA was unlikely to benefit Britain's long-term interests. By continuing the war, it may be that Churchill bankrupted Britain and mortgaged her future to the USA. It should be said that this was probably a better fate than putting trust in Hitler and becoming a client state of Nazi Germany.

In July, Churchill signalled his determination to fight on. He regarded the French fleet, anchored at Mers-el-Kebir, as a potential menace. Although the Franco–German armistice terms agreed that the fleet should remain in French hands, there was a real danger that Hitler might seize it. On 3 July, Churchill ordered its destruction. The British attack on July 5 resulted in three capital ships being put out of action. One thousand two hundred and fifty French sailors were killed. The US President, Franklin D. Roosevelt (FDR), approved Britain's action. It did much to convince him of Churchill's resolve to continue the war. Thus, Britain was worth supporting. The attack, nevertheless, soured Britain's relations with Vichy France. Petain's government broke off diplomatic relations with Britain.

Given that Churchill would not make peace, Hitler had little alternative but to make war. Still, he remained half-hearted about Sealion, so much so that he did not direct the campaign personally. Instead, after a whistle-stop tour of France, he returned to Germany to ponder the future. The German high command structure was such that when Hitler's attention wandered, there was no one with the drive or vision to pick up the reins. In historian A. J. P. Taylor's view, Sealion was a mixture of 'improvisation and bluff'. In Britain, however, the German threat was taken seriously. Home Guard units, armed with a variety of makeshift weapons, prepared for invasion. Army chiefs doubted whether they could hold up German forces once they had landed. Navy chiefs doubted whether they could prevent a landing if the *Luftwaffe* controlled the air. Thus, as the Chiefs of Staff reported, 'all depends on the air force'.

German thinking was much the same. The *Wehrmacht* was confident of conquering Britain if it could get its forces ashore. The German navy, decimated in the Norwegian campaign, was in no position to protect an invasion force. Only the *Luftwaffe* could prevent the Royal Navy destroying German landing forces. In late July, Hitler gave orders for a massed air offensive against Britain, to be followed by a cross-Channel assault in September, 'if we have the impression that the English are smashed'. Barges and coastal steamers were assembled in Belgium and northern France. The Germans were working to a tight schedule. British aerial resistance would have to be broken quickly, allowing time for the *Luftwaffe* to bomb the Royal Navy out of the Channel. By October bad weather would make an invasion impossible. Thus, everything depended on the conflict between the *Luftwaffe* and the RAF. This conflict, fought over the skies of southern England in the late summer and early autumn of 1940, is known as the Battle of Britain.

Göring was confident of success – with good reason. In July, the *Luftwaffe* had some 2,600 planes and 10,000 trained pilots, compared to the RAF's 1,000 planes and 1,500 trained pilots. Nonetheless, the *Luftwaffe* also faced serious problems. Given that it was making use of captured enemy airfields in Belgium and northern France, every local facility – of supply, repair, signals – had to be adjusted to German needs. Nor were *Luftwaffe* leaders clear on strategy. Was the aim to bomb British industry, population centres, radar stations, airfields or the Royal Navy, or was it essentially to destroy British fighters? German planes had to fly scores of kilometres before coming to grips with the RAF. German Messerschmitt fighters (Me109s and Me110s) lacked the range to operate over more than a corner of southern England. RAF Fighter Command, by contrast, was operating from home bases and over home territory. This meant its planes could stay aloft longer. Moreover, RAF pilots who had to bail out often lived to fight another day. German aircrews died or became prisoners.

Perhaps the main problem was that Göring and other German leaders underestimated the RAF's strength. They assumed that Britain could only produce 200 fighters per month. In fact, British factories turned out over 400 Spitfires and Hurricanes a month between July and November. (The Germans only built an average of 200 fighters a month in the same period.) Fighter Command thus fought the Battle of Britain on something like equal terms. It managed throughout to keep 600 fighters serviceable daily. The *Luftwaffe* was never able to concentrate more than 800 fighters against them. The RAF's main problem was lack of experienced pilots, not lack of aircraft. *Luftwaffe* leaders believed that their fighters were superior to both the Spitfire and the Hurricane. The reality was that the Hurricane was almost as good as, and the Spitfire technically superior to, the Me109 and the Me110 in speed and firepower. German leaders also underestimated the RAF's integrated warning system, not least the 50 radar stations which lined the British coast from the Orkneys to Land's End. These stations picked up incoming planes from a distance of about 120 kilometres (75 miles) and could make accurate estimates of their numbers and altitude. (Radar was a British invention, credit for which belonged to Robert Watson-Watt.) Once the planes reached the coast, they were followed by the Royal Observer Corps. Information was relayed to RAF Fighter Command Headquarters at Bentley Priory near London and then sent to the four Fighter Command Groups. Swift analysis of information enabled RAF fighters to be airborne by the time German planes were over their airfields.

Fighter Command was directed by Air Chief Marshal Sir Hugh Dowding. During the Battle of France, he had done everything possible to preserve Fighter Command for what he believed to be its essential role – the defence of Britain. Dowding's aim now was to stop the *Luftwaffe* winning air superiority. To this end, he deployed less than half of his fighters in southern England. His northern squadrons, out of range of German bombers, represented a reserve that he could feed into the battle. He believed that his prime task was to protect his airfields and his communications system. It was therefore essential to shoot down bombers before they released their bombs, rather than concentrating on their fighter escorts. There was opposition to Dowding's strategy from men like Air Marshal Leigh-Mallory and swashbuckling Squadron-Leader Douglas Bader. They believed Dowding should throw all his planes at the *Luftwaffe*'s fighters.

The Battle of Britain had no formal beginning or end, but most historians agree that it lasted from mid-July to mid-September. The opening round of the battle occurred over the Channel with attacks on British merchant shipping and western coastal towns. The Royal Navy, which had to be beaten if the *Wehrmacht* was to invade, remained untouched. Fighter Command, however, suffered heavy losses. The air war over the Channel showed that German tactics were superior and German pilots were better trained. Nevertheless, the RAF was quick to learn.

On 1 August, Hitler ordered the *Luftwaffe* to, 'overpower the English air force with all the forces at its command in the shortest possible time'. The objectives were planes, airbases, and aircraft factories. Göring fixed 'Eagle Day' for 7 August. Beset by bad weather, it stuttered into life on 8 August. Throughout the week, the Germans claimed that the 'exchange ratio' was in its favour. However, German losses were running so high that Göring now ordered the *Luftwaffe* to concentrate its efforts on airfields. He also increased the proportion of fighters to bombers. Bad weather delayed the start of this effort. Not until 24 August did the RAF feel its effect. In the following fortnight, airfields in the south of England suffered extensive damage. By early September, the RAF was perilously close to defeat. Between 24 August and 6 September, Fighter Command lost 290 aircraft. The *Luftwaffe* lost 380 aircraft, only half of which were fighters. For two weeks the RAF was losing more planes than it could replace. A serious pilot shortage was also developing: 231 pilots were killed or wounded with only half that number coming from training units.

At this critical moment, the *Luftwaffe* switched tactics and changed its target to airfields further inland and to bombing London. This was a major blunder. It was partly a retaliation for a British bombing raid on Berlin. The raid was ineffective but it enraged Göring (he had announced that he would eat his hat if a single bomb fell on the German capital). The change of strategy was also the result of poor intelligence. German leaders were convinced that the RAF was down to its last reserves. They hoped that an attack on London would force British fighters north of the capital to give battle. Consequently, dense formations of German bombers, protected by phalanxes of fighters, attacked London from 7 September. The diversion of the attacks gave the RAF a welcome respite. Moreover, London was a more distant target for the *Luftwaffe* than south-eastern airfields. This gave Fighter Command more time to marshal its fighters to intercept. It also reduced the flying time of the Messerschmitts. For ten days in mid-September, the skies of southern England were filled by German planes heading towards London to be intercepted by RAF fighters. On 15 September, the *Luftwaffe* sent the largest force yet – 200 bombers with a heavy fighter escort. Dowding threw all his planes into a counter-attack. The RAF destroyed nearly 60 German planes (not the 183 claimed at the time). The RAF lost 26 planes; it was clearly not beaten. German air supremacy had not been achieved. On 17 September, Hitler announced the postponement of Sealion. Nazi Germany had suffered its first defeat. The legacy of that defeat would be long delayed. However, the survival of Britain which it assured helped to determine the downfall of Hitler's Germany.

By simply remaining a viable force, the RAF won the Battle of Britain. The victory was largely due to 3,000 RAF pilots. The majority were British, but Canadians, Australians, New Zealanders, South Africans, Americans, Czechs and Poles also flew British fighters. 'Never,' said Churchill, 'had so much been owed by so many to so few.' The 'few' shot down 1,300 German planes between July and September. The RAF lost 800 planes (and 500 pilots). Moreover, the RAF lost more fighters than the *Luftwaffe*. It was the loss of 600 German bombers which made the balance sheet read so favourably for the RAF. While the Battle of Britain was won in the air, it was also won on the ground in the aircraft factories. Britain had more fighters ready for action in October than in July, despite the losses over the summer. Dowding, the main architect of British success, was shabbily treated. Churchill, convinced he lacked flair, replaced him in November. He was given 24 hours to clear his desk.

The *Luftwaffe* assault continued through September but instead of airfields, its main targets were now British cities. The aim was to break British morale. Between September 1940 and May 1941, the Germans dropped 35,000 tons of bombs, over half of them on London. After November, all the bombing was done at night. (Daylight raids resulted in heavy losses of planes.) The RAF had no effective defence against night bombers. Even with pilots stuffed full of carrots that were supposed to improve night vision, British fighters stood little chance of intercepting the bombers. Some 45,000 people died in the 'Blitz'- far less than had been feared. British propaganda depicted cheery and defiant citizens clearing up the debris after nights of heavy bombing. This image was part myth. The bombing often caused panic and confusion. Yet the 'spirit of the Blitz' was not all propaganda. German bombing did not shatter civilian morale. Indeed, arguably the British people became more united in the face of the shared peril. Nor did the Blitz cause major economic damage. Even in Coventry, which suffered one of the heaviest raids, most of the factories were in full production within a few days. All the Blitz succeeded in doing was generating a long-lasting anger among most Britons and a determination to seek revenge.

Bombing was not the only, nor perhaps even the most serious, threat that Britain faced. Its ability to continue to feed the population, arm the troops and supply its ships, aircraft and tanks with fuel depended upon being able to keep its shipping lanes open. There were various ways in which the Germans could threaten British shipping. German bombers, based in France and Norway, were soon taking a heavy toll. Mines, whether laid by aircraft, surface ship or submarine, were a constant menace. German battleships and cruisers provided the most spectacular but, given the Royal Navy's strength, least effective threat. The greatest threat came from submarines. In April 1941, nearly 700,000 tons of shipping was lost – far more than British shipyards could replace. So severe was the crisis in Britain, the scale of rations had to be cut. By mid-1941 Britain was near to losing what Churchill called the 'Battle of the Atlantic' and, thus, close to losing the war. (Chapter 10 deals with the U-boat threat in more detail.)

The search for allies

Churchill was sustained by a supreme confidence that the USA would come into the war. This confidence was not particularly well founded. Certainly, FDR sympathized with the British cause. In late 1939, he persuaded Congress to allow the Allies to purchase arms on a 'cash and carry' basis. He knew, however, that most Americans had no wish to get involved in war with Germany. Given the strong isolationist lobby in Congress, he had to proceed cautiously. For a few weeks after the fall of France, US military leaders were reluctant to send arms to Britain: if Britain surrendered, US supplies would fall into German hands and might eventually be used against the USA. Once it was clear that Britain intended to fight on, FDR determined to do everything possible to help. Most Americans agreed with him. They saw Hitler's success as a looming threat to the USA, and judged that Britain's survival was essential to the US's own security. In August 1940, America provided Britain with 50 destroyers in return for the right to establish bases in British possessions in the Caribbean. Although most of the US ships needed considerable repair, the destroyer deal was an important gesture and an indication of FDR's intent. That intent was kept under wraps in the autumn of 1940 in the run-up to the presidential election. His opponent Wendell Willkie played on the fear that FDR was leading the USA into war. FDR declared his determination to preserve peace, 'Your boys are not going to be sent into any foreign wars,' he said in the campaign. After his re-election success, FDR's support for Britain became more overt.

Churchill clamoured for war material. 'Give us the tools,' he declared, 'and we will finish the job'. Unfortunately Britain was not in a position to pay for the tools. By late 1940, she was out of dollars and yet dependent on US imports. In March 1941, Congress was persuaded to pass the Lend-Lease Act which gave FDR the power to make huge quantities of US resources available to Britain. Arrangements for repayment were to be made later. This, FDR explained, was like a man who lends his neighbour a garden hose to put out a fire. The USA, he announced, would become 'the great arsenal of democracy'. By mid-1941, the USA was hardly neutral. US troops had taken over from a British garrison in Iceland, and US warships were escorting convoys bound for Britain halfway across the Atlantic. However, most Americans still had no wish to get involved in the war. Hitler, having no wish to fight the USA, ignored US breaches of neutrality. Thus, there was no certainty when – or even if – the USA would join the war on Britain's side.

Churchill's other great hope was Russia. Despite his anti-Bolshevik record, the idea of an alliance with Russia appealed to his sense of history. Yet Stafford Cripps, sent to Moscow to try to improve Anglo-Russian relations, was kept at arms length by Stalin. Britain had nothing to offer Russia as adequate compensation for a break with Germany. Cripps wrote gloomily in August 1940 that if the Russians had to choose between the two sides, 'there is no doubt whatever they would choose Germany'. Nonetheless, German-Soviet relations did give Britain some hope. Stalin, who had hoped for a long war of attrition, was concerned by the quick fall of France. Determined to gain some advantage from the situation, he annexed the Baltic States and parts of Romania in June 1940. These acquisitions angered Hitler. He loathed communism and dreamed of winning *lebensraum* in the East. By September, his high command was considering an attack on Russia. Large numbers of troops were heading eastwards. Nevertheless, Hitler kept his options open. In November, he met Russian Foreign Minister Molotov in Berlin and proposed that Russia should join with Germany, Italy and Japan in dividing the world. Germany would take most of Europe, Italy the Mediterranean, Japan the Far East, and the USSR Persia and India. Molotov showed no interest. He was more concerned about the situation in Finland, Bulgaria and Romania, and determined to hold Germany strictly to the terms of the Nazi–Soviet Pact, which defined their respective spheres of influence in eastern and southern Europe. This was enough to convince Hitler that 'the final struggle with Bolshevism' was inevitable. The decision to attack Russia was fixed in December 1940. Six months were to elapse before the forces necessary to implement it were set in motion.

Meanwhile, Hitler had tried to find other allies against Britain. In October 1940, he met Spanish dictator Franco, hoping to persuade him to join the Axis and attack Gibraltar. The loss of Gibraltar would have seriously weakened Britain in the Mediterranean. Franco, not trusting Hitler, and under considerable economic pressure from the USA not to get any closer to the Axis powers, failed to be won over. Petain, whom Hitler met the following day, proved equally unresponsive. Nor did Japan join the war against Britain. However, the Japanese government did sign the Tripartite Pact with Germany and Italy in September 1940. This bound the signatories to come to each other's assistance if any of them were attacked.

Italy at war

Mussolini was Hitler's chief ally during 1940–1. He wished to emulate Hitler's success. France's collapse and British weakness provided huge opportunities, not least the prospect of turning the Mediterranean into an Italian 'lake'. Yet Mussolini's ambitions were greater than his strength. Italian forces were not ready for war. The army had carried out an expansion programme far beyond its means. The navy had good ships but neither the leadership nor industrial support required to operate them effectively. The air force had nothing but obsolete aircraft. Italian troops had fought poorly against France. Nevertheless, Mussolini was confident of success in Africa and the Balkans. After France's surrender, Italy's fleet of six battleships became the largest capital force in the Mediterranean. The Royal Navy had only five capital ships. Undeterred, British Admiral Sir Andrew Cunningham offered battle at Calabria in July 1940. The Italian fleet had all the advantages. It knew of British movement through radio decrypts; it had more, and better, ships; and the action took place close to Italy, ensuring the Italian ships had air support. In spite of this, the Italian fleet fled on contact, losing one battleship in the process. On 11 November, Royal Navy carrier-borne aircraft inflicted heavy damage on Italian battleships moored at Taranto. Britain now held the naval advantage in the Mediterranean.

In the summer of 1940, Italian troops from Ethiopia marched into frontier areas in the Sudan and Kenya and occupied British Somaliland. Italy had some 92,000 troops in Ethiopia and 250,000 native troops supported by 323 aircraft. Britain deployed only 40,000 troops, most of them local, and 100 aircraft. Furthermore, British forces were outclassed in equipment. However, Italy's Ethiopian army was timidly led and could not easily be reinforced or re-supplied. The British, by contrast, could build up their forces in the region by the transfer of troops from Egypt, India and South Africa. In January 1941, the British Commander in East Africa, General Alan Cunningham (Admiral Cunningham's brother), went on the offensive. He quickly expelled the Italians from their footholds on British territory and then, proclaiming support for Haile Selasie (the ex-Emperor of Ethiopia), carried the war into

Ethiopia and Italian Somaliland. Cunningham's main army, advancing from Kenya, found it hard to keep up with the retreating enemy. In April, Cunningham took Addis Ababa, Ethiopia's capital. Other Allied troops occupied Eritrea. The Italian empire in East Africa had collapsed.

Both Britain and Italy regarded Egypt as much more important than Ethiopia. Churchill feared that the conquest of Egypt and the loss of the Suez Canal might lead to the collapse of British power in the Middle East. Consequently, he sent troops and a third of Britain's tank strength to Egypt (where Britain had military rights) when Britain itself faced the threat of invasion. Even so, the 70,000-strong British forces in Egypt were easily outnumbered by the 200,000 Italian troops in Libya. Italy's numerical superiority plus greater ease of supply and reinforcement prompted Mussolini to order an offensive into Egypt in mid-September 1940. Italian forces did not advance far. After three days they set about building defences and were stationary for the next three months. In December, 35,000 British, Australian and Indian troops, with only 275 tanks, counter-attacked. The attack was planned more as a raid than as a serious assault. Amazingly, the Italian army crumbled. The British advance continued until February 1941. The Italians were forced back over 2,735 kilometres (1,700 miles). One hundred and thirty thousand Italian prisoners were taken, along with huge amounts of weapons, motor vehicles and tanks. Allied forces, led by General Wavell, lost fewer than 500 men dead.

Hitler had hoped to assign the Mediterranean to Mussolini: his mind was focused on Russia. However, he felt he had no option but to intervene. In February 1941, he sent Rommel and the Afrika Korps to rescue the Italians. Rommel – glory-seeking and courageous – was probably the outstanding battlefield commander of the war. Rather than defend, as the German high command expected, he went on the offensive. By mid-April, the British had lost all their gains in Libya apart from Tobruk. Rommel, whose supply lines were dangerously extended, was unable to do more. Wavell, goaded by Churchill, launched a premature offensive during May–June. This proved a costly failure. Rommel's well-positioned anti-tank guns destroyed nearly 100 British tanks. In July, Wavell was replaced by Claude Auchinleck.

figure 5 North Africa and the Balkans 1940–1

The Balkans and the east Mediterranean

In October 1940, Mussolini, anxious to expand and settle old scores, ordered an Italian invasion of Greece from Albania. He told his son-in-law Ciano, 'Hitler always confronts me with a fait accompli. This time I am going to pay him back in his own coin. He will find out that I have occupied Greece.' Perversely, Mussolini's attack on Greece was launched at the same time that large numbers of Italian troops were being demobilized. Greek troops, far more committed to the war than the Italians, held their mountain positions, inflicting heavy casualties on the Italians. In November, the Greeks counter-attacked and the Italian retreat turned into a rout. Greek forces threatened to occupy large parts of Albania. Italy's invasion of Greece gave Britain a pretext to occupy Crete and base some RAF units in southern Greece.

The Balkans was a sensitive area for Germany. Hitler was anxious to reduce Soviet influence there. In June 1940, Romania was forced to cede territory to Russia. It seemed possible that Romania might also lose Transylvania to Hungary. In August 1940, with Hungary and Romania close to war, Germany intervened, not least because Romania's oilfields were Germany's main source of supply. Germany persuaded Hungary and Romania to accept a compromise. The compromise pleased neither country. Romania lost land but Hungary was not satisfied with its gains. In Romania, King Carol abdicated and General Antonescu established himself as dictator. The country teetered on the verge of collapse, offering inviting possibilities to Russia. At Romania's request, Hitler sent a military 'mission' to Romania, ostensibly to strengthen the ties between Germany and Romania by bringing Romanian troops up to German standards. In reality, the force was there to protect the oil districts and keep Russia out. In November, Romania (and Hungary) joined the Tripartite Pact.

Italian disasters in Greece were a blow to Axis prestige. Moreover, a British presence in Greece put Romania's oilfields at risk of bombing attack. This could seriously compromise Germany's ability to wage war. Hitler felt constrained to rescue his ally. While he did not really want to be distracted from the attack on Russia, that attack meant he could not leave his southern flank exposed. The Greeks tried to persuade Hitler to maintain peace, assuring him that their only quarrel was with the Italians. Their pleas fell on deaf ears. Thus, in February 1941 the Greek government asked for British troops to be sent to Greece. There was an anguished debate within the British cabinet about whether these forces, which would have to be withdrawn from North Africa, should be sent. Churchill was not enthusiastic: he wanted to finish off the Italians in Libya. However, most of the cabinet favoured helping Greece. If Britain reneged on an obligation to help, this would have a bad effect on potential allies. In addition, the sending of troops to Greece might encourage Turkey and Yugoslavia to join Britain. Those troops began arriving on the Greek mainland in March.

Hitler was also active. Pressure was exerted on Bulgaria to join the Tripartite Pact (it did so on 1 March) and permit the deployment of German troops. Fourteen German divisions arrived in Bulgaria and were stationed along the Greek border. German military planners realized the importance of Yugoslavia if the Greek and British troops were to be crushed quickly. German pressure on Yugoslavia to accede to the Tripartite Pact was unrelenting. The Yugoslav government finally caved in and joined on 25 March. By late March, Germany's position in the Balkans was very strong.

Despite this, on the night of 26–27 March, a group of Serb officers denounced the Yugoslav-German treaty, seized Belgrade, forced the (pro-British!) regent Prince Paul to resign, and had King Peter installed as monarch. A government was set up under the leadership of General Simovic. The coup was little short of madness. It divided a precariously unified country and in particular set Serb against Croat. It was also bound to provoke the Germans, whose forces surrounded Yugoslavia. The new Serb government could call on no external assistance. Instead, it was encircled by hostile states – Italy, Hungary, Romania and Bulgaria – all of which had long-standing territorial disputes with Yugoslavia. Hitler, suspecting that the coup had been masterminded by Britain, told his high command that it was his desire to 'smash Yugoslavia'. Denouncing the new government as illegitimate, Hitler sent his troops into Yugoslavia on 6 April. The poorly equipped Yugoslav army was not fully mobilized. Most of the Yugoslav air force (450 mainly obsolete planes) was destroyed in an initial air attack. The *Luftwaffe* went on to bomb Belgrade, killing some 17,000 civilians. On 8 April, German, Italian and Hungarian troops cut through Yugoslav defences. The invasion enabled Croat and Slovene nationalists to proclaim independence from Serbian-dominated Yugoslavia. Many Croatian units mutinied and went over to the enemy. So feeble was the Yugoslavian army's resistance that the Germans lost only 151 dead in the course of the campaign. Belgrade fell on 12 April. Five days later Yugoslavia surrendered. The country had been destroyed in ten days.

Greece, which the Germans also invaded on 6 April, did not survive much longer. Greek morale was high after success against the Italians, and the Greeks had support from three British divisions. Yet Greek forces were suicidally positioned. German forces broke through the Monastir gap between the Greek armies in Albania and Salonika and pushed southwards. The Graeco–British front collapsed as one position after another was outflanked. Greek Prime Minister Koryzis committed suicide. British troops, harried by the *Luftwaffe*, fled south to find harbours to escape. Some British troops were still arriving as others were being evacuated. The Royal Navy, despite almost total Axis air superiority, managed to evacuate over 50,000 of the 62,000 British troops in Greece but precious equipment was lost. On 27 April, German forces occupied Athens. The sheer disparity in quality between the *Wehrmacht* and its Balkan opponents, coupled with the ineptitude of Greek and Yugoslav defensive arrangements, account for the German triumph. The Germans, after suffering only 5,000 casualties, now occupied most of Greece. Italy took much of the former Yugoslavia.

Hitler's military advisers now suggested an airborne attack on Malta. Capture of Malta would bar Britain's sea route to the Suez Canal. General Student, Commander of X1 Air Corps, convinced that Malta was too strongly defended, proposed instead an airborne assault on Crete. Hitler agreed. Five hundred transport aircraft and 100 gliders were made available to carry the 22,000 soldiers. Although Student expected to be outnumbered, he was sure that surprise, the high quality of his troops and German air superiority would ensure victory. His force was certainly superior in quality to the 30,000 Allied troops in Crete. Many of the troops, fugitives from the Greek fiasco, were disorganized and disheartened. They also lacked tanks, artillery and aircraft support. Nevertheless, it seemed inconceivable that the Germans could take Crete. First, they did not have command of the sea. Second, Ultra, the intelligence source derived from the interception and decryption of enemy ciphers, had revealed the targets and timing of the German attack to General Freyberg, the British Commander in Crete. Unfortunately, he made inadequate preparations, positioning many of his forces for a seaborne attack which did not materialize. Even so, German parachute losses on 20 May were appalling. Hundreds of men died in the air during the descent. The next day, however, German troops won control of the airstrip at Maleme, enabling the Germans to fly in reinforcements. Supported by the *Luftwaffe*, German troops quickly exploited the situation. It was the same old story. British troops were soon in headlong retreat.

Crete was a disaster for Britain. Two thousand troops were killed and a further 12,000 taken prisoner. The Royal Navy, attacked by German planes as it evacuated some 18,000 troops, lost three cruisers and six destroyers; two battleships, one carrier, six cruisers and seven destroyers were damaged. Crete was the costliest British naval engagement of the war. Furthermore, the loss of Crete was a severe strategic blow. Possession of the island would have provided Britain with a base to threaten the Romanian oilfields. Still, Crete was an ambiguous German victory. The Germans lost 4,000 elite troops and some 300 aircraft. Disappointed by the campaign – the first major parachute operation in history – Hitler concluded that parachuting in war was dicing with death, in which the odds were stacked against the parachutist (Allied commanders drew different conclusions). He thus abandoned any idea of an airborne attack on Malta.

Britain had more success in the Middle East. The 38,000 Vichy French troops in Syria, led by General Dentz, were something of an embarrassment. Dentz could threaten Egypt from the east. He could also support Britain's Arab enemies in Iraq. In April 1941, British intelligence revealed that German and Italy were planning to use Syria as a staging area from which to supply Rashid Ali who had overthrown the pro-British regent in Iraq. In May, German aircraft arrived in Syria (with Iraqi markings) and bombed British forces in Iraq. Nonetheless, British troops quickly crushed Rashid Ali and restored the Iraqi regent. As a result of Dentz's complicity in the Iraq episode, British and Free French forces entered Syria in June. Dentz soon surrendered. A Free French regime was set up in Syria, ensuring that Britain's hold over Egypt and Iraq was more secure.

Conclusion

By 1941 it was clear that Britain had survived. However, she was still not entirely safe. As Germany increased its U-boat fleet, it seemed possible that Britain would be starved into surrender. Britain was unable to put Germany under similar pressure. The only way Britain could strike at Germany was by bombing. Unfortunately, British bombing raids had little pattern, purpose or success. Casualties among the bomber aircrews were as high as German civilian casualties. In truth, Germany was stronger in June 1941 than in June 1940. Her forces were supreme on land. Whenever British and German ground forces had met, the Germans had been victorious. German success in Libya, Greece and Crete were serious blows to British morale. Fortunately for Britain, Churchill's decision to continue the war was about to be vindicated. In 1941 Britain was to get the major allies she needed.

04

Operation
Barbarossa

This chapter will cover:
- why Hitler launched
  Operation Barbarossa
- why Barbarossa was initially
  successful
- why Barbarossa ultimately
  failed.

Russian General Popel recorded what happened to him on 22 June 1941:

> Army Chief-of-Staff Varrennikov ... telephoned at 4.30 a.m. and told us that the German artillery was firing along the whole frontier, that Przemysl was under fire from close range, and that in places they were crossing the frontier ... And precisely at that moment, the heavy tearing roar of motors reached our ears. We all sprang out into the street. It was already light. "June 22, the longest day!" flashed across my mind. The sun was rising – and to meet it came Hitler's heavily-loaded bombers. They turned over the town and came down. The crosses on the wings – which we knew from the recognition albums and diagrams – could be seen with the naked eye. So could the black dots which separated from the aircraft. They bombed with precision: the railway station, the approach roads, the oil refinery, our barracks ... When they had dropped their bombs, they circled slowly over the town. Why should they hurry? Not one of our fighters was there; our anti-aircraft guns had not fired a single shot.

Similar events were occurring along the entire Russo–German border. At 3.30 a.m. on 22 June 1941, Hitler had launched Operation Barbarossa. Some four million German troops, with 3,600 tanks and 7,200 guns supported by 2,700 aircraft, attacked Russia. Why did Hitler launch Barbarossa? Why were the Russians taken by surprise? Why did Hitler's invasion not go entirely to plan?

Why did Hitler launch Operation Barbarossa?

It is easy with hindsight to see war between Russia and Germany as inevitable. In 1941, Hitler was at the height of his power. Almost all Europe was under his control. Only Britain stood defiant in the West. Russia remained independent, and potentially threatening, in the East. In attacking Russia, Hitler, generally portrayed as a man of consistent, brutal principles, is seen as fulfilling his life's mission – a mission he had spelled out in *Mein Kampf*. He hoped to destroy Bolshevism and win *lebensraum* for the German master race. Recently, however, there has been some questioning of the 'inevitable' claim for this attack. Was Hitler a man with a set plan that he pursued relentlessly throughout his career? Or did he, like most political leaders, change his plans as opportunities arose? Was he more a devious pragmatist than a great crusader? Why and when did he become committed to attacking Russia?

In 1940, Ribbentrop, Hitler's Foreign Minister, was opposed to an attack on Russia. Convinced that the first essential was to defeat Britain, Ribbentrop favoured an alliance of Germany, Italy, Japan and Russia against Britain and, ultimately, the USA. For Ribbentrop, the Nazi–Soviet Pact was more than a temporary expedient: it contained the possibility of a permanent understanding. He envisaged Japan dominant in the Pacific, Russia in the rest of Asia, Italy around the Mediterranean, while Germany controlled most of Europe. Hitler seems to have taken Ribbentrop's views seriously. Thus, in late 1940 Ribbentrop encouraged Japan to settle her central Asian disputes with Russia and worked hard to achieve an agreement on the spheres of influence between Germany and Russia. For some months, Hitler seems to have wavered between the options open to him, the Ribbentrop path or an attack on Russia. In the autumn of 1940, German policy was engaged in a last effort to establish whether long-term co-operation with Russia was possible. The failure of talks between Hitler and Molotov, the Soviet Foreign Minister, in November 1940 convinced Hitler that Soviet ambitions in eastern Europe were irreconcilable with Germany's.

Arguably, Operation Barbarossa was not a programme planned years previously, but simply a reaction to Russian expansionist moves. On the surface, the Nazi–Soviet Pact had proved advantageous for Germany and Russia alike, allowing both countries to carve up Poland. Soviet–German co-operation had continued smoothly thereafter. Soviet raw materials and foodstuffs poured into Germany in 1940. Yet by the summer of 1940, the German General Staff became worried by a build-up of Soviet forces on Russia's western frontiers. Moreover, in June 1940 Stalin had seized the Baltic States and the Romanian provinces of Bessarabia and Bukovina, thereby exceeding the terms of the Nazi–Soviet Pact. Hitler was concerned by Stalin's ambitions in the Baltic and the Balkans. He needed nickel from Finland, iron ore from Sweden, but above all oil from Romania. Romania was a crucial obstacle to continued Russo–German understanding since neither power was prepared to see it within the other's sphere of influence.

Stalin's policy during 1940–1 is difficult to explain. Germany's victories in the West did not please him. He had hoped for a long war between the capitalist powers that would wear them all out. Now he had a much more powerful Germany on his doorstep. He realized the qualitative weakness of his armed forces against Germany's but considered that their numbers would deter any ambition of Hitler's to destroy Russia. Stalin vacillated between defiance and co-operation, making territorial demands one day and assuring Hitler that essential supplies would continue the next. A natural bully, he found it hard to conciliate. Whether he knew it or not, his diplomacy invited Barbarossa.

Stalin was hardly a trusting sort of man, and it has long puzzled historians why he should have trusted Hitler. Recently, an ex-Soviet General Staff Officer, Victor Suvarov, has claimed that, far from trusting Hitler, Stalin was intending a surprise attack on Germany in 1941. The disarray of the Soviet defences and the fact that major Soviet troop concentrations were close to the borders, in the worst possible position for defensive operations, can be used to support Suvarov's claim. However, the weight of historical opinion is still against such an interpretation.

Hitler may well have dithered in the autumn of 1940. However, there is plenty of evidence to suggest that his mind – and certainly his heart – was set on attacking Russia. As early as June 1940, he instructed Brauchitsch, his Commander-in-Chief, to examine 'the Russian problem'. In July 1940, Hitler told his military chiefs to expect an attack on Russia in 1941. By attacking Russia, Hitler hoped to kill several birds with the same stone. There seems little doubt about his ideological commitment to 'race' and 'space' – destruction of Jewish Bolshevism and conquest of *lebensraum*. He had little but contempt for the Slavs whom he saw as crushed and brutish creatures of a Bolshevik tyrant. Hitler had no wish to share his hegemony of Europe with that tyrant. Nor did he wish to be dependent on Soviet raw materials. By June 1941, Russia had delivered 2.2 million tons of grain, one million tons of oil and 100,000 tons of cotton. These deliveries proved essential for Germany's war effort. Such dependence could lead to Soviet exploitation. The bottom line was that Hitler did not trust Stalin.

There was another factor. Hitler believed that the conquest of Russia would have important implications in the West. He was convinced (correctly) that Britain continued to fight because it hoped for the eventual intervention of Russia and the USA. In a host of previous wars Britain had found a continental ally to defeat whichever power threatened to dominate Europe. By 1940, only Russia had the power to challenge Germany. Hitler knew that an Anglo–Russian agreement would pose a serious threat. He also knew that Churchill was doing all he could (without much success!) to reach such an agreement. Hitler hoped that once Russia was defeated, Britain would accept that all hope of victory had gone. There was some logic in Hitler's view; but there was also a major flaw. By attacking Russia, he would inevitably force the country into Britain's welcoming embrace.

On 18 December 1940, Hitler signed Directive No 21 Case Barbarossa. This stated that, 'The German armed forces must be prepared, even before the conclusion of the war against England, to crush Soviet Russia in a rapid campaign'. Hitler was gambling again but this time, he thought, on a certainty. While Soviet forces were much larger (the German forces mustered to invade Russia were not much stronger in numbers than those which had invaded France), the *Wehrmacht* was stronger in operational skill. It had a better trained and more experienced Officer Corps, while the ordinary German soldier was more highly skilled and better equipped than his Red Army equivalent. German morale, after the triumphs of the last two years, was sky high, and most Germans were committed to the coming conflict. Although not all Germans agreed with Hitler's racial obsessions, most were nationalistic and anti-communist. Hitler could also count on support from Romania, Hungary and Finland. He was confident that the Soviet political structure would collapse after the first blows. Russia, he insisted, was less strong than she had been in 1914. Her economic system was in chaos, her leaders hated and her armed forces weak. Hitler was not alone in his low estimation of Soviet forces. All Germany's military leaders thought that the Red Army was incapable of fighting a modern war. Cripps, the British Ambassador in Moscow, gave the Russians a month. American experts thought that Russia would be beaten within three months.

There was some cause for this view. Stalin, in the late 1930s, had conducted a series of brutal purges. About ten per cent of the adult population had been killed or sent to prison camps in Siberia. The Soviet army leadership had been particularly savaged. By the autumn of 1938, three out of five marshals, 13 out of 15 army commanders and 110 out of 195 divisional commanders were dead. Consequently, the army's leadership consisted of new and untried officers. During 1939–40, the Red Army had performed terribly against Finland. Its weaknesses were clear: poor communication; poor use of tanks; a lack of initiative among junior officers and non-commissioned officers (NCOs); an unwieldy command structure; and a supply system that functioned sporadically. Stalin's greatest fear in the event of a German invasion was the unreliability of the Soviet peoples. He was not sure that he could trust them to resist. Given this fear, in the event of war he hoped to hold Russia's frontiers, ensuring the Germans did not break into the interior. Therefore, the Red Army was thinly spread out, in defiance of all military wisdom about defence in depth.

Nevertheless, German intelligence woefully underestimated Soviet military and economic capability. Fearing an attack from Europe's capitalist states, Stalin had created (as part of his Five Year Plans) a military-industrial complex of enormous potential. In June 1941, Russia had far more tanks, planes and men than Germany. Some lessons had been learned from the Finnish War and some efforts had been made to reform the Soviet army. Newer tanks, like the T-34, were first class. Soldiers of proven ability were promoted to high command – not least Zhukov who had won the battle of Khalkin-Gol in Russia's undeclared war against Japan on the disputed border of Mongolia in 1939.

Hitler set the tone of the campaign in a secret address to his generals on 30 March: 'The war against Russia will be such that it cannot be conducted in a knightly fashion; the struggle is one of ideologies and racial differences and will have to be conducted with unprecedented, unmerciful and unrelenting harshness'. He decreed that all political commissars in the Red Army should be shot. Behind the front line, *Einsatzgruppen* (special task force) units were to be responsible for ruthless policing actions, including the elimination of the Bolshevik elite and Jews. The racial and ideological aspects of the war were fully acknowledged by the army leadership which told its troops to fight 'energetically and without consideration' against 'Bolshevik agitators, partisans, saboteurs and Jews'. The army leaders were by no means weak-willed fellow travellers who grudgingly obeyed Hitler. Leading generals agreed with Hitler that the war would be a 'clash of two ideologies' and a 'war of extermination'. The vision of an ideological crusade spread through the *Wehrmacht*'s entire structure. German troops could be as violent as they liked with the civilian population. There would be no penalties for killing Soviet citizens. The Germans were coming to Russia as destroyers and enslavers, not liberators. Instead of enlisting the Soviet peoples in the effort to overthrow the hated communist regime, the Nazis were to adopt policies certain to drive potential allies into the arms of Stalin. Moreover, because of their contempt for Slavs, the German military, not just Hitler, consistently underestimated the staying power and sophistication of their opponents.

Hitler made a major mistake in his dealings with Japan. When Matsuoka, the Japanese Foreign Minister, came to Berlin in April 1941, he was told nothing of German plans and instead was urged to turn Japanese forces south against the British at Singapore. Matsuoka accepted Hitler's advice. On his return journey through Moscow he signed a Neutrality Pact with Stalin – a pact that both countries observed until August 1945. The fact that Hitler did nothing to try to get Japan to attack Russia was to have enormous consequences.

It has often been claimed that Barbarossa was fatally delayed by Hitler's decision to send German troops into the Balkans in early 1941 to save Mussolini. The evidence for this is not convincing. The Balkan campaign, which involved relatively few troops, was concluded more rapidly than the German high command had anticipated. Problems with supplies were the main reason for the delay of Barbarossa until June. The delay was probably fortunate. In May, the Russian soil was still heavy after the spring thaw. By June it had dried out and was better suited for the German panzers.

Given that the Germans hoped to take Stalin by surprise, the movement of vast numbers of men, weapons and supplies to the Russian borders caused the Germans major problems. The *Wehrmacht* had other problems. Although on paper it had double the panzer divisions it had in 1940, this was only achieved by halving the tanks in each division. The German army was generally lacking in motorized vehicles. Its trucks came from a variety of sources, not least captured Allied equipment and commandeered civilian vehicles. Its weapons were an even greater hodgepodge. Supplying and maintaining units that were equipped with dissimilar weapons and support vehicles was likely to prove a nightmare. Events would show that the Germans had not paid enough attention to logistics.

By June 1941, the Germans had three armies ready to attack. Leeb led the Army Group North whose objective was Leningrad. Bock's Army Group Centre would drive towards Moscow. Rundstedt's Army Group Southern would advance into the Ukraine, and from there to the Caucasus, Russia's main oil-producing region. Hitler and his army high command differed in their view of how Barbarossa should be fought and about the main objectives. General Halder believed that the capture of Moscow was essential. Hitler was more concerned with seizing as much Russian territory as possible, especially in the Ukraine. No clear decision was made about whether Moscow or the Ukraine should be the main target. The German plan was basically to invade, destroy the Red Army, and see what happened.

However clever the Germans were at deception, it was Stalin who ensured that Barbarossa would catch the Red Army completely by surprise. Stalin, well aware of German troop concentrations on his frontiers, had excellent intelligence about German intentions. Well-placed agents in Berlin, Switzerland and Paris warned him of Hitler's plans from autumn 1940. In May 1941, Richard Sorge, the Soviet master spy in Tokyo, gave Stalin the exact date of the German invasion. Britain and the USA gave him similar warning. Yet Stalin clung to the belief that Hitler would not attack. Amazingly he continued to meet the commitments of the trade treaty with Germany: the last goods train crossed the German border minutes before the *Wehrmacht* launched its attack. Soviet commanders on the frontiers, denied access to reliable intelligence and fearful of offending Stalin, did nothing to take precautionary action. Until the very end Stalin was obsessed with the idea that nothing should be done which might be interpreted as provocation by Hitler. When told on 21 June that a German deserter had said that the invasion would begin early next morning, he ordered the man to be shot for spreading 'disinformation'.

Operation Barbarossa June–July 1941

Operation Barbarossa was launched on 22 June. Stalin's actions assisted the German attack. Even after the German invasion had begun, he did not immediately declare a state of war or order a general mobilization. He still imagined that the situation could be saved by negotiation, and even turned to Japan in the forlorn hope that it might be persuaded to mediate. Not until midday did Foreign Secretary Molotov announce that Russia was at war with Germany. Later that evening, General Timoshenko issued an order calling for offensive action by the three Soviet armies on the Western Front. By then, Russian forces were staggering from a series of shattering blows. The task of the Germans had

figure 6 Operation Barbarossa

been made easier by the Soviet dispositions. Soviet aircraft in forward airbases were sitting targets for the *Luftwaffe*. One thousand five hundred Russian aircraft were destroyed on the ground on 22 June (and a further 300 in the air). Everywhere, German panzers cut through Soviet defences with ease.

Stalin seems to have suffered some sort of breakdown as the reality of the invasion dawned on him. He stayed silent and secluded at his dacha outside Moscow for several days, perhaps expecting to be overthrown. Finally, on 3 July he came out of isolation and broadcast to the Russian people for the first time in his life (most Russians were surprised by his Georgian accent). Calling for an all-out effort to rid the country of the German fascists, he appealed to deep-rooted Russian patriotism, and warned that there would be a merciless struggle against cowards and deserters. On 19 July, he became Defence Commissar and in August, Commander-in-Chief.

In the opening days of Barbarossa, it looked as though Hitler's gamble was justified. German tactics were similar to those employed during 1939–40. In a series of fast-moving pincer movements, panzer and armoured divisions broke through Russian defences and created a series of pockets. German infantry dealt with the pockets, taking huge numbers of prisoners. Soviet generals time and again played into German hands when they tried to obey Stalin's orders to counter-attack rather than retreat. The initial successes of the invasion led to euphoria in the German high command. On 3 July, General Halder predicted that the war would be over in two weeks.

The battles in late June and early July were fought with a brutality not yet displayed in the war. Soviet prisoners, unprotected by the Hague Convention which Russia had not signed, were often massacred. This proved counterproductive. It meant that Russians were more likely to fight to the death. Furthermore, Stalin instituted summary executions for those generals who retreated, and he deployed 'Special Sections' in the rear of the fighting units to shoot deserters. Desperate Russian forces fought on stubbornly, suffering enormous casualties in the process. Meanwhile, German Army Group Centre, which had the largest number of tanks, pressed eastwards. On 16 July General Guderian captured Smolensk. His men had advanced over 645 kilometres (400 miles) in three weeks, and were two-thirds of the way to Moscow. In the North, Leeb occupied the Baltic States and closed in on Leningrad. Rundstedt's Army Group South, which included Romanian and Hungarian divisions, made the slowest progress, partly due to the fact that Russian armies in the south had a high proportion of T-34 tanks. The Germans still triumphed. Part of Rundstedt's force headed for the Black Sea. The rest pushed towards Kiev. By late July, the Germans had won the 'battle of the frontiers'. The Red Army had lost millions of men and the vast bulk of the 15,000 tanks and 8,000 aircraft located in western Russia in June.

Yet the German position was weaker than it seemed. The advance of the three army groups pulled them further apart and wide gaps appeared between them. The infantry found it hard to keep up with the rapid advance of the panzers. There were not enough troops to deal with the pockets of resistance, the surrender of huge numbers of troops and the occupation of territory. More seriously, Red Army resistance was much fiercer than expected. The Russians had far more men than the Germans had calculated. Equally disturbing was the fact that Russian industry continued to churn out planes, guns and tanks. On 11 August, Halder noted, 'The whole situation shows more and more clearly that we have underestimated the colossus of Russia'. The commander of one panzer division remarked that Germany must reduce her casualties, 'if we do not intend to win ourselves to death'. By August, the Germans had lost 179,500 men. The tank strength of the panzer divisions, whittled down through battlefield attrition and wear and tear, had dropped by half. Front-line infantry units were exhausted. Between 22 June and 28 July, for example, 12th Infantry Division marched 900 kilometres (560 miles), an average of 24 kilometres (15 miles) a day in intense heat, carrying weapons and rations.

Operation Barbarossa August 1941– January 1942

In August, the German advance stalled. The main problem was that of getting supplies to front-line troops who were being attacked by Soviet reserves. These offensives were weak and unco-ordinated but they forced the Germans to fight, thus consuming more fuel and ammunition. Civilian trucks collapsed on the primitive Soviet roads. German lines of communication remained exposed to attacks. For a month, the Germans made slow progress on all fronts. It was this period of inaction, not the month before Barbarossa started, that was the vital loss of time in the campaign.

The enforced pause at least gave the Germans time to reach a solution to the problem implicit in Barbarossa from the first – whether to place the main weight of their attack in the centre or on the wings. Hitherto, they had evaded the problem by advancing on all three fronts at once. They could do so no longer. Their strength was running out. Most of the army command wished to head straight to Moscow, some 322 kilometres (200 miles) away. Hitler, increasingly interventionist (to the dismay of his commanders), was not convinced. His strategic goals remained the same: Leningrad and Soviet forces in the Baltic must be conquered; so must the Ukraine and the Donets basin, with its huge coal reserves. The debates between Hitler and his generals were long and bitter. 'Hours of gibberish, and the outcome is there's only one man who understands how to wage wars,' wrote Halder gloomily. Brauchitsch suffered a heart attack. Halder offered his resignation (it was refused). On 23 August, Hitler got his way. Army Group Centre was to halt. The two groups on the wings were to destroy the Soviet armies facing them. Then panzers from all three groups would unite for a final blow against Moscow before winter set in. After the war, many German generals claimed that this decision was wrong and that with it Hitler lost the war. In fact, Hitler's decision made sense and was to have considerable success.

In late July, Zhukov, Stalin's Chief of Staff, had suggested abandoning Kiev. Stalin exploded. Zhukov, one of the few men who dared challenge Stalin, offered his resignation. It was accepted. Stalin now planned a counter-attack on the Bryansk Front. The attack was a disaster. Russian forces simply advanced into a German trap. On 16 September, German panzers striking up from the south met Guderian driving down from the north 160 kilometres (100 miles) in the Russian rear. The huge Russian forces in and around Kiev were trapped. Kiev fell on 19 September. By the end of September, the Germans had taken 665,000 prisoners, 884 tanks and 3,718 guns – the largest single mass ever taken in an operation of war before or since.

The Germans were moving again. Further south, Germans and Romanians took most of the Crimea, the Donets basin and a further 400,000 prisoners. In the North, Leeb began a concerted effort to take Leningrad. Rather than engage in costly street fighting, Hitler ordered that the city should be starved into surrender. By September, Leningrad was virtually cut off. The situation in the city was desperate. There were no stockpiles of food or fuel, and no effort had been made to evacuate the young and old. Nonetheless, Lake Ladoga made Leningrad difficult to fully encircle. The city's population had also constructed defence lines, including 998 kilometres (623 miles) of earthworks, 644 kilometres (400 miles) of anti-tank ditch and 5,000 pillboxes. In mid-September, Zhukov arrived to energize the defenders. Under his resolute command, panzer attacks failed to break through Leningrad's defences. The water route across Lake Ladoga provided a tenuous lifeline (railway tracks were laid across the lake in November when it froze). Inside the city, conditions were appalling. German bombardment inflicted 4,000 civilian casualties a day.

The Germans showed little mercy to Russians in Leningrad or elsewhere. Rosenberg, a Nazi expert on Russian affairs, wanted to win over the inhabitants, dissolve the Communist Party, liberate the national minorities and return the land to the peasants. In the former Baltic states, this policy was applied successfully. A similar policy would probably have worked in the south where many Ukrainians initially welcomed the Germans as liberators. Hitler, however, was not interested in winning hearts and minds. He considered Slavs, whether Russians or Ukrainians, as subhuman. The SS took over the conquered areas, ruling with an iron hand. Russian prisoners of war (POWs) were also treated appallingly. A report of March 1942 on the possible use of Soviet prisoners for the German economy indicated that out of 3.6 million Soviet soldiers captured, only 100,000 were still capable of working. The rest were dead or dying.

In desperate need of help, Stalin looked to Britain for assistance. Churchill had declared in July that, 'the cause of any Russian fighting for his hearth and home is the cause of free men and free people in every quarter of the globe ... we shall give whatever help we can to Russia'. Within weeks, Britain and Russia concluded an agreement for mutual assistance. Britain now had an ally who was able to absorb the greatest weight of the German military machine. (It perhaps did not occur to Churchill that this ally would win the war against Germany – with awful consequences.) In spite of Churchill's promises, Britain was no more able to aid Russia militarily than it had been able to aid Poland. There was no easy way of sending material to Russia, and Britain had few spare supplies to send. In November, FDR extended Lend-Lease to Russia, but little Western aid reached the Russians in time to help them in the struggle to save Moscow.

Russia consequently faced the crisis of war alone. Stalin called on Russians to remember the heroes of the past. In September, he decreed the creation of new units of 'Guards', quintessential symbols of the old Tsarist regime. New distinctions were created for heroes and victors. Even the Orthodox Church, persecuted and vilified for two decades, was restored to favour as the servant of 'Mother Russia'.

After their success at Kiev, the Germans were in a position to move on Moscow. Halder was the driving force behind the attack – code named Typhoon. Army Groups North and South were to continue towards Leningrad and Rostov, while the Centre, with the bulk of the panzer divisions, was to take Moscow. Despite the lateness of the season, the lack of supplies, and the serious losses sustained since June, German forces set off on the last stage of the road to Moscow in late September. Initially the advance went well, with yet more pockets being created at Briansk and Vyazma in October. A further 660,000 prisoners, 1,242 tanks and 5,412 artillery pieces were taken. On 2 October, Hitler told the German people, 'the enemy is broken and will never be in a position to rise again'. However, the arrival of autumn rains turned Russia's dirt roads into seas of mud, slowing the German forces to a crawl.

Nevertheless, Stalin's position remained desperate. In European Russia he had only 800,000 men with 770 tanks and 364 planes. In Moscow there was panic. Muscovites rushed to the railway stations to flee eastwards. On 10 October, Stalin turned again to Zhukov, calling him south to aid the defence of Moscow. As at Leningrad, he mobilized the citizens. Two hundred and fifty thousand Muscovites dug anti-tank ditches outside the city. Meanwhile, Stalin concentrated all his reserve forces to defend Moscow. He had a fresh resource. Assured by intelligence sources that Japan was committed to war against the USA and thus would not attack in the Far East, Stalin authorized the transfer of 25 Soviet divisions from Siberia to the Moscow front.

In November, as the first frosts of winter hardened the ground, the panzers made faster progress towards Moscow. Their strength grew weaker by the day. In mid-November, the Germans had to decide whether to make a last dash or dig in for the winter. Hitler decided to press on. He hoped – understandably – that one last effort might finish the war. The final stage of Operation Typhoon began on 16 November. Panzers headed north and south, intending to surround the Russian capital. They came close, but not close enough, to success. At the end of the month, the tanks, some only 32 kilometres (20 miles) from Moscow, were forced to a halt. On 27 November, the German Quartermaster General reported, 'We have come to the end of our resources in both men and material'. On 2 December, German units reached the Moscow tram terminus. They lacked the strength to push further. The temperatures were now falling fast. German soldiers, without winter uniforms, froze to death at their posts. The cold was so intense that weapons often did not work and engines would not start. Hitler had not prepared for a winter war because he and his generals expected victory by the autumn.

On 5 December, Zhukov, with reinforcements from Siberia, launched a counter-attack. Russian troops, better equipped for the winter than their foe and close to their supply dumps, had some success. German troops were forced to retreat, abandoning all the territory won in the last stages of their drive on Moscow. To make matters worse for Hitler, Soviet forces in the south recovered Rostov – the gateway to the Caucasus. Army Group North was driven back from Itikhvin, which helped ensure that the Russians could provide supplies to Leningrad across Lake Ladoga. Russian success caused consternation among German commanders and generated calls for a major retreat. Many Army Group Centre divisions were dangerously exposed as Soviet spearheads lapped around their flanks. For a time it seemed as though the *Wehrmacht* would suffer the same fate as Napoleon's Grand Army in 1812. Hitler would have none of it. He dismissed large numbers of generals (including Bock, Leeb and Guderian), relieved Brauchitsch as Commander-in-Chief, took personal command of the army, and issued orders to his troops to stand and fight where they were. By force of personality and threat of professional extinction, he infused the generals at the front with a determination to hold. Fortunately for the *Wehrmacht*, instead of concentrating his forces on Army Group Centre where the Germans were wobbling, Stalin ordered a counter-offensive on every front from the Crimea to Leningrad. This dissipated the Red Army's strength, and it failed to achieve any decisive breakthroughs. Somehow the Germans regained their equilibrium.

Conclusion

Hitler's gamble had failed. That failure was far from preordained. Arguments put forward that Hitler should have learned from history – from Napoleon's fate – are too simplistic.

Russia was not unconquerable – 1917 indicates that. Hitler knew his European history, the vastness of Russian territory and the problems of the Russian weather. His mistakes were to place too much confidence in the ability of his forces to overcome these obstacles, and to underestimate the capacity of Stalin's regime. In 1941, the *Wehrmacht* confronted too much space with too few resources. The *Luftwaffe* had not enough planes to maintain total command of the air, an essential ingredient of earlier German victories. Barbarossa rested on the mistaken belief that once the Germans challenged Stalin, his rotten political edifice would collapse. Instead, Nazi brutality ensured that the Soviet people rallied to Stalin. Stalin deserves little credit for Soviet survival. His purges, his dishonest foreign policy, his dismissal of all the warning signs of invasion, and his military bungling resulted in catastrophe. In 1941, Russia lost between five to eight million people and huge swathes of territory, including the main source of its food supplies and industrial raw materials. While the Germans had failed to defeat Russia, Barbarossa had come close to success. The future of the Russo–German war still hung in the balance. The Germans had been stopped but not defeated. In January 1942, Hitler was already thinking of the campaign he would launch in the spring to destroy Russia for good.

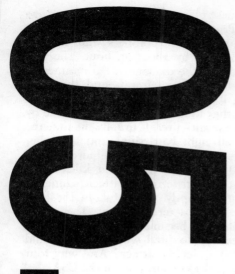

05

Pearl Harbor

This chapter will cover:
- Japanese expansion 1931–9
- Japanese and US policy 1940–1
- Pearl Harbor.

On 7 December 1941, Japanese planes from six aircraft carriers attacked the US fleet at Pearl Harbor in Hawaii. Japanese torpedo planes, dive bombers, level bombers and fighters attacked in two waves, separated by about an hour. The first wave of 183 planes did most of the damage in 30 minutes of attack. They focused on the military aircraft and the eight battleships anchored along Battleship Row. When the second wave of 170 planes arrived, they found their targets obscured by smoke and encountered intense anti-aircraft fire. By the time the two attacks had finished, all eight battleships and ten other warships had been sunk or seriously damaged, 349 aircraft had been destroyed, and 2,400 Americans had been killed. The Japanese lost 29 planes. In the short term, the attack, launched without warning, had been brilliantly successful. In the long term, Pearl Harbor was to prove a terrible error. The attack brought the USA into – what now became – the Second World War. Given that Japan's leaders doubted whether they could defeat the USA, why did they order the attack? And why four days after Pearl Harbor did Hitler declare war on the USA?

Japanese Expansion 1931–9

In the second half of the nineteenth century Japan adapted to Western technology with extraordinary rapidity. During 1894–5 she was strong enough to defeat China in war. In 1904–5, Japan defeated Russia, gaining Korea, and economic and military rights in the Chinese province of Manchuria. Japan fought against Germany during 1914–18, winning some of her Pacific colonies in the process. By 1918, Japan had a democratic system (of sorts), a growing population (of over 60 million), and a strong manufacturing base. In the 1920s, she pursued an international policy of co-operation rather than confrontation. However, Japan was far from a Western state. Many Japanese believed that the West had little to offer of spiritual value.

The world depression at the start of the 1930s pushed the Japanese economy into a severe downward spiral. High unemployment and declining incomes discredited the democratic process. Japanese political parties, riven by corruption, were blamed for their inability to tackle the economic problems. The depression also discredited liberal economics. Unlike Britain, Japan had no large empire from which to obtain cheap raw materials. Japanese nationalists thought Japan should obtain the resources she needed by conquest. China – divided and poorly governed – was the obvious source of supply.

On 18 September 1931, units of the Japanese Kwantung Army, which garrisoned parts of Manchuria, blew up some of the railway near Mukden. Blaming China for the incident, Japanese troops seized Mukden and went on to take the whole of Manchuria over the next few months. All this was the work of dissident officers, determined to force the Japanese government to reject the system of international co-operation. The government, aware that within Japan there was enormous support for the Kwantung Army's action, did not act forcefully against it. At the same time, China denounced Japan for breaching international law and called upon the League of Nations to act. The League sent a Commission of Enquiry to Manchuria, headed by Lord Lytton. His report condemned Japan – to little effect. Japan simply withdrew from the League and created the puppet state of Manchukuo in Manchuria.

In the 1930s, military leaders played a growing role in Japanese political life. There were parallels between the ethos that became dominant in Japan and Italian fascism and German Nazism. Japanese militarism shared with both an admiration of violence and force, and a hatred of both socialism and liberal capitalism. However, the similarities are probably less important than the differences. What made the Japanese militarist state so odd was the lack of strong leadership. Japan had no charismatic leader and no dynamic political party. She moved towards domestic authoritarianism, expansion and war without decisive leadership. Various parts of the government machine competed for control of decision making. A mature, forceful emperor might have controlled the situation but Hirohito, aged 25 when he became emperor in 1926, accepted his traditional non-activist role. Although his authority was theoretically absolute, his real power remained limited.

While the Japanese army gained increasing influence in the 1930s, it was bitterly divided. Some officers, imperialist and anti-communist, were committed to expansion in China and ultimately to war with Russia. Others urged caution abroad and revolution at home – a rejection of Western materialism and a return to dictatorial emperorship that would exalt traditional values. In the early 1930s, there was in-fighting between the army cliques, recurring political upheaval, and a spate of political assassinations by fanatical army officers. By the late 1930s, the continental imperialists held sway. In 1936, Japan signed the Anti-Comintern Pact with Germany, and later Italy – a vague alliance against Russia.

On 7 July 1937, Chinese troops of a local warlord fired on Japanese soldiers in Peking. The Japanese sent in more troops. So did Chiang Kai-shek, the Chinese nationalist leader. A full-scale war soon developed. While China had far more troops, its forces were poorly equipped and badly led. The heaviest fighting initially was in Shanghai. Following Chinese bombing of the town, Japan responded with a campaign of vengeance and extermination. In December, Japanese forces in Nanking went on a genocidal rampage, massacring some 200,000 civilians. Japanese aggression and atrocities united (for a time) the warring Chinese nationalists and communists. Japanese hopes of reaching agreement with Chiang, whereby they would control north China, failed. The war continued. By 1938, Japanese troops held northern China and most of China's coastline. Nonetheless, they found it hard to control such a huge area and crush Chinese resistance. The more they pushed into China, the farther they seemed from peace.

The Sino–Japanese war placed a huge strain on Japanese resources. Inflation increased, as did Japan's dependence on imported raw materials. The war justified increasing regimentation and repression within Japan. The international results of Japan's incursions were huge – not least a deterioration of relations with Britain and the USA. Japan's Prime Minister, Prince Konoye, announced in 1938 that Japan was fighting in China to uphold the rule of law and basic human decency. Japan, he said, would become the bulwark of a 'New Order' for Asia – the Greater East Asia Co-Prosperity Sphere. The New Order would end European imperialism, stop communism and unite Asians in a great cultural and spiritual alliance free of Western taint. Meanwhile, Japanese troops continued to commit terrible atrocities against the Chinese.

British Prime Minister, Neville Chamberlain, faced with a worsening situation in Europe, was desperate to avoid conflict with Japan. He appealed – in vain – for an end to the Sino-Japanese conflict. In the circumstances the best British hope was that Japan would get bogged down in a war of attrition in China – which was what happened. In conventional terms, Japan had won the war in China but it could not end it. Half of China's population (of 450 million) remained outside Japanese control.

Developments in Europe opened up the prospect of wider vistas for Japanese expansion. Some army commanders still favoured a northward attack on Russia. Yet in 1939, Japanese troops were defeated by Soviet forces in fierce clashes on the Mongolian border, discouraging those who were keen on war with Russia. The Nazi–Soviet Pact in August 1939 initially stunned the Japanese. The German, Italian and Japanese alliance against communism seemed to have collapsed. However, Japanese leaders soon realized that the Pact presented Japan with the opportunity of improving its relations with Russia. With its back secured against a Soviet attack, Japan could consider the possibility of an advance into South-East Asia. Takeover of French Indo-China, British Malaya and the Dutch East Indies would ensure that Japan had supplies of oil, rubber and other essential materials. German success in 1940 seemed to present Japan with huge opportunities. France and Holland were defeated and Britain was forced to concentrate its military resources in Europe. European colonial possessions were there for the taking. There was just one problem – the USA.

Japanese–American relations

From the start of the twentieth century, relations between the USA and Japan had been at best uneasy. After 1898, the USA controlled the Philippines. It also had extensive economic interests in China. Japanese expansion was therefore perceived as a threat. Nevertheless, drift and passivity were the main features of the USA's Far East policies in the 1930s. In fairness, FDR had to conduct US policy under considerable constraints. American outrage over Japanese conduct in China forced declarations of moral censure, while the strong isolationism in Congress limited his room for manoeuvre. FDR's moral condemnation had little impact on Japan. Not until 1939 did Congress approve a modest request of US$25 million in credits to help Chiang Kai-shek buy military supplies. This was the first concrete measure taken by the USA in an attempt to restrain Japanese expansion. After 1939, FDR, although still concerned not to move too far ahead of public opinion, assumed a more active role in foreign affairs. Hitler's conquest of western Europe stiffened his resolve to aid Britain and prevent further Japanese expansion. Aware that Japan was dependent on American raw materials (especially oil), FDR knew he could use the threat of economic sanctions.

In July 1940, Konoye returned to power in Japan. General Tojo, a fervent nationalist, became War Minister while Matsuoka, an ally of the army nationalists, became Foreign Minister. The presence of these two committed imperialists at the centre of power was to have important consequences. Matsuoka was determined to exploit the weakness of Britain and France to improve Japan's position in China. China was isolated from the outside world except by air and two primitive roads from British-controlled Burma and French Indo-China. Japan pressured Britain and the French colonial administration in Indo-China into closing the two roads in the summer of 1940. In September, the French were forced to grant Japan the right to base forces in northern Indo-China. These forces could operate against Chiang and also threaten the Dutch East Indies, Malaya and Burma.

Determined to strengthen Japan's ties with the Axis powers, Matsuoka signed the Tripartite Pact with Germany and Italy in September 1940. This bound the three countries to mutual support in the event of any one being attacked by a power which was not party to the Sino–Japanese dispute or to hostilities in Europe. The Pact, in Matsuoka's eyes, was a military alliance against the USA: only the USA fitted the treaty's description. Matsuoka, like Hitler, hoped that the alliance would deter the USA. Japan's star was now fixed to that of Germany.

US policy 1940–1

Matsuoka miscalculated. Far from being deterred by the Axis pact, FDR was determined to resist Japanese expansion in South-East Asia. When Japanese forces occupied northern Indo-China, FDR reacted by cutting off supplies of aviation fuel, lubricating oil and certain grades of scrap iron as a warning that Japan could not exploit the situation in Europe. In November 1940, Chiang Kai-shek's request for another loan of US$100 million won approval in Congress. FDR hoped that strong measures would deter Japan from further expansion.

FDR's main concern during 1940–1 was Europe, not the Pacific. He regarded Germany as a more serious threat than Japan. In December 1940, he warned Americans that, 'If Great Britain goes down the Axis powers will control the continents of Europe, Asia, Africa, Australasia, and the high seas – and they will be in a position to bring enormous military and naval resources against the hemisphere'. A totalitarian Europe would endanger what was left of democratic government. He was prepared to take whatever steps were necessary to prevent Axis victory. The Lend-Lease Act of 1941, which authorized FDR to 'sell, transfer title to, exchange, lease, lend, or otherwise dispose of' any 'defence article' to 'the government of any country whose defence the President deems vital to the defence of the United States', was effectively a declaration of economic warfare against the Axis. FDR provided Lend-Lease aid to both Britain and Chiang Kai-shek.

As the USA became, in FDR's words, 'the great arsenal of democracy', the USA edged towards an undeclared war in the Atlantic. FDR sought to ensure that US aid reached its intended destination and was not sunk by German U-boats. Joint Anglo–American naval planning took place. US warships now conveyed merchant ships halfway across the Atlantic while US forces occupied Greenland and Iceland. Opinion polls showed that most Americans were in favour of full support for Britain, even at the risk of war. However, 75 per cent still opposed a declaration of war.

In August 1941, FDR and Churchill met for the first time aboard ships off Newfoundland. They issued a statement – the Atlantic Charter – indicating common commitment to the preservation of democracy. Churchill reported to his cabinet that FDR had said he would wage war but not declare it. In September, a U-boat attacked the US destroyer *Greer*. FDR now issued orders allowing US ships to attack U-boats. US–German relations deteriorated further. By the autumn of 1941, there was a state of undeclared war in the Atlantic between the USA and Germany. FDR, with his eye constantly on opinion polls, was awaiting an incident that would give him an excuse to declare war on Germany. Hitler, his attention fixed on Russia, shrank from provoking war with the USA.

FDR wanted a war against Germany. He did not want a war against Japan as well. Most US military strategists believed that the USA lacked the resources to fight a war on two fronts. Appeasement of Japan thus made sense. Some Americans, notably Joseph Grew, the US Ambassador in Tokyo, called for a conciliatory policy. Grew opposed economic sanctions against Japan on the grounds that pushing her into a corner would make war more likely. Yet FDR and his Secretary of State, Hull, hoped that tougher economic sanctions would prevent further Japanese expansion. Determined to stand firm, they nevertheless supported peace talks with Japan which continued through most of 1941.

Pearl Harbor

Events in Europe in 1941 had a major impact on developments in the Far East/Pacific. Matsuoka was in Berlin in April 1941. Nothing was said of German plans to attack Russia. Hitler, confident of his ability to defeat Russia alone, was reluctant to share his victory. Instead of encouraging a joint attack, he encouraged a Japanese thrust to the south against Britain and the USA. Matsuoka, assuming Russo–German relations to be on a co-operative footing, went on to Moscow and signed a five-year non-aggression Pact with Stalin. Operation Barbarossa took Matsuoka completely by surprise. He was soon replaced. In the Japanese corridors of power debate continued about what to do next. Some militarists wanted to reject the non-aggression Pact and attack Russia. Others, not least War Minister Tojo, remained committed to southern expansion, especially as there was no longer a Soviet threat to Manchuria.

In July 1941, Japanese troops entered southern Indo-China. The USA reacted by tightening the economic screws, freezing all Japanese assets and imposing further embargoes on trade. The new sanctions effectively cut off 90 per cent of Japan's oil supply. Japan had only 18 months' supply of oil reserves. Either diplomacy would have to end the sanctions or the Japanese would have to seize the oil of the Dutch East Indies before sanctions hindered their ability to fight. For Japan, the clock was ticking. Konoye, fearful of the USA, was hesitant. Tojo argued that a 'go south' plan should begin as soon as possible.

Through the summer and autumn of 1941, Japanese leaders considered the possibility of war. While army leaders were confident that they could take the Allied colonies, navy leaders were not convinced of the wisdom of war. They knew that in their simulated war games, Japan invariably lost to the USA. Admiral Yamamoto, head of the Combined Fleet, had the task of designing a plan to defeat the USA. Most plans envisaged the Combined Fleet going on the defensive and luring the larger US fleet into a great battle in the western Pacific. Yamamoto thought differently. Encouraged by the success of the British operation at Taranto in 1940, he proposed to use his air carriers to eliminate the US Pacific fleet in Pearl Harbor by a surprise attack. If all went to plan this would even up the strengths of the two navies, giving Japan the opportunity to conquer South-East Asia.

In September 1941, Yamamoto's ambitious plans were submitted to the Naval General Staff. There were to be several simultaneous operations. On Z Day, amphibious forces would take Hong Kong and the US-controlled Wake and Guam Islands. Major attacks would also be launched on the Philippines and Malaya. Having accomplished their initial objectives, the Japanese intended to construct a chain of fortified bases running from the Kurile Islands, through Wake, the Marshall Islands, the Gilberts, the Bismarks, New Guinea, the Dutch East Indies and Malaya. They should then be able hold at bay any Allied force which threatened their defensive perimeter. The attack on Pearl Harbor was the key. Success here would ensure that the rest of the operations could go ahead without interruption. Roughly half of Japan's Combined Fleet was allocated to the Pearl Harbor Strike Force. To avoid being spotted, the fleet would approach Hawaii by a circuitous route, starting in the stormy waters of the Kurile Islands.

On 6 September, at a cabinet conference held in the presence of Emperor Hirohito, the Japanese alternatives were reviewed. The conclusion of the conference was to continue negotiating while preparing for war. Konoye, still hopeful of reaching agreement with the USA, suggested a meeting between himself and FDR. FDR refused. Tojo held out for an aggressive solution. On 17 October, Konoye, lacking army support, resigned. Tojo became Prime Minister. His objectives were clear: to establish Japanese primacy in the Far East and to defeat the Western nations which would not accept it. On 1 November, he agreed to a last effort to reach a settlement with the USA. Japan would offer to withdraw troops from southern Indo-China if the Americans would sell Japan a million tons of aviation fuel and stop sending supplies to Chiang Kai-shek. The next day, in the presence of the Emperor, Tojo expressed his fear that if Japan did not seize its advantage now, it never would. The Emperor did not intercede. The 30 November was the last day on which US concessions would be accepted. By 25 November, Japan would commence preparations for attack.

Unknown to Japan, since early 1941 the USA had been able to read Japanese diplomatic ciphers, as a result of a code-breaking operation known as 'Magic'. The Americans were thus aware that the Japanese were planning war at the same time that they were professing to talk peace. On 26 November, Secretary of State Hull bluntly presented the Japanese negotiators with the USA's ultimate position. Japan must withdraw its troops not only from Indo-China but also from China and accept the legitimacy of Chiang Kai-shek's government. The Hull note reached Tokyo on 27 November. Japanese leaders agreed that the US terms were unacceptable. While Tojo instructed his Washington emissaries to persist in their talks, Japanese forces proceeded to their attack positions.

On 26 November, the Pearl Harbor Strike Force – six carriers, two battleships, two cruisers and eleven destroyers, commanded by Admiral Nagumo – set sail from the Kurile Islands, maintaining strict radio silence. US intelligence failed to detect it. All the indicators suggested that the Japanese would attack Malaya and the Philippines. FDR and his senior military commanders knew that war with Japan was coming. (Warning to that effect was sent out on 27 November.) They believed that an attack on Pearl Harbor was inconceivable. Some conspiracy theorists still argue that FDR did know about Japan's intentions and deliberately allowed the attack on Pearl Harbor to go ahead as the pretext he needed to draw the USA into the war. This is ridiculous. FDR would not have begun a war by deliberately losing a large part of his vital Pacific fleet. He knew that Japan was up to something. He did not know what. There is no need to doubt his genuine shock when news of the Pearl Harbor attack reached him. Among the Americans there was much evidence of incompetence and miscalculation but not of conspiracy.

Soon after 7 a.m. on Sunday 7 December, the radar operative at Pearl Harbor detected the approach of a large concentration of aircraft some 220 kilometres (137 miles) away. However, the naval duty officer, when alerted, concluded that the echo on the screens represented a flight of US planes which were scheduled to land at Hawaii. He told the radar operative, 'not to worry about it'. At 7.49 a.m. the first wave of Japanese planes struck Pearl Harbor. Since June 1940, US forces there had undertaken three major alerts and many anti-aircraft and anti-submarine drills. For two months, the fleet had been at a permanent state of readiness. The length of the warning period had blunted the edge of preparedness. Moreover, in peacetime the Pacific fleet always observed Sunday as a holiday: the officers slept ashore and the crews woke to a late breakfast. Consequently, as the Japanese planes swooped into the attack, 75 per cent of the anti-aircraft guns on the US ships were unmanned. By 8.12 a.m. the Pacific fleet was largely destroyed. It was a humiliation without precedent in US history.

The disaster was not as great as it might have been. Three US aircraft carriers were away from Pearl Harbor – two at sea and one under repair in California. Nor did the Japanese destroy the naval dockyards or the vast oil stocks on Hawaii – arguably a more valuable target than the ships (most of which were raised from the shallow waters and quickly repaired). Japanese pilots wanted to go back for a third attack. Nagumo refused. The attack had succeeded beyond his wildest dreams. Concerned about the whereabouts of the US carriers, Nagumo thought the sensible course was to withdraw his fleet from danger.

Within hours of Pearl Harbor, Japanese forces attacked Wake, Guam, the Philippines, Malaya and Hong Kong – to stunning effect. British plans to defend its colonies in South-East Asia depended on the new battleship, *Prince of Wales*, and the old battle cruiser, *Repulse*. On 10 December, both ships were found by Japanese bombers and sunk in two hours. 'In all the war,' wrote Churchill, 'I never received a more direct shock'.

Denouncing the Japanese attack as a 'day of infamy', FDR asked Congress to declare war on Japan. On 8 December, Congress obliged. Contrary to the advice of some of his closest advisers, FDR asked for a declaration of war only against Japan, not against Germany and Italy. On 11 December, Hitler obliged those Americans who wanted war with Germany by declaring war himself (Mussolini did likewise). Why Germany declared war on potentially the most powerful state on earth has long puzzled historians. Germany had, after all, previously ignored the USA's overt support for Britain, and had been careful to avoid provocation. Nor was the war in Russia going well. Ribbentrop, who had a better appreciation of the USA's strength than Hitler, stressed (in vain) that the terms of the Tripartite Pact did not bind Germany to go to Japan's assistance. Hitler seems to have concluded that the USA was effectively at war with Germany, or soon would be, and decided that it was better to act first. His declaration of war was undoubtedly a colossal mistake. Without it, FDR might have found it hard to persuade Congress to enter the European war – an unwelcome diversion for most Americans who were determined to avenge Pearl Harbor.

Conclusion

By 1941, FDR's conviction that Germany and Japan had to be stopped had been translated into acts which both countries could justifiably claim were hostile. At this point, FDR did want a war with Germany. Accordingly, he should not have wanted war with Japan. Arguably, his policies forced Japan into a corner. Given that he was primarily concerned about the situation in Europe, involvement in a Pacific war might be seen as careless. However, all efforts at negotiation had failed. Japan was expansionist, and Japanese expansion was a threat to US economic and strategic interests. Japanese leaders surely deserve more blame than FDR. Underestimating the US ability to wage war, the attack on Pearl Harbor was an immense blunder.

Japan's decision to attack the USA instead of Russia was the decisive decision of the Second World War. Had Japan attacked Russia when Hitler launched Barbarossa, Russia would probably have been defeated. Furthermore, US entry into the war would not have been precipitated. Japan's decision was very much influenced by German actions. Hitler's belief that Germany could defeat Russia without Japanese assistance was a crucial misconception.

Events in December 1941 appeared to link the fortunes of the Axis partners and to turn a European and a Far Eastern war into a world war. Yet little thought had been given in Berlin and Tokyo about how the Axis powers might co-operate; indeed there was to be little harmonization of strategy. The war in Europe and the war in the Far East were to remain largely separate, connected only by the active involvement of Britain and the USA in both.

From Britain's point of view, the important thing was that the USA was now in the war. Churchill wrote later, 'Hitler's fate was sealed. Mussolini's fate was sealed. As for the Japanese, they would be ground to powder. All the rest was merely the application of overwhelming force'. Nevertheless, it would take time for the USA's 'overwhelming force' to make itself felt. The immediate outlook was bleak. Germany controlled most of Europe, while Japan was on the point of dominating South-East Asia. Whatever Churchill might think, Allied victory in 1941 was far from certain.

06

the turning of the tide

This chapter will cover:
- the war in the Pacific 1941–3
- the war in North Africa 1941–2
- the war in Russia 1942–3.

In June 1941, the war had been an unequal struggle between Britain and German-dominated Europe. By December 1941, it had become a world war. All the great powers and many of the smaller ones had been sucked in. The problem for the Axis powers was that the Allies had potentially much greater resources. The Axis thus had to win quickly or not at all. In early 1942, Axis forces triumphed almost everywhere. Yet in the second half of 1942, the tide began to turn. Japanese expansion was held. In Russia, the German drive south stalled at Stalingrad. Rommel was driven back from Egypt. Why did Axis forces have so much success in the first half of 1942? Why were the Allies able to turn the game round in the second half?

Japanese expansion 1941–2

Within days of Pearl Harbor, Japan struck at a number of targets in South-East Asia. Most of the smaller objectives – Guam, New Britain, Bougainville and Buka – fell quickly. Anglo–Canadian troops in Hong Kong, and US marines on Wake Island provided some resistance but both places were in Japanese hands by Christmas. The collapse of Malaya was one of the most shameful British defeats of the war. After staging multiple landings in northern Malaya, Japanese commander Yamashita cut south down the peninsula to Singapore. Although outnumbered by more than two to one, his experienced troops outfought the Anglo–Indian forces. Time and again British positions were encircled or bypassed. At the end of January 1942 the Japanese, having advanced 805 kilometres (500 miles), reached Singapore. British Commander Percival dispersed his 130,000 troops to defend the 48-kilometres (30-mile) long northern shore of the island. Yamashita, by contrast, concentrated his 35,000 men (who were desperately short of ammunition and food). During 8–9 February, Japanese forces crossed the narrow waters of the Johore Strait, capturing the city's water reservoirs. On 15 February, Singapore surrendered – the most discreditable capitulation in British history. In only 70 days, at a cost of 10,000 casualties, Yamashita had captured Britain's main Far East base and opened the way to the Dutch East Indies.

At the same time, other Japanese forces attacked the US-controlled Philippines. The US–Filipino forces were led by 60-year-old General Douglas MacArthur. His defence of the Philippines turned him into an American hero – for no very good reason. While it is unlikely that any US general could have saved the islands, MacArthur made a number of errors. On 8 December, Japanese aircraft found US planes still on their runways nine hours after the war had begun. MacArthur, with much less excuse than the commanders at Pearl Harbor who were cashiered for their supposed negligence, lost over half his planes. Thus, Japanese troops faced no serious air threat when they began landing two days later. Outnumbering the invaders by more than two to one, MacArthur determined to hold Manilla. However, he was soon forced to retreat into the Bataan peninsula. Properly defended, Bataan might have resisted attack indefinitely but little had been done to prepare it for resistance. The 80,000 Filipino–US troops, along with 26,000 civilians, found it hard to survive in a malaria-ridden jungle without adequate food, medical supplies and ammunition.

US forces clung on to Bataan through January but their numbers shrank alarmingly from disease. In February, US General Wainwright reported that only a quarter of his men had the energy and resources for another fight. MacArthur, whose main base was underneath the island bastion of Corregidor, did little to help. Determined to galvanize FDR into sending reinforcements, he bombarded the world with press communiqués that misrepresented his own role and hid the dire condition of his army. As Wainwright's army wasted away, MacArthur announced that he planned to win or die on Corregidor. Not wishing to turn MacArthur into a martyr, FDR ordered him off the island. He left the Philippines on 12 March, famously saying, 'I shall return'. He was given command of a new theatre of war in the South-west Pacific and, for no obvious reason, awarded the Medal of Honor, an award his father had won in the Civil War. On Bataan, there were no rewards for US–Filipino troops surviving – or not – on 1,000 calories a day. Surrendering on 9 April, they were marched off to a prison camp in central Luzon. Some 600 Americans and 20,000 Filipinos died on the Bataan 'Death March'. Most died from exhaustion or disease. Some were brutally murdered. The garrison on Corregidor held out for another month before surrendering on 6 May.

The dogged defence of the Philippines did not slow the Japanese conquest of the Dutch East Indies. A mixed Allied fleet was annihilated by the Japanese navy in the battle of the Java Sea during 27–8 February. Java capitulated on 12 March. The Indonesians, delighted to be free from Dutch rule, were to prove

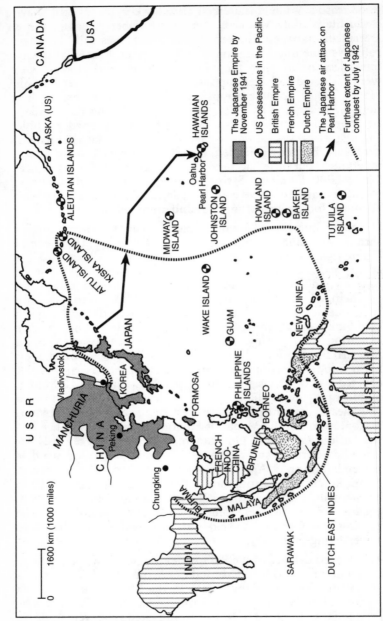

figure 7 Japanese expansion 1941–2

among the most enthusiastic of collaborators in Japan's 'New Order'. For the Japanese, the East Indies was a treasure house of oil, rubber, rice, timber and tin.

Japanese victory continued in Burma. With the help of Burmese collaborators, the Japanese drove back British and Chinese forces, and by May occupied the whole of Burma, cutting off Chiang Kai-shek from the outer world. Only the arrival of the monsoon prevented a Japanese advance into India. In April, Japanese carriers sailed into the Indian Ocean and their air groups raided ports in India and Ceylon, sinking two British cruisers and a carrier.

Japanese success on land had been achieved with very small forces, much smaller than those of their opponents. Some 1.75 million troops – the major part of Japan's army – were bogged down in China. However, Japan's considerable naval strength was committed to the Pacific. Not one of her 11 battleships, ten carriers or 38 cruisers had so far been seriously damaged. Many Japanese naval leaders now favoured a defensive strategy, luring the main US fleet towards Japan and then destroying it in a great battle. Admiral Yamamoto disagreed. He had little confidence in Japan's ability to win a long war, and believed that only a daring attack might give his country a chance of success. As he recognized, the balance of strength was still against Japan. She was up against the two greatest naval powers in the world. Moreover, Japan's success had been won against a USA virtually at peace. Now she had to face a USA mobilizing for war. Indeed, the USA still had a powerful Pacific fleet. It was this fleet that Yamamoto wanted to destroy.

FDR knew that only US air and naval power could roll back the Japanese from their Pacific outposts and liberate South-East Asia and China. Yet he agreed with Churchill that the defeat of Germany was far more important than that of Japan. Holding to the 'Europe first' strategy, he resisted US navy leaders' calls for a major offensive against Japan. Nevertheless, more resources were sent to the Pacific than envisaged. From the ashes of defeat, the USA prepared to hit back. It would have to fight with the old navy until the new navy under construction was ready. Despie this, it did enjoy one substantial advantage – its growing skill in collecting and analysing enemy radio traffic.

US carriers, given a breathing space by Japan's incursion into the Indian Ocean, tested themselves with raids on Japanese island bases. The raids created a new media hero – Admiral

Halsey. Halsey's task force pulled off the first US coup of the war – a bombing raid on Tokyo. The raid – dreamed up by FDR and Chief of Naval Operations, Admiral King – aimed to 'bring the war home to the Japanese'. On 2 April, US carrier *Hornet* set sail with 16 long-range B-25 bombers on its flight deck commanded by Colonel Doolittle. Halsey aimed to approach to within 805 kilometres (500 miles) of Japan, launch the B-25s, and then retire while the planes bombed Tokyo and flew on to land in China. On 18 April, *Hornet* was 1,046 kilometres (650 miles) from its destination when it was spotted by the Japanese. Halsey launched the B-25s, knowing they would be at the extreme limit of their range. All the planes took off safely. Thirteen bombed Tokyo and three bombed other targets; four landed in China, one in Russia and the rest were abandoned by their crews who parachuted down over China. Of the 80 fliers who went on the raid, 71 survived to return to the USA.

The Doolittle raid caused negligible damage but had major repercussions. At the moment the Doolittle bombs dropped, a debate was raging between the Japanese Naval Staff and the Combined Fleet over future strategy. The Naval Staff, keen to menace Australia, were committed to capturing New Guinea and the Solomons. The Combined Fleet, represented by Yamamoto, wanted a strategic victory. Yamamoto believed he could provoke a decisive battle with the US carriers by mounting an invasion of Hawaii's outlier, Midway Island, for which he was sure the USA would fight. Doolittle's raid ended the argument. Japan's leaders, horrified at the thought that US bombers might kill the Emperor, decided the US carriers had to be dealt with. After helping cover landings in New Guinea, the Japanese fleet would attack Midway.·

US naval intelligence officers listened to the Japanese fleet redeploy after its return from the Indian Ocean. Relatively certain that the Japanese intended to strike Port Moresby (New Guinea), Admiral Nimitz sent two carriers – *Lexington* and *Yorktown* – to meet a three-carrier Japanese force. The result was the Battle of the Coral Sea, the first sea battle where the opposing fleets were never within each other's sight. The attacking was done entirely by aircraft. The US lost 33 planes. *Lexington* was sunk and *Yorktown*'s deck damaged. Japan lost over 60 planes. One of its carriers was sunk and another badly damaged. The battle proved that US carriers and pilots were at least the equals of their foes.

Yamamoto now set in motion his main plan. He hoped to lure the US fleet north by a preliminary attack on the Aleutian Islands. Two carriers were sent to cover this attack. Meanwhile, the main Japanese fleet – four carriers, 11 battleships, 16 cruisers and 53 destroyers – headed for Midway Island. Thanks to the interception of Japanese radio signals, Nimitz knew where and when the enemy were preparing to attack. He did not fall for the Aleutian ruse. Nor did he intend to defend Midway. Instead, he directed his carriers to seek out and attack the Japanese carriers. Even so, the odds seemed stacked against the Americans. The US navy had only eight cruisers and 15 destroyers to support its three carriers – *Enterprise*, *Hornet* and *Yorktown* (which left Pearl Harbor after speedy repairs on 30 May).

On 4 June, Japanese Admiral Nagumo, failing to locate the US carriers, sent his planes to attack Midway. The attack was successful, destroying large numbers of US planes on the ground. Nagumo ordered his returning planes to prepare for a second strike, unaware that the US carriers, some 282 kilometres (175 miles) away, had launched 150 strike aircraft. At 9.30 a.m. US planes found the four Japanese carriers, their decks crowded with refuelling and rearming aircraft. US torpedo bombers attacked – to no avail and no hits. Thirty-five of the 41 US planes were shot down. Nagumo now prepared to launch his own aircraft to find and destroy the US carriers. However, his fighters, drawn down to sea level to attack the torpedo bombers, had left the sky open to US dive bombers. These now appeared, more by luck than judgement. One group had taken a wrong course and reached its target by shrewd guesswork. At 10.25 a.m. it was exactly placed to deliver the most decisive blow in the history of naval warfare. Its leader, Lieutenant-Commander McClusky, attacked with 37 dive bombers. The Japanese carriers' flight decks were still cluttered with planes. In five minutes, three Japanese carriers were destroyed. The fourth, *Hiryu*, survived to launch a retaliatory strike that put *Yorktown* out of action. Later that day, US bombers found *Hiryu* and damaged it so badly that it was scuttled. As the Japanese fleet fled, US pilots sank a cruiser and damaged another. At a cost of one carrier (*Yorktown* was sunk by a torpedo three days after Midway), a destroyer and 147 aircraft, US planes had destroyed four carriers, a cruiser, and 322 planes.

Midway was not quite the turning point in the Pacific war. Japan still had the edge in carriers (seven to four). Nor was the

Japanese offensive quite over. They still planned to move against New Guinea and the southern Solomons. Nevertheless, the material setback for Japan offered the USA an opportunity to take the initiative. While US strategy remained 'Europe first', the temptation to take limited offensives against Japan reflected political pressures that FDR could not ignore. Few Americans could forget or forgive Pearl Harbor or the Bataan Death March. When it was clear that there would be no 'Second Front' against France in 1942, US military chiefs also pressed for offensive action against Japan. The question was where to attack. Japan itself was not yet in the frame. She lay 3,218 kilometres (2,000 miles) from America's Pacific bases. In between was a strong chain of Japanese island fortresses. Was it better to proceed by taking the large islands of the East Indies or to 'island hop' across the tiny atolls of the central Pacific? MacArthur, who headed the South-West Pacific Area, was set on returning to the Philippines. Nimitz, who led the Central Pacific Ocean Area, aimed more directly at Japan. In July, Nimitz's plan – to hit the Japanese at the extreme point of their advance by capturing Guadalcanal (one of the Solomon Islands) – became the main priority.

US marines landed on Guadalcanal on 7 August, swiftly overcoming the Japanese garrison. The Japanese, concerned at a major breach in their defences, determined to recapture the island. The result was a bloody and long, drawn-out fight, involving ground, air and naval forces. Once the marines were ashore, the US navy had to re-supply them. Japanese naval forces were similarly committed to pouring men and supplies on to the island. Between August and November, there were a number of major naval battles. The Battle of Guadalcanal (12–15 November) was the greatest clash of battleships since Jutland in 1916. The Americans won – just. Two major Japanese ships were sunk. Yamamoto now decided to cut his losses and hold the Combined Fleet for a more favourable fleet engagement. Over the four months of fighting, the US navy had suffered severe losses – two carriers, seven cruisers, 15 other warships, 134 planes and almost 5,000 sailors – a loss so traumatic that for years afterwards the navy refused to reveal its casualties. Japanese losses had been similarly heavy – two battleships, one carrier, four cruisers, 17 other warships, 14 troop transports, 500 aircraft and 3,500 sailors. In the battle for air superiority, the Americans emerged victorious. On land, both sides displayed supreme bravery but while the Japanese were ultimately dependent upon their concept of honour in sustaining their resistance, the Americans could call up overwhelming firepower. The Japanese finally withdrew from Guadalcanal on 9 February 1943. They had lost 25,000 troops. The Americans had lost 2,500 soldiers in combat. All the US services, which did not yet command overwhelming advantages in numbers and technology, had shown they could defeat the best of the Japanese armed forces.

With most of Japan's naval and air power focused on the Solomons, MacArthur began operations in New Guinea. Bad weather, disease, difficult terrain and stubborn Japanese resistance slowed his advance. On the Asian mainland, the demoralized and poorly equipped Anglo–Indian army could not mount a serious challenge to the Japanese. Britain also faced the prospect of upheaval in India. The Congress Party now declared India free of the British raj. The imprisonment of Gandhi and other Congress leaders sparked off widespread rioting.

FDR was more concerned with China than India. His government had long sung the praises of Chiang Kai-shek and found it hard to swallow the criticisms of General Stilwell, Commander of US forces in China. Stilwell thought that Chiang and his men were a 'gang of thugs' who did little to threaten the Japanese, and used US money and equipment to pursue their own selfish ends. British leaders shared Stilwell's views. (Churchill was more impressed by Madame Chiang's shapely legs than by her husband's ability.) In June 1942, Chiang proposed that the USA should build an air force of over 500 planes in China. This force would then attack Japanese supply lines and bases along China's coast. FDR, aware that the USA lacked the capacity to fly in sufficient equipment, rejected the plan. However, still hopeful that Chiang might tie down much of the Japanese army, he promised to increase US airborne supplies.

The war in North Africa 1941–2

The importance of the war in North Africa has often been played down. Certainly the scale of the fighting cannot be compared to that in Russia. From Hitler's point of view, North Africa was a sideshow. Nonetheless, the area was strategically important. If Allied forces controlled North Africa, they would be in a position to land anywhere in the Mediterranean. Conversely, if Axis forces could drive the British from Egypt, the Middle East and its oil reserves would be threatened.

Rommel led the Axis forces. Bold and energetic, he rarely missed the opportunities that his opponents provided. His mission was simple: to protect Libya and keep the British occupied. Anything else was a bonus. Rommel hoped to win that bonus despite two major problems. The Italians, who made up a large part of his army, were dispirited by earlier defeats, badly equipped and conscious that they were German cannon fodder. His real Achilles heel, though, was supply. British air and naval forces, operating out of Malta, and with good intelligence of Axis intentions, savaged Italian convoys.

The British forces in North Africa in late 1941 were led by General Auchinleck. Churchill urged him to attack: 'It is impossible to explain to Parliament and the nation how it is our Middle East armies had to stand for four and a half months without engaging the enemy while all the time Russia is being battered to pieces'. Men, weapons and supplies were poured into Egypt, enabling Auchinleck to attack in November 1941. British forces, with a two to one superiority in tanks, proceeded to waste the advantage. Unable to grasp the basics of modern warfare, British officers dispersed their tanks rather than concentrating on powerful hammer blows. Rommel nearly won a major victory. Eventually, however, he was forced to retreat to Libya.

Rommel remained confident of success – with good reason. Increased German air and submarine support in the Mediterranean, coupled with some Italian naval successes, meant that more Axis convoys got through. In January 1942, Rommel attacked, driving the British back to Gazala where they established a defensive line. For four months, the front stabilized. Churchill demanded another offensive; Auchinleck urged caution until he had built up his reserves. Rommel struck first. During 26–7 May, he moved south around the Gazala Line. At one stage he personally led a tank raid into the British lines, trusting to enemy minefields to secure his flanks. The British forces, extricating themselves from danger, retreated to El Alamein, 97 kilometres (60 miles) from Alexandria. Tobruk surrendered on 21 June, after only a week's siege. Thirty-five thousand prisoners were taken. Churchill was horrified, 'Defeat is one thing,' he said, 'disgrace is another'.

Rommel, promoted to Field Marshal, now planned to advance into Egypt. Hitler, dreaming of German armies driving through the Middle East and joining with armies advancing through Russia to the Caucasus, supported him. Despite Rommel's

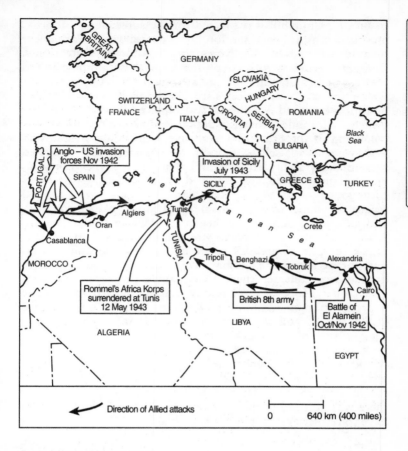

figure 8 North Africa in 1941–3

optimism, the Afrika Korps faced major problems. Its supply
lines, running across 1,609 kilometres (1,000 miles) of desert,
were far too long, and British planes were again inflicting heavy
losses on Italian convoys sailing to Tripoli. Moreover, the British
had taken up strong defensive positions at El Alamein. Lying to
the south was the Qattara depression, a great salt desert,
impassable to tanks. The British positions could be carried only
by direct assault. In early July, Auchinleck halted a series of
German attacks in an engagement known as the first battle of El
Alamein. Although British counter-attacks later in July failed
miserably, Rommel had suffered a serious defeat.

In Britain, Churchill was blamed for the surrender of Tobruk, and there was a formal motion of no confidence in Parliament (it was defeated by 476 votes to 25 with 40 abstentions). Churchill needed victories to bolster his position at home and to boost Britain's standing as an ally to the USA and Russia. Failing to realize Auchinleck's success in July, Churchill blamed him for inertia and Auchinleck was replaced (on 15 August) by General Alexander. General Bernard Montgomery took over command of the 8th Army. Abrasive, vain, always right, and with a genius for self-promotion, Montgomery also possessed some military ability. Arriving in Egypt, he was wise enough to adopt plans initiated and approved by Auchinleck. (Afterwards Montgomery insisted that the plans were his own.) On 30 August, Rommel, desperately short of tanks, planes and fuel, and suffering from jaundice, began an offensive to the south of Alam Halfa Ridge. It failed. Montgomery refused to counter-attack, despite Churchill's prodding. Instead, he built up his own forces, letting the Germans wear themselves out. Rommel, literally worn out, returned to Germany for medical treatment. By October, Montgomery had advantages of nearly four to one in troop strength (230,000 to 80,000), three to one in tanks (1,500 to 500) and nearly four to one in aircraft (1,200 to 350). Judging that his men lacked the flair to beat the Germans in tank warfare, he planned an infantry-artillery assault which would destroy the enemy's defences. Only after this 'dogfight' would he launch the main body of his armour. Given that Allied forces were about to land in Morocco and Algeria, arguably there was no need to fight a battle at all. The Germans would have to retreat even without a British attack.

On 23 October, a heavy artillery bombardment began the second battle of El Alamein. Infantry were then sent forward to create corridors through the German minefields. The infantry attack soon stalled. Efforts to force tanks across the minefields had no more success, while diversionary thrusts to the south failed to draw enemy forces away from the crucial sector. By 26 October, Montgomery had suffered heavy losses. Things might have been worse. Rommel's replacement died of a heart attack as the battle began, and Rommel did not arrive back in North Africa for nearly 48 hours. The Germans thus missed several opportunities for counter-attacks. Meanwhile, Montgomery kept on pummelling the Germans, to considerable effect. By early November, the Afrika Korps was down to 30 tanks. On 4 November, the British finally broke through. Rommel, hopelessly outnumbered, conducted a masterly retreat, helped by Montgomery's extreme caution. Nevertheless, no one could deny Montgomery his victory. The British took 30,000 prisoners. Their own casualties were 13,500.

On 8 November, the strategic situation in North Africa changed fundamentally with Operation Torch – the landing in Morocco and Algeria of Anglo-American forces under the command of General Dwight D. Eisenhower. Eisenhower's performance in staff positions over the previous two years had brought him to the attention of General George Marshall, Chief of Staff of the US army. Eisenhower's jovial personality led many to underestimate his iron will and extraordinary intelligence. One of his greatest talents was getting men to work together as a team. Operation Torch reflected the triumph of British strategic arguments over Americans, like Marshall, who wanted an early invasion of northern France. The British felt that the Americans overlooked the enormous difficulties in mounting a full-scale invasion across the Channel (not least the lack of landing craft). The Americans felt that the British were traumatized by the horrors of trench warfare in the First World War and by the humiliating defeats during 1940–1. They also felt they were being drawn into a sideshow to protect British interests in the Middle East and Mediterranean. It took a direct order from FDR overruling Marshall to commit US troops to North Africa. FDR wanted action somewhere. If France was ruled out, then North Africa was the only place that fitted the bill.

A convoy of 850 ships transported the forces which landed at Oran, Casablanca and Algiers. The poorly equipped Vichy French troops in North Africa did not mount serious resistance. Admiral Darlan, Petain's right-hand man, agreed to collaborate with the Allies as he had already done with the Germans. He was helped to this decision by news that German forces had entered unoccupied France on 11 November and that the Vichy government had lost its last shreds of independence. Darlan's order to French forces to cease fighting was obeyed. Yet the fact that a German collaborator had been put back in power caused an outcry in Britain. Few tears were shed when Darlan was assassinated by an extreme French royalist in December.

Rommel retreated to Tunisia. Caught between Montgomery advancing from the east and Eisenhower advancing from the west, his position seemed unenviable. Hitler and Mussolini rushed 250,000 troops to Tunisia to help.

The Eastern Front 1942–3

By March 1942 operations in Russia had slithered to a halt in the spring mud. Little could be done until May. Both sides made use of the time to repair their losses. Stalin planned to increase the strength of the Red Army to nine million men. The Germans had to scrape the barrel to replace the 900,000 men lost in 1941. They were increasingly dependent on Italian, Romanian and Hungarian troops. However, Hitler was confident that he could finish off Russia. In April he issued his plans for Operation Blue. The main German thrust was to be in the south. In the Crimea, the 11th Army, led by Manstein, would destroy the Russian army in the Kerch peninsula and take Sevastopol. Army Group South, now led by Bock, was to enclose Voronezh on the River Don and capture Stalingrad on the River Volga. Finally, German forces would drive into the Caucasus. Capture of the Caucasian oilfields would cripple the Soviet – and enhance the German – war effort.

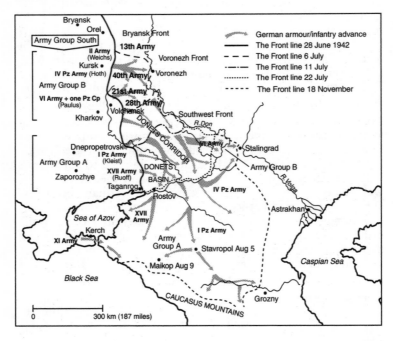

figure 9 German advance in 1942

Stalin believed that the Germans would renew their attack on Moscow. His forces thus concentrated on the Central Front. They also mounted an ill-conceived and unsuccessful offensive. The worst disaster was the attempt to take Kharkov in the Ukraine. Hitler, overruling his generals, ordered a German counter-attack on 17 May. It was hugely successful. By the start of June, the Soviets had lost 300,000 men and 1,200 tanks. German victory at Kharkov was another indication to Hitler that his judgement was superior to that of his generals. It was also clear that he was going to meddle in the conduct of Blue to an even greater extent than he had in Barbarossa.

At the same time, Manstein began operations in the Crimea. By 19 May, he had completed the conquest of the peninsula, destroying or capturing 175,000 men, 4,646 artillery pieces and 496 tanks. On 2 June, the Germans began a massive bombardment of Sevastopol. The town was captured on 4 July, the Germans netting 90,000 Russian troops.

On 28 June, the main German offensive began, taking the Soviets completely by surprise. Breaking through the Russian defences, Bock sent 4th Panzer Army to attack Voronezh while 6th Army, led by General Paulus, headed to Stalingrad. Disappointed by Bock's performance, Hitler replaced him with General Weichs in mid-July. Hitler also divided his forces. While Army Group A pushed on towards the Caucasus, Army Group B was to thrust towards Stalingrad, 'to smash the enemy forces concentrated there, to occupy the town and to block land communications between the Don and Volga'.

For the first time, Stalin allowed his commanders to retreat. Most did so, trading space for time. This meant that the German advance yielded only modest numbers of killed and captured Soviet troops. On 9 August, troops of Army Group A sighted the first oil derricks at Maikop. In the Caucasus, the Russians were vulnerable since many of the local peoples welcomed the Germans as liberators. Maikop fell but the Soviets had so thoroughly destroyed its oil wells that this did not help the Germans. As German tanks reached the foothills of the Caucasus, lack of supplies forced them to a halt.

The 6th Army, also suffering from supply problems, advanced on Stalingrad. On 21 August, Paulus smashed through Soviet forces to the west of the Don, and two days later reached the Volga, north of Stalingrad. Hitler's determination to capture the city made little strategic sense. The Germans had already cut the Russian traffic on the Volga. The city – the largest of many called after Stalin – was essentially a prestige symbol. For the same reason, Stalin refused to abandon it. Men and materials were rushed to its defence. The city, which ran for some 32 kilometres (20 miles) down the west bank of the Volga (1.6 kilometres (one mile) wide at this point), could not be easily besieged. Consequently, it had to be taken by direct assault. By early September, *Luftwaffe* attacks had left much of the city in flames. In mid-September, German troops began the fight for Stalingrad. Russian troops defended bravely, and through the autumn a street-by-street struggle was fought in wrecked houses and factories. Zhukov, who now took supreme control of the Southern Front, fed in sufficient forces to maintain a tenacious hold on the ruins. The fighting was horrendous. A German panzer division officer wrote during October:

We have fought for fifteen days for a single house with mortars, grenades, machine-guns and bayonets. Already by the third day 54 German corpses are strewn in the cellars, on the landings, and the staircases. The front is a corridor between burnt-out rooms; it is the thin ceiling between two floors. Help comes from neighbouring houses by fire-escapes and chimneys. There is a ceaseless struggle from noon to night. From storey to storey, faces black with sweat, we bombed each other with grenades in the middle of explosions, clouds of dust and smoke ... Stalingrad is no longer a town ... it is an enormous cloud of burning, blinding smoke; it is a vast furnace lit by the reflection of the flames.

By mid-November, the Germans had battered the defenders back to a strip of land along the Volga. By then, virtually all the German reserves had been sucked into the city. The kernel of the Stalingrad operation was German: the shell was not. Poorly equipped Romanian, Hungarian and Italian forces protected Paulus's flanks. The Soviets, well aware of the German weakness, planned two major operations. Operation Uranus was to encircle the German forces fighting on the Volga while Operation Mars was to take out the exposed Rzhev salient in Army Group Centre. Zhukov assembled a million men, 900 tanks and over 1,000 planes for his counter-attacks. Operation Mars, which began in November, was a failure. The German 9th Army, led by Model, a master of defensive warfare, inflicted over 300,000 casualties on the Red Army. Operation Uranus was another matter. On 19 November the storm broke. Over 3,500 Soviet artilleries opened up on Romanian positions north of Stalingrad. By noon, Soviet forces had broken through the Romanian defences, advancing some 80 kilometres (50 miles) before the day was over. The next day, Soviet forces crushed Romanian forces to the south of the city. Hitler, returning from Bavaria to his East Prussian headquarters, was out of contact for much of the 21 and 22 November. Without guidance, those on the scene did little. Perhaps there was little they could do. The fighting for Stalingrad had so eroded 6th Army's strength that even had it pulled out, it may have been in no condition to fight a major battle outside the city. Even so, General Zeitzler, who had replaced Halder as Chief of Staff, argued furiously with Hitler that he should allow the 6th Army to retreat. Assurances from Göring that the *Luftwaffe* could supply Paulus with the 500 tons of supplies per day he needed persuaded Hitler to stand fast. On 23 November, the Soviet pincers encircled the 6th Army, trapping 220,000 Germans in Stalingrad.

It was soon apparent that the *Luftwaffe*, already heavily committed to supplying Rommel, lacked sufficient planes to provide an effective airlift. In spite of heroic efforts, it managed to deliver only 105 tons of supplies on average a day. Some claim that this served only to prolong German agony for little purpose. This is mistaken. The planes succeeded in evacuating 42,000 wounded. More importantly, the fortunes of Army Group A in the Caucasus depended upon Paulus holding out as long as possible. Paulus's best hope of deliverance was Manstein who was given the job of relieving Stalingrad. On 12 December, Manstein's relief force set out. The first two days went well. Cutting through Russian defences, the lead panzers got to within 56 kilometres (35 miles) of Stalingrad. Manstein urged Hitler and Paulus to order 6th Army to break out and join up with him. Hitler refused. Whether Paulus's troops could have fought their way out of the city remains debatable. On 16 December, the Russians launched Operation Little Saturn, destroying Italian and Romanian forces along the River Don, north-west of Stalingrad, and forcing Manstein to abandon his efforts to reach the city. The Russian advance also threatened to cut off Army Group A, still deep in the Caucasus. Hitler grudgingly agreed that his troops should withdraw from the Caucasus.

These events sealed Stalingrad's fate. On 22 December, the Russians captured the last German airfield in the city. Now 6th Army could only be supplied by parachute drops. Paulus's army continued to defend stubbornly. On 7 January, the Russians sent emissaries into the city to demand surrender. The German high command refused, insisting that 6th Army fight to the end, thus preventing Stalin from redeploying forces from the Volga to battles farther west. Three days later, the Russians began a massive offensive, bombarding the city with 7,000 guns, the largest concentration of artillery in history. The expenditure of 911,000 artillery shells, 990,000 mortar shells and 24,000,000 rifle and machine-gun rounds by the Russians in January gives some indication of the ferocity of the battle. By 24 January, 6th Army, out of fuel and low on ammunition, had been split in two. Paulus asked permission to surrender. Again Hitler refused. Instead, he promoted Paulus to Field Marshal, hoping he would continue to fight. No German field marshal had ever surrendered. On 31 January, Paulus broke that tradition. He and his southern forces capitulated. His northern troops surrendered two days later.

Stalingrad was a major defeat for Hitler. Some 147,000 Germans and Romanians died in the fighting for the city and 110,000 became prisoners: of these only 5,000 survived captivity in Soviet camps. The *Wehrmacht*'s reputation for invincibility was destroyed. Dr Joseph Goebbels, Hitler's propaganda minister, spun the defeat as best he could, proclaiming three days of national mourning and the coming of 'Total War'. In truth, Stalingrad's importance may have been exaggerated. Far from being a turning point of the war, it was not even a totally catastrophic defeat. The Soviets had suffered 500,000 casualties – more than the Germans. Nor had the sacrifice of 6th Army been totally in vain. By holding out for so long, they enabled Army Group A to withdraw from the Caucasus. In March 1943, the Germans still held the territory they had at the start of 1942.

Conclusion

In the first half of 1942, the military advantage and strategic initiative lay with Germany and Japan; the skill and daring of their forces won impressive victories. However, the second half of 1942 witnessed a major shift in fortunes. With hindsight it is easy to see that the Japanese overreached themselves strategically and logistically in the Pacific. The Germans did the same in Russia and North Africa. But it was a close run thing. If a small group of US dive bombers had not been in exactly the right place at the right time on 4 June, Japan might have continued to hold the initiative in the Pacific. If the *Wehrmacht* had not got bogged down in Stalingrad, the Eastern Front might have had a very different complexion. As it was, Japan and Germany created opportunities for successful Allied counter-attacks. In 1943, the initiative would rest with the Allies. The balance of power was swinging irrevocably in their favour as mobilization of human resources accelerated and war production increased. Yet the Axis powers were still not defeated. At the end of 1942, Japan held more territory than it had at the end of 1941. German forces remained deep inside Russia. Rommel held out in North Africa. The Axis powers could still hope to split the Allied coalition apart, starve Britain into surrender, or discover a secret weapon. The game was still on and still to be won.

07

Axis retreat 1943–4

This chapter will cover:
- the war in North Africa in 1943
- the invasions of Sicily and Italy
- the war in Russia 1943–4
- the Pacific/Far Eastern war 1943–4.

By 1943, the odds were stacked heavily against Axis victory. However, if the Axis powers could successfully prolong the war, they could perhaps split the Allies and thus avert defeat. FDR called the three Allied powers the 'United Nations'. In reality, the three nations were far from united. Stalin, in particular, had little in common with FDR and Churchill. A deal between Stalin and Hitler (as in 1939) was not inconceivable. Given such a deal, it is difficult to see how the USA and Britain could easily have defeated Hitler, and this would have impacted negatively on their war effort against Japan. Even if no deal was struck, the Axis powers in early 1943 still had some prospects. In the event, the period between January 1943 and June 1944 was to be hugely successful for the Allies. By 1944, Italy had surrendered and Germany and Japan were no longer in control of events. What went wrong for the Axis powers? Why were the Allies so successful?

North Africa 1943

In January 1943, FDR and Churchill met at Casablanca to plan future strategy. The immediate question was not where to fight: Anglo–American forces were already engaged in North Africa. The key question was what to do once Axis forces had been expelled from Africa. Stalin was still urging the Western Allies to open up a Second Front in northern France. FDR's main advisers, not least Chief of Staff George Marshall, supported this strategy. From the start, Marshall had contended that the Western Allies, rather than dispersing their forces in the Mediterranean, should concentrate on one simple, massive blow at northern France. Once an Allied army was landed in France, it could head towards Germany. This would provide relief for Russia; without such relief Hitler might still triumph. It was also possible that if the Western Allies were not seen to be helping him, Stalin might reach some agreement with Hitler.

The key issue was whether a Second Front was feasible in 1943. American leaders, with far greater resources to commit to the war than Britain, saw an early Second Front as an opportunity rather than a risk. Churchill, by contrast, was not inclined to risk Britain's limited potential in what could be a costly failure. The Dieppe Raid on 19 August 1942 had proved that a cross-Channel invasion would be a hazardous enterprise. More than two-thirds of the 5,000 troops who landed at Dieppe failed to return. As Britain still had more forces in the European theatre than the USA, Churchill was able to play a more equal role in the discussions than would be the case at later conferences. He persuaded the Americans that an immediate Second Front was impossible. He was right to do so. None of the preconditions for a successful landing in France existed. The Allies first needed to win the Battle of the Atlantic, destroy the *Luftwaffe*, and build sufficient landing craft.

Given the postponement of an early Second Front, the Western Allies had to do something to divert German strength from the hard-pressed Russians. For the moment, the only place where they could confront their European enemies was in the Mediterranean theatre. The campaign in North Africa had still to be won. Once that was achieved, Sicily and Italy would be open to attack. Indeed, Churchill had developed a Mediterranean strategy that envisaged not only the invasion of Italy but also landings in the Balkans. He thought (incorrectly) that Italy and the Balkans were Germany's 'soft underbelly'.

On the last day of the Casablanca meeting, FDR announced that 'unconditional surrender' by the Axis powers was the only term on which the Allies would end the war. Anxious to avoid the troubles that President Wilson had run into by agreeing to peace with Germany on the basis of the Fourteen Points in 1918, he also wanted to give Stalin some guarantee that the Western powers would not make a compromise peace. It has been claimed that unconditional surrender was a mistake, and that it ensured Germany and Japan would fight to the bitter end and prolonged the war by preventing a negotiated peace. Such arguments are not convincing. The Axis powers were unlikely to yield until they had been totally defeated. A coup against Hitler was improbable. So with whom were the Allies supposed to negotiate? They were certainly not prepared to do so with Hitler.

In early 1943, Rommel was holed up in Tunisia and it seemed only a matter of time before he was forced to surrender. Hitler, however, was determined not to sell Tunisia cheaply. Two hundred and fifty thousand men were sent to reinforce Rommel and 400 planes were withdrawn from the Eastern Front to help supply them. This made little strategic sense. Given Allied aerial dominance, the supply route was certain to be tenuous at best.

The winter weather put paid to Allied hopes of a quick assault on Tunisia. By February when it became possible to move again, the 1st Army held a strong position along the coast. The US Second Corps held the line further south. The 8th Army, which had chased Rommel all the way from El Alamein, was approaching Mareth. Although surrounded, Rommel was in a position to strike at one or more of his enemies from a strong central position. On 14 February, he attacked the US Second Corps in southern Tunisia, causing initial mayhem. British reinforcements and the nature of the terrain helped to stop the German advance. US troops, well led by General George Patton, eventually pushed Rommel back to where his attack had begun. The Americans quickly learned the lessons of the fighting at Kasserine. Henceforward, the US army would be a far more effective organization.

Rommel now turned his attention to the British 8th Army on the Tunisian–Libyan border. In spite of four determined Axis attacks, Montgomery held his ground. Rommel, still sick, handed over his command to General Arnim and left Africa for ever. Back in Germany, he warned Hitler that it was 'plain suicide' for Axis forces to stay in Tunisia. His words had no effect. Hitler told him that he had lost his nerve. By now the Allies had total control of the skies. Informed by Ultra of virtually every Axis air and naval movement, Allied air attacks devastated the transport crossings to North Africa. At the end of March, Montgomery broke through the Mareth Line and edged northwards. In early May, the Allies captured Tunis. Arnim, with fewer than a hundred tanks still running, had to resort to distilling fuel from wines and spirits. On 13 May, he surrendered. Some 250,000 Germans and Italians were taken prisoner. This was the largest capitulation yet inflicted on Axis forces, a humiliation for Hitler and a disaster for Mussolini who had committed his destiny to the creation of a great Italian empire in Africa. The Desert War, which had cost the Axis powers over one million casualties, 8,000 planes and two million tons of shipping, was over.

The invasions of Sicily and Italy

At a meeting in Algeria in May 1943, Churchill and Marshall agreed to invade Sicily (Operation Husky). This had always been envisaged. Certainly, there was little else that the Allied forces in North Africa could do to engage the enemy. It was too late to move them back to Britain in time for a 1943 Second Front. If Husky went well, Allied forces could go on to invade Italy. While Churchill was almost alone in believing that Italy could become the back door into Germany, many Allied leaders did think that Italy's defeat would bring a decisive change in the balance of power. The field commanders were confident that the conquest of Sicily would be swift. It could and perhaps should have been swifter. There were few German troops in Sicily in June. Nevertheless, Allied leaders spent over two months preparing for the invasion. In one sense, the time was used profitably. A massive air campaign destroyed much of the capability of the *Luftwaffe* in Sicily and Italy.

Eisenhower was supreme commander of the invasion of Sicily. The invading force was to comprise the British 8th Army, led by Montgomery, and the American 7th Army, led by Patton. Eisenhower's tact and patience helped ease the friction between his quarrelsome generals. The Royal Navy devised a clever ruse for deceiving the Germans about Allied intentions. A dead body dressed as a British officer was placed in the sea off Spain with details of a bogus plan to attack Greece and Sardinia. The plan worked: the false information was fed to Hitler by Spain. Accordingly, German warships sailed from Sicily to Greece, and a panzer division was sent from France to the Balkans. The Axis powers were thus taken by surprise when, on 10 July, Allied forces invaded Sicily in what was to be the largest single day amphibious operation of the war. One hundred and fifty thousand troops landed from nearly 3,000 ships, protected by over 1,000 aircraft. The 8th Army landed in the south-east, the US 7th Army in the west. The objective of both armies was to reach Messina as quickly as possible, preventing as many Germans as possible from escaping to the Italian mainland across the Messina Straits. Patton, driving east, had farther to go. Montgomery, who devised the plan, had given pride of place to his 8th Army. However, German troops put up dogged resistance in the foothills of Mount Etna and slowed down the British advance. To Montgomery's chagrin, Patton reached Messina on 17 August, a few hours before him. Due to a mixture of bad luck and poor co-ordination of Anglo–American air, sea and ground forces, 40,000 Germans and 70,000 Italians were ferried safely to Italy. To make matters worse, Patton, the hero of the campaign, displaying a characteristic lack of self-control, slapped two US troops suffering from shell shock and malaria. The incidents almost ended his military career, and resulted in his replacement by the less-effective Omar Bradley.

In hindsight, Operation Husky was poorly planned and poorly executed. Yet, the capture of Sicily was no empty victory. The southern Mediterranean was now open to Allied shipping. By shortening the route to the Middle and Far East, some four

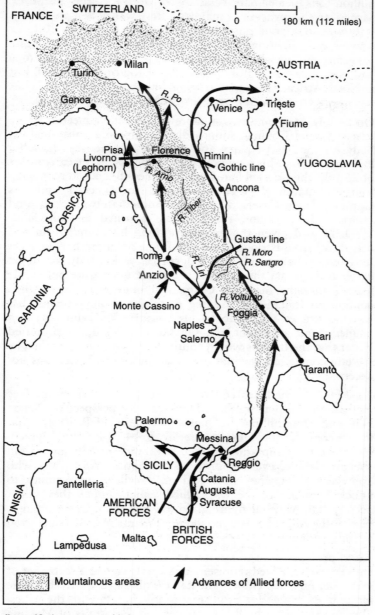

figure 10 the conquest of Italy

million tons of merchant vessels were freed for other purposes. Moreover, the invasion of mainland Italy was now a possibility. Italy was in a poor position to defend herself. Over 200,000 Italians were fighting in Russia. Nearly 600,000 were fighting partisans in Yugoslavia and the Balkans. Some 160,000 men had been killed or captured in Sicily, on top of the 200,000 lost in North Africa. The Italian economy was approaching collapse. Its cities were hit both by strike action and Allied bombers.

On 24 July, Mussolini was summoned to attend a meeting of the Fascist Grand Council, supposedly the supreme policy-making body for the Fascist party and so Italy. In practice, Mussolini had always made his own policy. Nonetheless, in the early hours of 25 July, the Council had a vote of no confidence in him. King Victor Emmanuel was appointed to succeed him as Commander-in-Chief. The King immediately sacked and imprisoned Mussolini. Few Italians mourned his fall. Since 1940, he had given the Italians nothing but humiliation and defeat. Marshal Badoglio, the new Prime Minister, hoped to get Italy out of the war. He believed, correctly, that Italy would get better terms from the Allies if she made a separate peace. He feared, though, that the Germans would resist any Allied landing on Italian soil. Aiming to minimize the damage that warring armies might do to his country, Badoglio played a tangled game of diplomacy. On the one hand, he promised Hitler that the Italians would continue to fight. On the other, he secretly conducted negotiations with the Allies. Hitler was not deceived.

As Marshall had feared, the Americans found themselves increasingly drawn into a Mediterranean perspective. When FDR and Churchill met in Quebec in August, FDR insisted that the Second Front must occur in 1944. Churchill agreed. However, the temptation to take advantage of Mussolini's fall was irresistible, even to previously sceptical Americans who appreciated that they now had an excellent opportunity to knock Italy out of the war. Allied leaders hoped they might occupy Italy without fighting. So did Badoglio. Unfortunately, neither the Allied high command nor the Italian leadership acted quickly enough.

After protracted negotiations in Lisbon between Badoglio's emissaries and Allied representatives, Italy signed a secret act of surrender on 3 September. The Italians obtained relatively gentle terms in exchange for promising to co-operate with the Allies. On the same day, the 8th Army crossed the Straits of Messina and landed in Calabria. Five days later, the news of Italy's surrender was broadcast. The Germans, who had anticipated the event, immediately occupied Rome, forestalling a planned Allied airborne attack. Badoglio and the King fled south as German forces occupied central and northern Italy. In Greece and Yugoslavia, Italian troops were disarmed by the Germans. In those instances where they resisted, the Germans took savage revenge. On 12 September, Mussolini, rescued by a brilliant airborne operation, was reinstalled as dictator. He was very much Hitler's puppet. For all practical purposes, northern Italy was a German-occupied country. A vicious war between anti-fascist partisans and Mussolini's fascist militia, backed up by German forces, was soon underway in northern Italy.

The Allies hoped to reach Rome by the end of 1943. The September landings in Calabria went well. Resistance was light as the Germans retreated northwards. On 9 September, another Allied army led by US General Mark Clark landed at Salerno, 48 kilometres (30 miles) south of Naples. Kesselring, the overall commander of German forces in the Mediterranean, determined to oppose the landings. Clark's forces therefore faced stiff resistance. Vastly superior firepower ensured that the Allied forces secured a bridgehead. Kesselring, unable to drive the Allies back into the sea, decided to make them pay the highest possible price for every metre of Italy. His main allies were the Appennine Mountains and the miserable autumn weather which turned the land into a sea of mud. Kesselring made his first stand on the Volturno River, north of Naples. He then retreated to a much stronger defensive position – the Gustav Line. Essential to this position was the mountain-top monastery of Monte Cassino, the birthplace of the Benedictine Order. By the end of 1943 Allied forces had advanced only 113 kilometres (70 miles) beyond Salerno. They were still 129 kilometres (80 miles) short of Rome.

German defences seemed so strong that the Allies hit on the idea of a landing at Anzio on 22 January 1944, a few kilometres south of Rome and nearly 97 kilometres (60 miles) north of the Gustav Line. The Anzio landings took the Germans totally by surprise. However, instead of breaking out, the Allied Commander, General Lucas, spent over a week consolidating his bridgehead. This gave Kesselring precious time. When Lucas tried to advance, he faced fierce German resistance and made no headway. Indeed, Allied forces were soon on the defensive as Hitler ordered (costly) German counter-attacks. A stalemate ensued. Over the winter of 1943-4 the Allies made no impression on the Gustav Line. Allied planes bombed Monte Cassino to little effect: German forces were not in the buildings. After the bombing they did occupy the monastery's ruins which were better for defence purposes than the intact building. Finally in mid-May, Free French forces captured the key mountain Petrella Peak. This helped Polish forces capture Monte Cassino on 18 May. On 23 May, Kesselring gave up the Gustav Line and retreated northwards. The same day, the Anzio garrison advanced out of its beachhead. General Clark, more interested in his 5th Army being the liberator of Rome than destroying the *Wehrmacht*, allowed the retreating Germans to get away and consolidate a new line just north of Florence – the Gothic Line. Clark's entry into Rome on 4 June had few consequences. Fearing some kind of German countermeasure, few Romans turned out to welcome the Allies. The Pope highlighted his ambiguous war record by asking that the Allies keep black troops out of Rome.

Allied progress in Italy had been slow and disappointing. This was partly due to faulty conception. Italy was more a backbone than a 'soft underbelly'. Churchill's notion that Allied troops might push over the Alps and burst into central Europe was whimsical in the extreme. Allied leadership in Italy did not help matters. General Alexander, the overall commander, was unable to control his subordinates effectively. Thus the Anglo–American armies in Italy fought their own battles. Clark – ambitious, ruthless and more impressed with style than substance – was to prove one of the most disappointing American commanders of the war. It is easy to be critical of the Allied campaign in Italy. Yet it did tie down some 35 German divisions in Italy and dozens of other divisions elsewhere in south-east Europe, placed to anticipate further amphibious landings. These divisions might otherwise have fought on the Russian Front or helped defend France in 1944. The campaign eliminated the Italian armed forces from the war. It also provided the Allies with airfields from which to bomb targets in the Balkans, central Europe and southern France. It is not clear, even now, whether these gains were worth the price paid for them.

Russia 1943-4

The German surrender at Stalingrad is often seen as marking the end of Hitler's hopes of victory in Russia. In January and

February 1943, the Germans had been pushed back along the entire front. They retreated in something approaching confusion from their gains in 1942 to the line from which they had started the previous summer. However, Stalingrad did not spell the certainty of Soviet victory. The *Wehrmacht* remained formidable. In February, Manstein contained the Russian offensive in the south, counter-attacking when the Russians were running out of fuel and ammunition. He recaptured Kharkov and established a new defence line along the Donets River. Stalin now showed interest in a negotiated peace. This would have involved Germany evacuating all Russian territory. Hitler, confident that he could hold on to his conquests in Russia, showed no interest.

Hitler rejected the advice of Manstein and others that the *Wehrmacht* conduct a mobile, fluid defence in 1943 as a means of conserving resources while wearing down the enemy. Instead, he insisted on an offensive – Operation Citadel. Aware that Germany would have to fight Anglo–American forces in the Mediterranean or France, he needed a decisive victory in the East. He thought he knew where he could win one. Having retaken Voronezh, Russian troops occupied a large salient, (161 kilometres (100 miles) deep and 241 kilometres (150 miles) wide), centred on the town of Kursk. The Kursk 'bulge' offered the possibility for a German encirclement. A northern army (led by Kluge) would head south from Orel, while a southern army (led by Manstein) would drive north-east from Kharkov, trapping the Russians within the salient.

The Russians were well aware that the salient was likely to be a great temptation to the Germans. The Red Army General Staff was confident that a mixture of in-depth defences and well-planned counter-attacks could thwart German attack. By now a whole generation of younger Russian commanders had started to emerge – combat-hardened men who were proving themselves the equal in every respect to their German counterparts. Stalin too had learned lessons – not least that he could trust Zhukov. He was persuaded by his military leaders to allow the Germans to make the opening move in 1943. The Russians undertook a massive programme to prepare Kursk's defences, while also deploying substantial reserves to be thrown into the battle at the decisive moment. The Soviets kept most of their measures hidden from the Germans. Conversely, intelligence from British and other sources allowed Stalin to anticipate where the main German blow would fall.

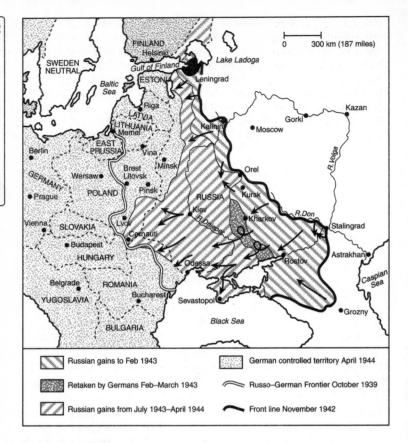

figure 11 Russia 1943–4

Citadel, planned initially for May, was postponed until July. Hitler's reasoning was sound. Throughout the Russian campaign, the Russian T-34 tank had proved better than German armour. The Germans had now developed new, more formidable tanks – not least the heavy Tiger and the medium Panther. Hitler delayed Citadel to increase the numbers of these tanks. What he did not know was that two new Russian tanks, the SU122 and the SU152, were as good as anything the Germans had produced. Hitler's uncharacteristic insistence on delay – in previous campaigns he had consistently backed surprise over preparation – probably destroyed Citadel's chances of success. While more German tanks did become available, the Russians had more time to prepare their defences. By July, the Russian defence lines around Kursk were sown with half a million mines. In an unusual admission of foreboding, Hitler told Guderian just before Citadel began that every time he thought of the operation he felt sick. He perhaps comforted himself with the thought that the Germans had always won in the summer even though in general winter had been too much for them.

The Battle of Kursk – the climactic battle of the war – began on 5 July. The Germans, with 435,000 men, 9,960 artillery pieces and 3,155 tanks, attacked the salient from north and south. The Russian defensive positions were manned by over a million troops with 13,013 artillery pieces and 3,275 tanks. In reserve were an additional 449,133 soldiers, 6,536 artillery pieces and 1,506 tanks. In many ways, David was attacking Goliath. As the Germans advanced, they encountered intense resistance and had difficulty clearing a path through the minefields. In the air the *Luftwaffe* and Red Air Force fought a desperate struggle for superiority which neither side won. On 12 July, with the German pincers still 80 kilometres (50 miles) apart, Zhukov launched a counter-attack on the German positions around Orel. A day-long tank battle, involving some 1,300 tanks on each side, ensued – the world's greatest tank battle until the 1991 Gulf War. In losses the conflict was a draw: the Soviets lost 400 tanks and the Germans 320. But the Soviets held their ground and had far more tanks to lose. That evening, Hitler, for once acting decisively, called off the offensive, overruling Manstein who pleaded for the remaining tanks in the reserve to be thrown into battle. Manstein's belief that he could break through to Kursk was wishful thinking: the Russians were threatening to annihilate most of Germany's remaining armoured divisions. Kursk, not Stalingrad, was the turning point in the war. It ended Hitler's hopes of holding on to the bulk of his conquests in Russia. From now on, Germany would be permanently on the defensive on the Eastern Front.

By the summer of 1943, the Red Army enjoyed a significant numerical superiority: 5.75 million troops, 7,855 tanks and 21,000 anti-tank guns against three million German troops with 2,088 tanks and 8,000 anti-tank guns. The Soviets also possessed advantages in intelligence gathering and in operations' execution. Soviet deception methods consistently misled the Germans about where the next strike would come.

The Red Army was helped considerably by the Lend-Lease programme: US trucks gave the Russians speed and flexibility over German troops who were still very reliant on horses.

In the summer and autumn, the Soviets launched offensives to the north and south of Kursk which the Germans were unable to block. The Soviets focused their attention on the Ukraine. Disregarding Hitler's orders to hold on to Kharkov, Manstein was forced back to the line of the River Dnieper. The long, drawn-out battle for the Dneiper continued through October to December. On 6 November, Kiev was taken. By the end of December, Russian forces had cut off the German army in the Crimea, which had been forbidden by Hitler to evacuate.

Rather than trying to encircle the Germans, the Russians tried to find weak points to attack. Whenever they encountered strong resistance, they broke off and renewed their advance elsewhere. This continual pressure kept the Germans permanently off balance, always responding to one desperate situation after another. Soviet forces were led by elite Guard divisions, armed with tanks, artillery and rockets. Once a breakthrough was achieved, the mass of infantry followed, often undisciplined and living off the countryside. They were true cannon fodder. (After the war Zhukov told Eisenhower that the best way to clear minefields was simply to march infantry over them.) After the infantry came another elite corps: the military police who restored order and drove the infantry forward to fresh assaults.

The heavy fighting in the summer and autumn further wore down German divisions and increased the imbalance between the opposing forces. However, the German front did not break. Only 98,000 Germans were taken prisoner in the four months of campaigning between August and December. German troops fought desperately, inculcated with the values and assumptions of Nazi ideology. Nazi indoctrination was backed up by a military justice system whose ruthlessness was only exceeded by the Soviet army. In the First World War the German army had executed only 48 of its soldiers for breaches of discipline. In the Second World War it executed between 13,000 and 15,000 soldiers as a direct result of courts-martial for subversion, desertion and disobedience. This total does not include the tens of thousands ordered to serve in penal battalions, which was almost the equivalent of a death sentence.

There was relatively little activity in the north in 1943. In September, the Germans began construction of defences – the

Panther Line – stretching from the Baltic to the swamps south of Pskov. German engineers, helped by thousands of slave labourers, laid 201 kilometres (125 miles) of barbed wire and dug vast trench systems and anti-tank ditches. Yet Army Group North had not pulled back to the new positions when the Red Army struck in mid-January 1944. The Red Army's 60 divisions faced 20 German divisions and had a six to one advantage in tanks. Within four days, the German situation was desperate. Nevertheless, Hitler ordered his troops to fight where they stood rather than retreat to the Panther Line. They did not pull back until February. German forces survived but at an exorbitant cost. Had German troops withdrawn in January, Hitler could have saved substantial reserves for use in the south. The Russian advance meant that the siege of Leningrad was finally lifted. The city of three million people had been besieged by the Germans for 890 days. Some 200,000 inhabitants had been killed by German shells. Another 630,000 had died of cold or starvation.

The Russians kept up the pressure in the south. Their vehicles were able to cope with the mud better than German tanks and lorries. Hitler declared a number of towns as fortresses in which the troops would fight to the death. This had little effect. By April 1944, Soviet troops had reached – and breached – German defences along the river Dnestr. In May, the Crimea was finally liberated.

Thus, by April 1944 the Russians had recovered virtually the whole of pre-war Soviet territory. Between July 1943 and April 1944, the Red Army had advanced 965 kilometres (600 miles) in some places. The future looked grim for Hitler. The initiative was firmly with the Russians who could concentrate their superior forces in a particular sector while much of the German army was static. In May, there was some reprieve for the Germans as operations came to a temporary halt. The fighting had exhausted the Soviet armies. Moreover, Stalin, like Hitler, was now awaiting the opening of the Allies' Second Front in France. Soviet action thereafter would depend on the outcome of the amphibious operation.

The Pacific 1943–4

While the pace of the war against Japan was to a large extent dictated by the 'Europe first' strategy, Allied forces were strong enough to go on the offensive in 1943. As in Europe, there were strategic differences between Britain and the USA. There was also tension between US commanders, caused partly by disagreements over strategy (not least between the army and navy), and partly by personal ambitions and enmities. Admiral Ernest King was the foremost champion of war against Japan. Aged 64 in 1943 (past the age of mandatory retirement), even his admirers could find little nice to say about his character. He made life miserable for anyone around him, including his wife and seven children. Yet his mastery of every aspect of naval warfare and administration made him indispensable. King knew that the USA was building ships at a rate Japan could not match. By late 1943, the USA had a 10:4 advantage over Japan in heavy fleet carriers, a 9:5 advantage in light carriers, a 35:3 advantage in small escort carriers and twice as many battleships. The US superiority would be even greater in 1944. In addition, the new US carriers had planes that outclassed the best Japanese aircraft. The USA also maintained its intelligence advantage. This reaped considerable reward, not least on 18 April 1943 when US planes were able to intercept and shoot down Admiral Yamamoto's plane. His death was a significant blow to the Japanese.

In 1943, King won formal recognition from FDR and Churchill that the war with Japan could be won only by a US naval campaign in the Pacific, not by an American–Chinese–British coalition force based in Asia. King's basic strategy was to island hop, capturing Japanese-held islands on the way towards Japan itself. The problem was which islands to 'hop' to. While General MacArthur wanted to advance along the northern coast of New Guinea towards the Philippines, Admiral Nimitz proposed a sweep through the chain of small atolls in the central Pacific – the Gilberts, the Marshalls, the Carolines and the Marianas – towards Formosa. In spring 1943, the Joint Chiefs of Staff agreed to support both MacArthur and Nimitz. US forces thus advanced on two fronts. The Pacific campaigns ultimately depended on how closely the opposing forces could integrate air, land and naval operations, since no element of military power by itself could prove decisive. Both sides found it hard to get inter-service co-operation. However, the Japanese problem was more serious. While the Joint Chiefs could and did enforce US co-operation, the Japanese army and navy often fought essentially different wars. The lack of ports and airfields in the Pacific remained a serious problem for the Americans. A staggering 4.5 tons of material was needed to deploy one US soldier abroad and one ton a month thereafter to maintain him.

There was a pattern to US 'island hopping'. Initial sea battles often decided the long-term outcome of campaigns by preventing the Japanese from reinforcing their island garrisons. Consequently, the Battle of the Bering Sea (March 1943) decided the fate of the Aleutian Islands. During the Battle of the Bismarck Sea (March 1943), US bombers sank eight troopships and ten warships bringing reinforcements to Japanese defenders in New Guinea and the Solomons. Thereafter, the Japanese dared not risk sending transports to points under siege, making it possible to use the tactic of neutralizing Japanese strongholds with air and sea power, and moving on, leaving them to die on the vine. (Admiral Wilkinson called it 'leapfrogging'.) The first strongpoint left stranded by this strategy was Rabaul. By late 1943, MacArthur's US and Australian forces controlled most of Papua, New Guinea. Halsey's marines had been similarly successful in the Solomons. In November, an amphibious force seized part of Bougainville in the northern Solomons, enabling US planes to attack Rabaul on a daily basis. A Japanese fleet that moved to challenge the operation was beaten in the Battle of Empress Augusta Bay. When the Admiralty Islands were taken in March 1944, Rabaul's isolation was complete and 100,000 Japanese were stranded. MacArthur now had the Philippines firmly in his sights.

In the central Pacific, Nimitz orchestrated attacks on successive chains of islands. In November 1943, the Americans assaulted Makin and Tarawa in the Gilbert Islands. Makin, where the Japanese had only a small force, was soon cleared. Nearly 1,000 Americans lost their lives on Tarawa, rooting out 4,000 Japanese who refused to surrender. Makin and Tarawa provided airfields from which to soften up strongpoints in the Marshall Islands. These islands were taken by US forces in February 1944. The US navy then turned its attention to the major Japanese base at Truk, 1,931 kilometres (1,200 miles) to the west in the Carolines. On 17 and 18 February, a carrier force dropped 30 times as much explosive on Truk as the Japanese had dropped on Pearl Harbor. Truk was then unusable and, like Rabaul, was bypassed as Nimitz turned his attention to the Marianas.

In India, the new British Commander-in-Chief, General Wavell, set about reorganizing the Indian army for an assault on Burma. As part of his strategy, he formed the Chindits. Led by General Wingate, their job was to penetrate behind Japanese lines and cause as much trouble as possible. The Chindits' first expedition in February 1943 lost nearly 1,000 men but severely harassed the Japanese for four months. In October, Admiral Lord Mountbatten was appointed to command the newly-formed South East Asia Command. There were few more glamorous (and ineffective) wartime commanders. General Bill Slim, commander of the new British–Indian 14th Army, was far more effective. Over the winter of 1943–4, both the Japanese and British prepared to take the offensive. The Japanese attacked first in March 1944. Advancing quickly, they soon threatened the key towns of Imphal and Kohima. Surrounded and cut off from each other, Slim's forces fought tenaciously, withstanding sieges which lasted from April to June. Slim was able to use his aerial superiority to keep both towns supplied. By June, Japanese attempts to take Imphal and Kohima had cost them 60,000 men. The 14th Army lost 16,700. The Japanese were forced to lift the two sieges and retreat back into Burma. Slim's forces now prepared to go on the offensive.

The war in China went better for Japan. For most of 1943, FDR maintained his high regard for Chiang Kai-shek. The US view was that China was capable of playing a major role in the war against Japan, and that it was essential to send Chiang as much equipment as possible. During 1943, it became increasingly clear that Chiang had little appetite for offensives against the Japanese. FDR's confidence in Chiang was therefore already dented by the time a major Japanese offensive in China in the spring of 1944 wiped out whole Chinese armies and captured many US airbases. Chiang's troops and the US 14th Air Force had no option but to retreat deeper into China.

Conclusion

The various campaigns during 1943–4 suggested that the dazzling successes of blitzkrieg were giving way to an attritional struggle in which brute force counted for as much or more than operational or tactical skill. Germany and Japan could not match the combined capacities of their adversaries. However, it was not just a question of resources and big battalions. Allied commanders in 1943–4 displayed a more skilled approach to war – an approach learned by hard experience. By early 1944, it was clear that the tide of war was flowing fast in the Allies' favour. Italy had surrendered. German forces were in helter-skelter retreat on the Eastern Front, and the commitment of her allies – Romania, Bulgaria, Hungary and Finland – was uncertain. US forces in the Pacific were getting ever closer to the home islands of Japan. The main question was not 'if' but 'when' would Germany and Japan be defeated. Much depended on the long anticipated Allied cross-Channel invasion of France.

08

resistance and collaboration

This chapter will cover:
- Hitler's 'New Order'
- Resistance movements in Europe
- Japan's 'New Order'.

On 10 June 1944, troops of the SS 'Das Reich' Division, hastening north to the fighting in Normandy, occupied the French village of Oradour-sur-Glane, 26 kilometres (16 miles) from Limoges. The troops, angered by the fact that they had been constantly held up by sniping and demolition, determined on vengeance. Oradour's entire population of some 650 people was ordered to assemble on the fairground. The men were taken in groups of 20 to a nearby farm and shot. The women and children were herded into the village church. Soldiers then brought in a large box, which they placed near the altar. Within minutes, the box which contained explosives blew up, setting fire to the church. Women and children were shot as they tried to climb out of the windows. Only ten people, most badly burned, managed to feign death and escape. The ruins of the village, which has never been rebuilt, remain a testament to the brutal action taken by the Germans against those who resisted their rule. The Japanese took similar action in Asia. After 1945, it was convenient to assume that most Europeans and Asians were resistors of one sort or another. The truth was more complex. In many areas the conquerors encountered little resistance. Indeed, some peoples and regimes proved keen to collaborate with their new rulers. How much collaboration was there? What was the extent of the resistance?

Hitler's 'New Order'

Hitler's ultimate intention was to create a 'New Order' organized on racist principles. He considered western Europeans to be acceptable, in a way that Slavs in eastern Europe were not. German rule in the West was thus very different to German rule in the East. German control in western Europe was something of a patchwork. Greater Germany, which by now comprised virtually all the German-speaking peoples of Europe, annexed very little territory. While there were military governors in (occupied) France and Belgium, Norway, Denmark and Holland were granted some rights of self-administration. Vichy France, like Croatia and Slovakia, was very much a German satellite state. Provided there was no opposition, Hitler was content to leave national governments in office and rule through the existing structures of authority. He even conceded rights of parliamentary government to the Danes who conducted a democratic election as late as 1943.

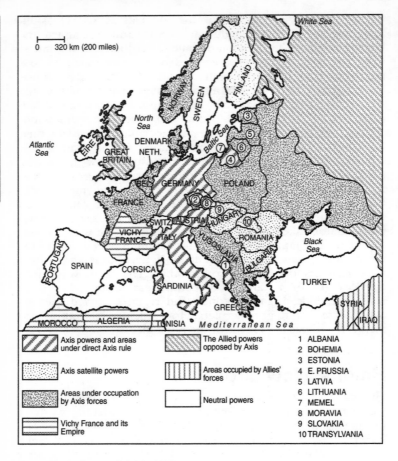

figure 12 the German Reich in 1942

Something of a veil has been drawn across the extent of
collaboration with Germany in western Europe. Collaboration
varied according to location, circumstance and time. At one end
of the spectrum, there were members of indigenous fascist
groups, eager to take their place in the New Order. At the other
were those who adopted a live-and-let-live philosophy. Between
the extremes there existed varying degrees of collaboration. The
number of fascist collaborators was relatively small. Though a
few figures such as Vidkun Quisling in Norway were placed in
important positions, in general the Germans were not

enthusiastic about local Nazis. They realized that the new governments in western Europe would have to have some credibility with the local people if German interests were to be served. Relatively few west Europeans were prepared to fight for the Germans (for example, in Waffen SS units) but some pro-Nazi collaborators were effective in helping maintain order at home. There were other active, non-fascist, collaborators. The mass unemployment of the 1930s had led to a widespread disillusionment with capitalism and liberalism. Many Catholic Europeans accepted authoritarianism and had little sympathy with parliamentary democracy, widely discredited as corrupt, divisive and inefficient. Many Europeans were hostile both to communism and the threat from the USA and Britain – the archetypical liberal-capitalist states. Given the reasonably widespread desire to protect European civilization from communism and Americanization, there were opportunities for Germany to gain adherents for a European unity programme.

Hitler, however, had no vision of a Europe that was anything other than a façade for German domination. Economically, western (like eastern) Europe was organized for exploitation by Germany. Occupied countries were supposed to serve the German economy by providing food and raw materials while Germany concentrated on industrial production. By 1944, there were eight million foreign workers in Germany – a quarter of the workforce. While some of these came voluntarily from countries which were (purportedly) Germany's allies, most came involuntarily from occupied countries. Foreign workers' treatment was largely determined by their racial origins. While Russians and Poles were usually little better than slave labourers, west Europeans were usually better treated. Nevertheless, the transportation of people to Germany was extremely unpopular in western Europe. Those conservatives, who hoped that Hitler's New Order would usher in an era of western European co-operation which would protect European culture from Russian or Anglo-Saxon influence, were soon disillusioned.

Passive collaboration was more common than active collaboration. German occupation forces established working relationships with local victuallers and police, while individual Germans struck up personal relationships with local women. Businesses and industries reoriented themselves to provide for the German market. Vichy France and other semi-satellite regimes sought, with varying degrees of enthusiasm, to accommodate to the New Order while promoting their own interests. The bulk of west Europeans, through acceptance of the German presence were, in effect, passive collaborators. There was little else they could be.

Barbarism in eastern Europe

In the East, racial and political ideology resulted in a descent into barbarism on a scale unknown in the West. In Hitler's view, the Slavs were an inferior race occupying living space that would be better utilized by superior German stock. In Russia, moreover, a regime existed based on communism – a political philosophy that was the very antithesis of national socialism. This had a considerable impact on how conquered peoples were treated. Except in the Baltic States of Latvia, Estonia and Lithuania, there was little scope for collaboration in eastern Europe.

As the *Wehrmacht* advanced in September 1939, SS *Einsatzgruppen* (the special task force) followed behind. Their job was to systematically find and kill known Polish patriots, as well as other 'undesirable elements'. Thousands were shot. Western Poland was incorporated directly into the Reich. In order to make way for ethnic German settlers, a million Poles were evicted and dumped in the General Government, which comprised the remainder of German-occupied Poland. Under the rule of Hans Frank and the SS, the native population was rapidly reduced to the status of subhuman slaves whose native culture was to be eradicated. The area was systematically plundered for food and other resources. Harshly governed labour camps were established. Even without taking the Jewish population into account, several million Poles died as a result.

What had been started in Poland was continued on a grander scale in Russia. Russians and Ukrainians were treated appallingly by their new rulers. Mass executions, deportations of thousands of inhabitants, confiscation and destruction of property, and plundering of food and other resources were systematically undertaken. Millions of Soviet civilians died as a result of Nazi occupation policies.

In the West, the ideological dimension of the war and its effect on behaviour was limited. POWs were treated with at least a modicum of respect and adherence to international law. The murder of POWs in cold blood was rare. The same was not true in the East. Many captured Russian troops were simply shot as vermin or in retaliation for hard fighting or imagined (and actual) murder and mutilation of Germans. A policy of malevolent neglect meant that the majority of those who were taken prisoner died of starvation, exhaustion and disease while confined in vast holding pens in transit to permanent POW labour camps. Over three million Soviet POWs died. The Russians treated German prisoners equally savagely. Those POWs who were not killed outright were sent to the East to perform hard labour without adequate food, clothing or shelter. Over a million German POWs died.

German ruthlessness was counterproductive. It simply encouraged resistance. Furthermore, the Germans lost potential support. Most Ukrainians, for example, desperate to see an end to Stalin's brutal rule, might well have collaborated with the Germans. However, the brutality of Nazi occupation made accommodation difficult. Even more carelessly in the East than the West, Germany threw away the possibility of gaining mass support.

Resistance in Europe

In Britain's darkest hour in July 1940, Churchill established the Special Operations Executive (SOE). Its aim was to support resistance to Hitler's rule in occupied Europe. Churchill's dream of setting Europe 'ablaze' was not without foundation. Few Europeans welcomed German rule. Some fled either at the time of invasion or later and created forces supported by the Allies, such as the Free French, led by de Gaulle. There were also those left behind who were prepared to resist. Their numbers grew as the exploitive nature of Hitler's New Order became clear. In 1941, for example, the Germans looted Greece of much of its foodstuffs: mass famine (in which over 40,000 Greeks died) was the inevitable result. Thereafter, no self-respecting Greek was willing to co-operate with Germany. The pitiless nature of the German occupation of eastern Europe provided more than enough reason to resist. In western Europe, the growing demands for labour to be sent to Germany in the latter part of the war, combined with the increasingly harsh measures taken by the Gestapo and other security forces, drove some off the fence and into the resistance camp. In southern France, for example, some Frenchmen took to the hills and joined the resistance movement known as the Maquis rather than be shipped off to Germany as forced labourers. Resistance grew as the tide of war turned in the Allies' favour. The SOE and the US Office of Strategic Services (OSS) provided logistical support when and where they thought appropriate. Moscow did the same on a more limited scale.

Resistance movements, however, faced grave problems, not least the fact that they were split into communist and anti-communist groups. After the 1939 Nazi–Soviet Pact, European communist parties, through the influence of the Comintern, had not joined in resistance activities. Operation Barbarossa changed everything. Russia now ordered all communist parties to initiate subversive activity. Sometimes the communists collaborated with non-communist groups. Elsewhere there was creative competition. De Gaulle, alarmed by the prospect that his Free French movement might fall under communist control in France, created a pan-resistance 'Secret Army' led by a National Resistance Council under his authority. This helped to unite and strengthen the (relatively small) French resistance movement. Nevertheless, the French communists had their own agenda and only co-operated with other resistance groups when it suited their interests. At times, as in Greece and Yugoslavia, there was civil war between left and right resistance groups.

Harsh punishment deterred many from getting involved in resistance movements. The German authorities, supported by domestic police forces and satellite security forces, resorted to extreme measures to retain control, including retaliatory mass reprisals. A classic example was the extinction of the population of the village of Lidice in the Czech Republic in May 1942 after the assassination of Reinhard Heydrich, Himmler's deputy. The Germans' general policy was to execute ten civilians for each German killed by guerrilla activity. Fear of reprisal encouraged informing, which in turn increased the efficiency of German control. Most resistance organizations had to devote a high proportion of their energy to combating informers, nowhere with complete success.

The German system of control was efficient and economic. It is unlikely, for instance, that there were more than 6,500 German security forces in France at any stage during the war. Between 1940 and 1944, the number and size of armed groups in France were small and there were few major acts of sabotage. The French resistance only came into its own in the summer of 1944 after the Allied invasion of Normandy. Resistance fighters in Brittany wrested much of the region from the Germans ahead of the Allied advance. Other resistance groups were responsible for the destruction of railways, power and telephone lines. Yet the French resistance's role should not be exaggerated. Even in July

1944, it deployed at most 116,000 armed men. In July, the Germans determined to make an example of the several thousand Maquisards on the Vercors plateau in the Grenoble region. German forces cordoned the plateau while SS troops landed by glider on the summit. Between the 18 and 23 July they brutally killed everyone they found there. The resistance fighters lacked the training and heavy weapons needed to engage professional troops.

The degree of success of any resistance movement was determined by geographical factors. Eastern Europe had terrain – mountain, forest and swamp – well suited for partisan activity. Such areas, though, lacked the resources necessary to support armed guerrillas and were too distant from Allied bases for supplies to be easily sent. Most of occupied western Europe was unsuited to irregular operations. (Denmark, Belgium, Holland and northern France are flat, treeless and densely inhabited.) The only part of western Europe in which the terrain favoured resistance activity was northern Norway. Nonetheless, the population was so sparse and the density of German occupation troops so high (Hitler, fearing a British invasion, grossly over-garrisoned Norway throughout the war), that all guerrilla activity had to be organized outside the country. While internal Norwegian resistance was of limited significance, Norwegian resistance fighters from Scotland did succeed in destroying the heavy-water plant at Vermork in February 1943, thus crippling the German atomic weapons programme. The Italian Alps and Appennines were regions favourable to partisan activity, and there was considerable Italian resistance to German rule after 1943.

Risings against the German occupation forces invariably met with disaster. In July 1944, German forces crushed an insurrection by Slovaks in eastern Czechoslovakia. In Poland the 'Home Army', under the direction of the government in exile in London, unleashed the Warsaw rising in August 1944. The Home Army hoped to seize Warsaw before the arrival of the Red Army led to the installation of a Polish communist regime. The gamble failed. Stalin halted his forces outside Warsaw, content to see his Polish enemies slaughtered by the Germans. In seven weeks of combat, tens of thousands of Poles died. The rising did not force Hitler to seriously reduce his front-line strength. Far from demonstrating what insurrections might contribute to Hitler's defeat, Warsaw stood as a warning of how dangerous it was, even in 1944, for subject peoples to take up arms against the *Wehrmacht.*

Hitler faced sustained guerrilla resistance in only two areas: first in the rear of the Eastern Front, in vast forests and in the impenetrable Pripet Marshes; and second in Yugoslavia. The Russian partisan formations were initially composed of surviving regular troops who retained the will and some of the means to fight on. For recruitment they depended upon volunteers from the local population. By the summer of 1944, there were tens of thousands of partisans who, in the face of ferocious German repression, carried out useful acts of sabotage. Despite this, the losses inflicted by partisans, whether on the personnel or the material of the *Wehrmacht*, did not seriously damage the German war effort.

The most effective partisan warfare was in Yugoslavia. Its mountainous terrain and long coastline which gave easy access to SOE's supply units was ideally suited to irregular warfare. Hitler's aggression in April 1941 outraged Serb national pride and by its suddenness left thousands of military units in possession of weapons and territory which provided the basis for irregular operations. The first to rise in revolt were Serbian monarchists, led by Mihailovic. His Chetniks waged war in border areas that had been stripped from Yugoslavia and given to Hungary, Bulgaria and Albania. They were also at odds with the Germans (who had imposed a puppet regime in what remained of Serbia), and fought against the Croatian Ustashi (who made common cause with the Italian occupation forces). The Chetniks were not the only Yugoslav resistance group. Anti-monarchist guerrillas – 'Partisans' – also emerged. These were led by a Comintern agent, Josip Broz, whose pseudonym was Tito. Mihailovic refused to co-operate with Tito in creating a national resistance movement. In fact by November 1941, Chetniks and Partisans were fighting each other for control of western Serbia. Mihailovic soon entered into local truces with the Italian occupying forces to avoid casualties, and to acquire arms to fight Tito. He also tried, not always successfully, to spare the Serb population from atrocity at the hands of the Germans. Tito's Partisans, undeterred from action by even the most brutal of reprisals, waged war ferociously in pursuit of their goal – the creation of a communist Yugoslavia. By late 1943, Tito had established himself in the eyes of SOE as the most effective of the Yugoslav guerrilla leaders. Lack of support from Britain drove Mihailovic into closer co-operation with the Germans so that he could continue the civil war against Tito. This only confirmed the Allied prejudice against him. By 1944, all British aid was sent to the Partisans.

Until 1943, 20 Italian divisions were stationed in Yugoslavia and Albania, along with six German divisions. When Italy signed an armistice with the Allies in September 1943, Tito acquired large quantities of Italian weapons. This enabled him to increase his forces to over 100,000, take control over much of the area relinquished by the Italians, and launch ambitious attacks against the Germans. Hitler, committing seven additional German divisions to Yugoslavia, mounted large-scale pacification operations against the Partisans. Tito was forced in May 1944 to seek British rescue. He quickly returned to continue the fight. In August, he visited Stalin, 'granting' permission for Russian troops to enter Yugoslavia. They began to push in from Romania in September. Hitler's evacuation of Greece and southern Yugoslavia in October transformed the Partisans' position. Belgrade fell to a joint force of Red Army and Partisan forces on 20 October. In 1945, Tito was hailed as the only European resistance leader to have liberated his country by guerrilla effort. Some even suggested he diverted such numbers of German and satellite troops from other battlefields as to have affected the war's outcome. In truth, Yugoslavia's liberation was the direct result of the arrival of the Russians. Nor did Tito hold down vast numbers of Germans. Most German troops in Yugoslavia were of poor quality. From Germany's point of view, Tito was simply a nuisance value. He did not mount much of a threat to lines of communication with Greece or the area from which she drew essential materials.

By the end of 1944, as the Germans retreated, almost everyone claimed to be a member of the resistance including many, like Mitterand (a future French premier), who had been in the middle management of Vichy. The truth is that the vast majority of western Europeans prudently held aloof from opposing German occupation. There were probably more western European collaborators than armed resistance fighters. The publication of underground newspapers and the running of intelligence networks, whose subsidiary activities included the smuggling of crashed aircrews out of occupied territory and occasional acts of sabotage, were largely irrelevant. Even in eastern Europe, resistance had a negligible impact on the outcome of the war. While bands of partisans were able to use swamps, forests and mountains to good effect, most of these areas had little strategic importance. Most serious uprisings failed with a price of great suffering to the brave patriots involved but at a trifling cost to the German forces that put them down. Among Hitler's army of 300 divisions deployed across Europe in June 1944, fewer than 20 were committed to internal security duty. Most of these were of poor calibre. Outside central Yugoslavia, parts of western Russia and pockets of defiance in mountain Albania and southern France, occupied Europe lay inert under the jackboot. The peoples of Europe did not liberate themselves. They needed to be liberated.

The 'New Order' In Asia

In 1942, Japan ruled an enormous area – eastern China, Manchuria, the Philippines, French Indo-China (present Laos, Vietnam and Cambodia), British Burma and Malaya, and the Dutch East Indies (present Indonesia). In territorial terms, the extent of Japanese power was one and a half times greater than the area Hitler controlled at the height of his conquests in 1942. Japan did not come to empire unprepared. It had ruled Korea for over 30 years and had ten years' experience of administering Manchuria. More important, it had a theory of empire which was by no means hostile to or unpopular with all the peoples whom it 'freed' from European colonial rule. The idea of a Greater East Asia Co-Prosperity Sphere had taken root in Japan before the war. At one level, it was merely a cloak for imperial expansion; at another it clothed a genuine belief in Japan's mission to lead other Asians to independence from foreign rule.

Like Germany, Japan had opportunities for enlisting support in the occupied territories and, like Germany, did not exploit them successfully. Japanese victories during 1941–2 dented the prestige of the 'white' imperial powers, and provided Japan with an opportunity to pose as a liberating power capable of reorganizing eastern Asia under benign leadership. Many educated Asians – Burmese, Malays and Indonesians – were ready, even eager, to co-operate with Japan. However, while Japanese propaganda made much of anti-imperialism, it soon became clear that one imperial regime had been replaced by another. Supposedly independent governments in the Philippines and Burma were no more independent than the puppet regimes set up in Manchuria and China. In practice, the Japanese military organized conquered territory. Japan's exploitive treatment of the Co-Prosperity Sphere soon exposed her claim to benign leadership as false. Nevertheless, the Japanese encountered little resistance from most of the occupied Asian populations. Only in the Philippines was there a large-scale, anti-Japanese guerrilla movement.

Barbarism in the Second World War was not confined to eastern Europe. In the Far East, the Japanese were capable of terrible atrocities, particularly against the Chinese. In Nanking (during 1937–8), a quarter of a million people were slaughtered. Unit 731 in Manchuria conducted experiments in bacteriological warfare in which thousands of human guinea pigs died horrible deaths. A Japanese soldier who allowed himself to be taken prisoner was regarded as a man without honour and therefore no longer human. Not surprisingly, the treatment of Allied POWs was brutal, showing utter contempt for the conventions of war. The inmates of the 300 POW camps were starved, beaten and denied medical treatment. Prisoners slaved in the coal and sulphur mines of Manchuria or on the roads and railways that were built through malaria-infested jungles. In parts of Burma and Thailand, local labour was conscripted to work in harsh conditions with Allied POWs: 90,000 out of 270,000 Asian labourers died on the construction of the Burma railway (compared with 12,000 out of 61,000 POWs).

Conclusion

After 1945, a curtain was drawn over the extent of support for both Hitler's and Japan's New Orders. Active collaborators were portrayed as small and unrepresentative cliques, while the role of the resistance movements was exaggerated. This helped salvage national respect and enabled post-war reconstruction to employ the same civil servants and industrialists that had co-operated with the New Order. In reality, there was far more collaboration, albeit mostly of a passive rather than active nature, than resistance. Indeed, it may be that both Germany and Japan could have made better use of the territories they overran, forging their New Orders into economic and political units with a productive capacity that might have made up for the Axis's disadvantages compared to her enemies. An orchestration of the concept of Europe or Asia might have secured the positive support of other nations. The ruthless and selfish nature of the German and Japanese regimes ensured that this did not happen.

09

the Holocaust

This chapter will cover:
- Nazi treatment of Jews 1933–41
- genocide
- responsibility for the Holocaust.

At 11.00 a.m. on 4 August 1944, half a dozen Gestapo and Dutch police arrived at the offices of 263 Prinsengracht in Amsterdam. They had information that Jews were concealed in the building. Two office workers were forced at gunpoint to reveal the Jews' hiding place – an annexe at the back of the building, the entrance to which was hidden behind a bookcase. The annexe had been specially constructed by Otto Franks, the building's owner. He and the rest of his family – his wife Edith and their two daughters, Anne (aged 15) and Margot (aged 18) – had been in hiding since July 1942. Four other Jews had joined the Franks in the annexe. Everything the Franks needed was smuggled to them secretly by loyal employees. Throughout the years of their self-imposed 'captivity', Anne Frank kept a diary. Her last entry was made on 1 August 1944. The Franks' family were sent to Auschwitz. Anne and Margot were later moved to another camp, Bergen-Belsen. Both died of typhus in March 1945, a few weeks before British soldiers liberated the camp. Edith Franks died in Auschwitz in January 1945, three weeks before Russian troops freed the surviving prisoners. Otto Franks was among the Auschwitz survivors. When he returned to Amsterdam in June 1945, a loyal employee gave him Anne's diary, rescued from the annexe. It was eventually published, selling millions of copies. It tells the story of what happened to just one Jewish family caught up in the Holocaust.

In late 1941, Hitler was committed to a plan to murder all of Europe's Jews. This plan is usually referred to as the 'Final Solution' or the 'Holocaust'. The problem with the term Final Solution is that the Nazis had several 'final solutions', not all of which intended to annihilate the Jews, before the final 'Final Solution'. Holocaust is thus possibly a better word. While the Holocaust was possibly not the worst crime against humanity in the twentieth century (Stalin and Mao Zedong probably killed more people in the name of economic determinism than Hitler killed in the name of racial determinism), it was a terrible lapse into barbarism. There are still some who deny that it happened, claiming that it was a myth created by Jews and communists to damn the Nazis. The deniers' case collapses, however, because there is overwhelming evidence, from survivors and from perpetrators alike, that the Holocaust did occur. The key questions are why, how and who was to blame?

Nazi treatment of Jews 1933–41

In 1933, there were some 500,000 Jews in Germany, less than one per cent of the population. Anti-Semitism was an article of faith for Hitler and for many of his supporters. While he had not prepared a step-by-step anti-Jewish programme, Hitler certainly had in mind the major lines of future action. From 1933, there was a flood of laws excluding Jews from specific jobs. In 1935, Hitler introduced the Nuremberg laws: marriage and sexual relations between Jews and Germans were prohibited; and Jews lost their German citizenship. By making their lives difficult, the Nazis hoped to encourage Jews to emigrate. However most Jews, barred from taking any of their assets out of Germany, were reluctant to leave. Moreover, there were few countries willing to accept them. In 1937 Herman Göring, officially responsible for Nazi policy towards Jews, began issuing decrees which shut down most Jewish businesses. The hardening of anti-Semitic activity was possibly accelerated by the Nazi takeover of Austria in March 1938. Nazis beat up and humiliated many of Austria's 200,000 Jews, and looted Jewish homes and businesses. In August 1938, Adolf Eichmann set up a Central Office for Jewish Emigration in Vienna. This allowed would-be emigrants to complete procedures in one day which in Germany took many weeks. Jews left the Central Office with an emigration visa and little else. Virtually all their property was confiscated.

On 7 November 1938, a German official in Paris was shot by a Polish Jew. Two days later, Propaganda Minister Joseph Goebbels called for the official's death to be avenged. Nazi activists took him at his word. During 9–10 November – *Kristallnacht* (the night of broken glass) – 8,000 Jewish businesses were destroyed; 200 synagogues burned down; hundreds of Jews beaten up and over 90 killed. Some 30,000 Jews were herded into concentration camps. Most were later released but only after agreeing to leave Germany. Over the winter of 1938–9 many new laws against Jews came into effect. From 1 January 1939 Jews were forbidden to undertake any form of independent business activity. They were also banned from visiting theatres, cinemas and circuses. In January 1939 Göring commissioned Reinhard Heydrich, right-hand man of SS chief Heinrich Himmler, to bring the, 'Jewish question to as favourable a solution as present circumstances permit'. The solution was forced emigration. Heydrich copied Eichmann's methods. Tens of thousands of Jews were 'encouraged' to leave Germany.

It is possible to claim that Nazi anti-Jewish policy before 1939 was erratic and improvised, with Hitler accepting whatever 'solution' to the Jewish problem was currently in vogue. More likely though, Hitler was the chief – if not always the sole – driving force of anti-Semitism. Party activists, who urged him to take radical action against the Jews, urged him in a direction he wanted to go. Arguably, Nazi goals had been systematically pursued and rapidly achieved: by September 1939, about 70 per cent of Germany's Jews had been driven to emigrate. Just where Hitler's policy was leading is debatable. In a speech to the Reichstag in January 1939, he said:

> Today I will once more be a prophet: if the international Jewish financiers in and outside Europe should succeed in plunging the nations once more into a world war, then the result will not be the Bolshevizing of the earth, and thus the victory of Jewry, but the annihilation of the Jewish race in Europe.

The fact that Hitler expressed such views cannot be taken as proof that he was already set on genocide. Indeed, given the emphasis on emigration, it seems unlikely that he was yet contemplating mass murder.

The German conquest of Poland was to have dire consequences for Poles in general and for Polish Jews in particular. Hitler made his brutal intentions clear from the start. In 1939, a special task force – or *Einsatzgruppen* – was set up. Its role was to combat 'all anti-German elements' and to 'render harmless' the leadership class in Poland. Thousands of doctors, teachers and landowners were executed. By defeating Poland, Germany won territory containing over 17 million Poles and two million Jews. Roughly half this area was incorporated directly into the Third Reich. The rest was formed into the General Government, ruled by Hans Frank and the SS. German rule was based on terror. Jews had to wear the Star of David on pain of death, and many were sent to labour camps. Himmler hoped to create a reservation for Jews within the General Government, and over the winter of 1939–40, thousands were deposited in the Lublin area. However, transportation problems, arising from the build-up for Operation Barbarossa, resulted in the Lublin plan being postponed.

The concentration and isolation of Jews in Polish cities became part of Nazi policy in 1940. Was this 'ghettoization' policy a conscious first step for annihilation? It certainly helped the (later) implementation of the Holocaust. Yet there is plenty of evidence to suggest that the Nazi leadership had not really thought through its policies. Ghettoization was introduced at different times in different ways for different reasons on the initiative of different authorities. The first 'sealed' ghetto was established in Lodz in April 1940. The Warsaw ghetto was not sealed until November 1940. It soon housed about 500,000 Jews. This resulted in six people sharing a single room. In Warsaw, the food rations for Jews fell below an average of 300 calories a day (compared with 2,310 for Germans). Fuel was also in short supply. In consequence, the health of most Jews deteriorated. Some 500,000 Jews probably died in the ghettos and Polish labour camps between 1939 and 1941.

Hitler's victories in 1940 brought Dutch, French, Belgian and Danish Jews under German control. In July 1940, the Germans began to promote the notion of sending western European Jews to Madagascar, a large island off the east coast of Africa. There was apparent enthusiasm for the Madagascar plan at every level, from Hitler downwards. The continuation of the war with Britain though, ensured that the plan was never put into effect.

Another plan suggested that Jews were in danger. In 1939, Hitler introduced a euthanasia programme – a euphemism to camouflage the killing of mentally and physically handicapped people. The aim was partly financial: it would help conserve medical resources. Nonetheless, Hitler's desire to create a pure race was probably more important than economic considerations. He empowered certain doctors to grant 'a mercy death' to those suffering from 'incurable' illnesses. A central office was established in Berlin at Tiergarten Strasse No. 4 to oversee the euthanasia programme: it thus became known as Operation T-4 or simply as T-4. All institutions holding mental patients had to provide specific information about their patients. On the basis of this information, three 'experts' decided who should die. Those selected for death were transferred to wards in six special hospitals. Killings got under way in the autumn of 1939. At first, most victims died by means of a drug overdose but T-4 doctors soon decided that carbon monoxide gassing was more efficient. Most of the T-4 staff, managers, doctors and nurses were loyal Nazis and had no moral qualms about what was going on. Meanwhile, a small team of doctors and bureaucrats worked out the methods of implementing child euthanasia. Midwives and doctors were ordered to report all infants born with severe medical conditions. Those babies selected to die were transferred to special clinics where they were given drug overdoses or starved to death. While great efforts were made to maintain secrecy, the euthanasia programme became public knowledge. In 1941, a number of church leaders denounced the killings. Fearful of alienating public opinion, Hitler ordered a stop to the programme. By then over 70,000 people had been killed.

Hitler had shown no mercy to the Polish elite or to handicapped Germans. Given that he regarded the Jews as far more dangerous, he was unlikely to find it hard to order the Holocaust. However, Nazi policy pre-June 1941 does not seem to have been set on genocide. The forced emigration of Jews, whether to the Lublin area or to Madagascar, remained the 'final solution'.

Genocide

Operation Barbarossa, launched in June 1941, also launched the Holocaust. Hitler was now set on destroying Jewish Bolshevism. In March 1941, he had issued a directive to his army high command insisting that 'the Bolshevik-Jewish intelligentsia' must be 'eliminated'. Germany's army leaders accepted Hitler's call for unprecedented brutality. Most shared his hatred of Bolshevism and Judaism (which they saw as one and the same) and his belief that the enemy had to be beaten, whatever the cost. Implementation of most of the initial dirty work was left to four *Einsatzgruppen*, each of about 1,000 men. Although the officers had been briefed by Heydrich in June, the precise content of their orders is a matter of controversy. *Einsatzgruppen* actions during June–July suggest that there was no pre-invasion genocide order. Generally they rounded up and shot communist leaders and some, but by no means all, Jewish men. Relatively few Jewish women and children were killed. A few thousand policemen, untrained in mass killing techniques, were unlikely to be thought sufficient to kill five million Russian Jews.

Some historians think that an elated Hitler, confident that victory over Russia was at hand, ordered the mass killing of Soviet Jews in mid-July, and at the same time asked Himmler to come up with plans to kill all of Europe's Jews. On 31 July, Göring, who was still officially responsible for the Jewish question, charged Heydrich with, 'making all necessary preparations ... for bringing about a complete solution of the Jewish question within the German sphere of influence in Europe'. Arguably, this is evidence that a genocide order had been given. It is equally possible, however, that Hitler finally decided on total genocide more out of a sense of desperation than of elation. By September, Barbarossa was not going according to plan. It may be that Hitler decided in late September or early October that the Jews should pay for the spilling of so much German blood. Given the scarcity of documentation, debate about Hitler's motivation is likely to continue. Nevertheless, there is little doubt that the decision was Hitler's. Himmler was not acting on his own initiative, although it is conceivable that Hitler authorized him to produce a (violent) solution of the Jewish question without enquiring too closely into what that would involve.

From mid-August 1941, the killing of Soviet Jews was on a different scale to what it had been before. Jewish women and children were now routinely massacred. In July, most of the victims were shot individually by firing squad. By August, hundreds of victims were forced to lie in or kneel at the edge of a trench before being shot in the back of the head. Karl Jager, head of a unit of *Einsatzgruppen A*, kept gory records. In July 1941, his unit killed 4,293 Jews of whom only 135 were women. In September 1941, by contrast, his unit killed 56,459 Jews – 15,104 men, 26,243 women and 15,112 children. Not only the *Einsatzgruppen* carried out the killings. Auxiliary forces, recruited from people of the Baltic States and the Ukraine, were also willing executioners. So were ordinary German soldiers. The killing continued through 1942–3. By 1943 over two million Russian Jews had probably been murdered.

In August 1941, Himmler commissioned his SS technical advisers to test different ways of killing and recommend those which were more efficient and more 'humane'. Not surprisingly they soon hit upon the idea of gas: the T-4 programme had ensured that the executioners were trained, the technology proven, and the procedures worked out. Jews of the Lodz ghetto were among the first to be gassed. Over the winter of 1941–2 an SS team converted an old mansion at Chelmno into a barracks and gas chamber. Chelmno began operations in January 1942. It was a pure killing centre. By the time it was destroyed in March 1943, some 140,000 Jews (and a few thousand Gypsies, Poles and Russians) had died there. At the same time, Himmler selected Odilo Globocnik to oversee the killing of Polish Jews. Dozens of SS and ex-T-4 men were assigned to Globocnik in the autumn of 1941. Their task was to construct and run a number of death camps in the Lublin area.

figure 13 the killing centres

Co-ordination of various agencies, both within Germany and in the occupied countries, was required if thousands of Jews were to be transported to the killing centres in Poland. Accordingly, a meeting of top civil servants was held at Wannsee in January 1942 to discuss logistical and other matters. The conference, chaired by Heydrich, formulated common procedures whereby all of Europe's Jews were to be 'resettled' in the East. The conference minutes, prepared by Eichmann, did not spell out extermination. At his trial in 1960, Eichmann was franker than he was in the minutes: 'the gentlemen ... talked about the matter without mincing their words ... the talk was of killing, elimination and liquidation'. The Wannsee conference was not the starting point of the Holocaust: that was already underway. Yet it was the moment when it was endorsed by a broad segment of the German government.

The mass gassing of the Jews in the General Government is usually known as Operation Reinhard, after Reinhard Heydrich. Heydrich was the 'brains' behind the killing. Ironically, he was assassinated by Czech partisans in May 1942. Belzec, the first functional Operation Reinhard camp, opened in

March 1942, Sobibor in May and Treblinka in July. The basic layout and procedures were the same at all three camps. Each was divided into two parts. Camp 1 contained barracks for undressing. Camp 2 contained the gas chambers. A path known as the 'tube', bordered by a wire fence, linked the two camps.

Jewish leaders had the job of finding people for 'resettlement'. Warsaw had to supply 10,000 a day from July 1942. The transportation experience was horrific. People were crammed into freight cars without food or water. Once the transports arrived at Belzec, Sobibor or Treblinka, the camp authorities aimed to kill all but a few of the deportees within two hours. Males and females were separated, forced to undress, and then to run down the 'tube' to the building signed 'Baths and Inhalation Rooms'. They were pushed into chambers which could hold hundreds of people. A diesel engine pumped in carbon monoxide gas. After 30 minutes, the engine was switched off and the Jewish 'death brigade' (or *Sonderkomando*) had the job of disposing of the bodies. Although the Operation Reinhard camps were simply death camps, a Jewish workforce of several hundred was employed in the various steps of the killing process. The work-Jews, poorly fed and ill-treated, found that their reprieve from death seldom exceeded a few months.

During 1942–3, Himmler's goal of exterminating all the Polish Jews had been largely achieved. By November 1943, all the Operation Reinhard camps had been dismantled. Some 500,000 Jews died at Belzec; 150–200,000 at Sobibor; and 900–1,200,000 at Treblinka. Himmler thanked Globocnik, 'for the great and unique service which you have performed for the whole German people by carrying out Operation Reinhard'.

The killing reduced Germany's potential labour pool at a time when it was suffering from a desperate shortage of manpower. As a result of protests by the army, industry and civilian authorities, there were phases during which the extermination was slowed down to permit the exploitation of Jewish labour. During 1941–2 two camps, Majdanek and Auschwitz, began to serve a dual purpose. On the one hand, they were extermination centres; on the other, they were labour camps in which some Jews received a stay of execution.

By 1941, Auschwitz had expanded into a vast labour camp, mainly for the utilization of Russian prisoners of war. Camp Commandant, Rudolf Hoess, told by Himmler that Auschwitz was to be a principal centre for killing Jews, had no moral

figure 14 the Jewish dead

qualms. A fanatical Nazi, he was determined to carry out his orders to the best of his ability, and hit upon the idea of using Zyklon B as the gassing agent. First tested on Russian prisoners, it killed in half the time required by carbon monoxide. Hoess shifted the gassing to a new, more secluded camp at Birkenau. It began operations in 1942. With good railway connections, Auschwitz–Birkenau quickly grew into the largest of the Nazi death camps. The process of killing was slick and streamlined. As the trains arrived, SS doctors decided who was fit and unfit. The unfit, the old, the sick, and young children were condemned to immediate death in the gas chambers. The fit (usually about a third of each transport) were taken to one of Auschwitz's many labour camps, most of the inmates of which were non-Jews. As in camps across German-occupied Europe, inmates were stripped of their individuality, poorly fed and brutally treated. Few survived for more than a few months. In total, over one million Jews from all over Europe probably died at Auschwitz.

During 1944–5, concentration camps in Germany, hitherto used mainly for non-Jewish prisoners, were used to house Jews evacuated from the East. (Tens of thousands lost their lives on the marches, perishing from cold, hunger, disease and periodic shootings.) Allied soldiers who liberated these camps after April 1945 were appalled by what they found.

The exact number of Jews who died in the Holocaust will never be known. Most historians, accepting the findings of the Nuremberg Tribunal, think that over five million died. Most of the killing was in 1942. In mid-March 1942, some 75 per cent of all the eventual victims of the Holocaust were still alive; some 25 per cent had already died. By mid-March 1943, 75 per cent of all the eventual victims were dead.

The Jews were not the only non-combatants to die at the hands of the Germans. Millions of non-Jewish Poles, Ukrainians and Russian civilians died as a result of German occupation, reprisal and deportation policies. Of 5.7 million Soviet prisoners, some 3.3 million died in German custody; 25,000 Gypsies and 6,000 Jehovah's Witnesses were also killed by the Nazis.

Who was to blame?

Immediately after 1945, most historians believed that it was Hitler's aim all along to exterminate European Jewry. He simply sought the right moment to act. By no means do all historians today agree. It is possible to claim that improvization was usually the name of the game in the 'authoritarian anarchy' that was the Third Reich. Some think that the Holocaust arose simply as a result of the chaotic situation in eastern Europe after 1939, not from Hitler pursuing long-term ideological aims. Relatively few historians now think that Hitler envisaged and planned the Holocaust from 1933 onwards. However, most agree that his fervent anti-Semitism played a central role in the evolution of Nazi policy. While not always personally concerned with the detailed moves to achieve a 'solution of the Jewish question', he gave signals that established goals. Hitler's actions pre-1941 do not indicate that he was planning genocide. Nevertheless, given his hatred of Jews, the potential for a Holocaust was always present. Once Germany was at war with Russia, it made sense (by Hitler's standards) to kill all Russia's, and then all Europe's, Jews. No order signed by Hitler containing an explicit command to exterminate the Jews has ever come to light. It is unlikely to do so. Incredible though it may seem, the order to kill millions of people was probably little more than a nod from Hitler to Himmler.

While Hitler was the ideological and political author of the Holocaust, it was translated into a concrete strategy by Himmler, a fanatical racist and the ultimate bureaucrat. As a result of the SS's powerful position in Poland and Russia, Himmler was able to take control of anti-Jewish initiatives. There is no doubt that the SS was a perfect instrument for mass murder. However, it could be that the SS has become Germany's 'whipping boy'. In truth, relatively few SS men were directly involved in the Holocaust. Nor was the SS the only organization responsible for the killings.

The army high command accepted the need for harsh measures against Jews in Russia. German officers and men believed that Jews were behind partisan activity, and accordingly were happy to shoot them in retaliation. Police battalions also played a crucial role. Their task was to scour occupied Russian territory, shooting every Jew they could find. Historians have focused attention on the members of Reserve Police Battalion 101. The men were a good cross-section of German society. Few were fanatical Nazis. Some were devout Christians. Thus, they were not a promising group from which to recruit mass murderers. Yet this is what most became – killing women and children, not in a depersonalized way but at very close quarters. Refusal to take part in the slaughter did not result in punishment. Most of the men seem to have been proud of their actions. Historian

Daniel Goldhagen thinks that because the men of Police Battalion 101 were so typical of German society, the 'inescapable truth' is that most of their fellow Germans would also have served as Hitler's 'willing executioners'.

A strong case can be made against the German people. Very few Germans were critical of anti-Semitic action at any stage between 1933 and 1945. Knowledge about the mass shootings in Russia was fairly widespread. Germans who took part in the killings often told their families. Goldhagen claims that 500,000 Germans may have been directly implicated in the Holocaust and that many Germans approved of it. Despite this, his 'willing executioners' case is not proven. The fact that Hitler tried to preserve the Holocaust's secrecy suggests that he felt he could not rely on popular support. The gassings involved small numbers of men and occurred out of sight of most Germans.

It has been suggested that Jews might have done more to resist. Most seemed to have yielded to their fate with minimal resistance. Some Jewish historians have even blamed Jewish leaders for collaborating with the Germans. Such charges are unfair. Few Jews were aware in 1942 of what 'resettlement in the East' meant. Successful armed resistance was virtually impossible. Over three million Russian POWs died while in German custody. There was no serious uprising among these prisoners. If men of military age and training were unable to resist, Jewish old and sick men, women and children stood little chance. The most serious Jewish resistance came in the Warsaw ghetto during April–May 1943. Some 60,000 Jews, who knew their probable fate, tried to fight German troops who had moved into the ghetto to make Warsaw Jew-free. With one rifle for every 150 men, the Jews had no illusions about the final outcome, but they chose to die fighting rather than die in the camps. By May 1943, the Warsaw ghetto was virtually liquidated: over 56,000 Jews had been killed or transported to the camps. Only 16 Germans died in the fighting.

From 1940 to 1944, Germany dominated most of Europe. The Germans pressed virtually all their allied and satellite states for Jewish deportation, claiming Jews were needed as forced labourers in the East. There were varying degrees of co-operation. After 1945, non-German collaborators at the highest level protested their innocence, claiming they were unaware of the ultimate intentions of the Germans or that they had little option but to obey German orders. All the German satellite states in central and eastern Europe – Slovakia, Croatia,

Romania, Bulgaria and Hungary – introduced measures against Jews in some form or another. These measures pleased Hitler and placated indigenous anti-Semitic groups. However, the various states were not uniformly hostile to Jews, and each responded differently to the varying degrees of German pressure. The Slovakian government, led by Jozef Tiso, a Catholic priest, agreed to the deportation of the country's Jews. The pro-German leaders of Croatia happily introduced discriminatory legislation against Jews. Some 30,000 Croatian Jews were shot or died in Croatian concentration camps. The Croatians also ethnically cleansed their new country of Serbs. Some 400,000 Serbs were deliberately killed by the Croats using measures similar to the *Einsatzgruppen*. Over 100,000 Romanian Jews died. No other country beside Germany was involved in the massacre of Jews on such a scale. Yet as the defeat of Germany became a distinct possibility, Romanian dictator Antonescu rejected German pressure to deport native Romanian Jews to the Nazi death camps. This allowed him to claim after the war that he had saved most of the 300,000 Romanian-born Jews, a claim which obscured the other half of the story. Bulgaria refused to hand over Bulgarian Jews. More Jews were alive in Bulgaria in 1945 than in 1939. Until 1944, the Hungarian government was deaf to Germany's deportation requests. Hungary thus seemed something of a safe haven for Jews fleeing from Germany and Poland. (Hungary's Jewish population increased from 400,000 in 1939 to 700,000 in 1944.) Nonetheless, many Hungarians were anti-Semitic and some Jews suffered terribly in Hungarian labour battalions. In 1944, German forces occupied Hungary and some 430,000 Jews were sent to Auschwitz.

The situation was similarly patchy in western Europe. Once Jewish deportations began in 1942, the Germans relied heavily on native police and bureaucrats. The degree of co-operation varied considerably and this, in part, determined the widely different Jewish losses – from 75 per cent of Jews in Holland to only five per cent in Denmark. France had a strong anti-Semitic tradition and the Vichy government introduced measures to eliminate Jewish economic and political influence. Many Jews were interned in special camps. For those French officials who collaborated with the Germans in 1942, the deportations were simply a continuation of a programme deemed by the Vichy government to be in France's national interest. About half of France's 300,000 Jews did not have French citizenship. These Jews were the ones most likely to be deported. The Vichy government actually resisted Germany's attempts to deport French-born Jews, restricting the total number of Jews deported to under 80,000. Unlike the Vichy government, Danish leaders were opposed to all aspects of anti-Semitism. Until 1943, the Germans did not interfere much in internal Danish affairs and so Jews remained relatively safe. When the German authorities finally insisted on Jewish persecution in late 1943, most of Denmark's 8,000 Jews escaped to Sweden in an armada of small boats. The Nazis encountered serious obstacles in Italy where anti-Semitism had never been strong and where most of the 50,000 Jews were fully integrated into Italian society. Italian Jews were only in danger after the German takeover in 1943.

Some 40 per cent of west European Jews were killed in the Holocaust. Holland, with 105,000 Jews deported, suffered the greatest loss both in absolute and relative terms. The extent to which west European collaborationists were in a position to say 'no' to the Nazis remains debatable. The claim that the situation would have been much worse without the collaborationists is plausible. In France, for example, far more Jews survived the Holocaust than perished. This was in part due to delaying tactics adopted by the Vichy authorities.

There were no collaborationist governments in Nazi-occupied Poland and Russia to facilitate or hinder the Holocaust. Here, German authorities determined their own priorities. However, the attitude of local people to Jews had some bearing on the Holocaust. Most Poles were anti-Semitic and seem to have done little to help, and much to harm, Polish Jews during the war. Some Poles actually approved of the Holocaust. Many people in the Ukraine and the Baltic States were also vehemently anti-Semitic. Regarding Jews as Soviet agents, they were ready to collaborate with the Germans. The Lithuanians were particularly enthusiastic: over 90 per cent of all Lithuanian Jews were killed; some two-thirds were possibly killed by Lithuanians.

There is no doubt that the strength of European anti-Semitism eased the Nazi implementation of the Holocaust. The intensity of anti-Semitism in any particular country also had some effect on how far the destruction process went. In the final analysis though, the degree of Nazi control, rather than the strength of local anti-Semitism, was the decisive factor in determining the number of Jews who were killed.

Despite German efforts to maintain secrecy, word about the Holocaust quickly leaked to the outside world. The governments in Britain and the USA were aware of the situation in 1942. Some historians have attacked Allied leaders (especially FDR) for 'abandoning' the Jews. Such attacks are probably unfair. FDR did not appreciate the full extent of Nazi policies until late in the war. Like most contemporaries, he thought that the genocide stories were anti-German propaganda, and he was reluctant to accept as gospel truth second- and third-hand reports, especially when they came via Russia. Once FDR and Churchill accepted the horrible truth, there was little they could do. Ransoming Jews was a non-starter: Allied leaders had no intention of being blackmailed by the Nazis. The Allies lacked the military capacity to bomb Auschwitz before 1944; even had it been bombed successfully, this would have come too late to save most of its victims. Jewish organizations opposed the bombing of Auschwitz on the grounds it would kill more Jews than it saved. Allied leaders were convinced – rightly – that the best way to help the Jews was to win the war as quickly as possible.

Serious charges have been levied against Pope Pius XII for not condemning either the Holocaust or the massacres of Serbs in Croatia. The Vatican, with its unrivalled net of informants all over Europe, was aware of what was going on. Although Pius's policy of neutrality was in line with the longstanding tradition of Vatican diplomacy, it is difficult to defend his silence. Many Germans and Croatians were sincere Catholics and a papal appeal not to co-operate with the Nazis might have had some effect. Instead, Pius XII, who feared the threat of communism more than the threat of fascism, expressed no views on the great moral issue of the century.

Conclusion

Although the Holocaust was an enterprise to which countless people throughout Europe contributed, it was essentially a German enterprise. The easy way for the Germans to escape collective responsibility after 1945 was to lay all the blame at the door of Hitler. He was a convenient scapegoat. His personality, leadership style and ideological convictions shaped the nature of the Third Reich. German – indeed European – anti-Semitism may have been a necessary condition for the Holocaust but it was not a sufficient one. It was Hitler who made the difference. While Hitler probably did not always harbour the intention of literally exterminating the Jews, extermination was always a possibility, especially in the event of war. And Hitler wanted war. He probably did not want the war he got in 1939 but he certainly got the war he wanted in 1941. Barbarossa was the key to the Holocaust. The war against Russia gave him the opportunity of destroying Jewish Bolshevism and he took it with a vengeance. What to most people now seems irrational and evil, seemed to Hitler logical and good. At the very end of his life, he claimed that the extermination of the Jews was his legacy to the world.

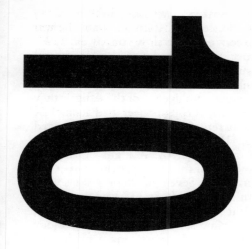

10 war at sea and in the air

This chapter will cover:
- the Battle of the Atlantic
- why the Allies won the Battle of the Atlantic
- early strategic bombing 1939–42
- the combined bomber offensive 1943–5
- the effectiveness of Allied bombing.

In mid-March 1943, three convoys, two fast and one slow, headed to Britain across the central Atlantic. Twenty-eight escort vessels protected the convoys. The slow convoy SC 122 – with 60 merchant ships, successfully manoeuvred past a patrol line of German U-boats (submarines). The two fast convoys – HX 229 with 40 vessels and HX 229A with 38 – were directly behind SC 122. Warned by naval intelligence of the danger, they also avoided the U-boats. Then, through sheer bad luck, HX 229 was spotted by a U-boat returning home with a damaged engine. It informed the U-boat high command which concentrated ten U-boats on the convoy. A night of carnage ensued. U-boats sailed in and out of the convoy, firing torpedoes at merchant ships and escorts alike. Seven merchant vessels were sunk. Allied bad luck continued. As U-boat 338 was rushing to join the attack on HX 229, it ran into SC 122. In less than ten minutes, it fired five torpedoes and sank four ships. A three-day running battle ensued, in which the U-boats sank a further 21 ships. Only the arrival of long-range aircraft from Northern Ireland prevented a worse catastrophe. This U-boat victory was one of many in early 1943. In March 1943, it appeared that the U-boats were winning what Churchill called the 'Battle of the Atlantic'. The outcome of this battle was crucial. If it was lost, Britain might be forced to surrender and the USA's contribution to the European war would be jeopardized. In the event, the U-boats did not triumph. By May 1943, the Battle of the Atlantic had turned in the Allies' favour. Why did the Allies win?

The Battle of the Atlantic 1939–42

In 1939, both sides hoped to strike decisively at the other by imposing a blockade at sea. This had been an effective British strategy against Germany in the First World War. However, the extent of German conquests during 1940–2, coupled with the development of a range of substitutes for imported materials such as rubber, made the British surface blockade of German ports less effective than during 1914–18. In the Second World War, it was Britain that was most vulnerable to naval blockade. Britain was dependent upon imports of goods from overseas to feed her population and to provide raw materials for her factories. If her British merchant navy was unable to deliver the goods, Britain might be starved into surrender. In 1939, Britain had the largest merchant fleet in the world, comprising some 4,000 vessels. To protect this fleet, the Royal Navy deployed over 200 vessels – destroyers, sloops and corvettes.

Prior to the war, Hitler had given little thought to the German navy. In 1940, with Britain's refusal to surrender, he focused his attention on how Germany might threaten British shipping. After mid-1940, German bombers based in France and Norway took a heavy toll. Mines, whether laid by aircraft or surface ship, were a constant menace. Surface raiders – battleships and cruisers – provided the most spectacular but, given the Royal Navy's strength, the least effective threat. In 1941, the German navy lost two of its few capital ships: in May the *Bismarck* was sunk after a chase by most of the British Home Fleet; and a month later the *Lutzow* was sunk by a torpedo. Thereafter, German surface ships were confined to Norwegian waters and the Baltic.

The greatest threat to Britain came from the German submarines. Churchill admitted later that, 'the only thing that really frightened me during the war was the U-boat peril'. The man who controlled Germany's U-boat fleet, Admiral Karl Donitz, had long seen the potential for submarine warfare but Raeder, his superior, had favoured the construction of a surface fleet, and U-boat development had been neglected. It continued to be neglected during 1939–40. In 1939, Germany had only 57 U-boats and, fortunately for Britain, only 27 were ocean-going. Until mid-1940, U-boats thus posed no major threat. Yet the conquest of Norway, Holland, Belgium and France opened up all sorts of possibilities for U-boat deployment. The capture of French ports, like Brest and La Rochelle, meant that U-boats could now strike out into the Atlantic Ocean. Although there were rarely more than ten U-boats stationed in the Atlantic in 1940, they inflicted heavy damage: 217 British merchant ships were lost in the second half of 1940. Britain, concentrating her fleet in home waters in case of German invasion, had few vessels available for escort duty. Donitz believed he could strangle Britain with 300 submarines. In July 1940, Hitler belatedly ordered an intensive U-boat building programme, with a production target of 25 a month for 1941. Whereas capital ships took a great deal of time and money to construct, submarines could be produced quickly and cheaply.

Learning from the hard experience of the First World War, Britain introduced the convoy system almost immediately war broke out. Nonetheless, convoys offered only partial protection. Amazingly, the Royal Navy had shown little interest in developing anti-submarine devices prior to 1939. Asdic, the echo-sounder used to detect submerged U-boats, was ineffective beyond 914 metres (1,000 yards) and reflected only range and bearing, not depth. Depth charges were a hit or miss weapon. (They usually missed.) After 1939, both the Royal Navy and the RAF established research and development programmes which eventually led to improved radar and sonar for all anti-submarine vessels and better depth charges.

In 1940, the U-boats adopted a 'wolf-pack' strategy, dispersing on a patrol line across likely routes to maximize the chances of interception. Once a convoy was sighted, radio contact was made with other U-boats which then converged to mount a concentrated attack. These attacks were usually made by surfaced U-boats at night. In April 1941, nearly 700,000 tons of shipping was lost – far more than British shipyards could replace. In 1938, Britain imported about 68 million tons per year. By 1941, this was down to 31.5 million. To make matters worse, Germany was adding to its U-boat numbers at a considerably higher rate than it was losing them. By mid-1941, Britain was near to losing the Battle of the Atlantic.

British countermeasures, however, proved reasonably effective. More destroyers and corvettes were made available for escort duty, ensuring that convoys were not such easy prey. The establishment of bases in Iceland and Newfoundland helped to extend the range of escort vessels and air cover. US navy escorts also took some of the strain in the western Atlantic in the autumn of 1941. Ultra, monitoring signals sent between U-boats and from Donitz's headquarters, provided the best defence. Intelligence of U-boat location enabled the Admiralty to re-route convoys – a crucial factor in deflecting the U-boat offensive. By the end of 1941, Britain was just about able to contain the U-boat threat. More could have been done. The RAF was reluctant to devote air power to the Atlantic. Yet statistics were clear: convoys which had air cover suffered far fewer losses than convoys which did not. Defending the convoys would have been a better use of air power in 1941 than bombing Germany.

The situation changed in December 1941 when the US joined the war. Donitz immediately transferred the weight of his effort to the US coast where the U-boats enjoyed a 'happy-time' sinking unescorted US vessels lit up by the lights on the shoreline. During February 1942, 73 ships were sunk; 95 in March; 69 in April and 111 in May. (The US navy failed to sink a single U-boat until April.) Aware that it was short of escort vessels, the US navy was slow to introduce convoys. When they were finally introduced in May, losses quickly fell. With US air cover now in place along the Atlantic seaboard, the U-boats moved south to easier pickings in the Gulf of Mexico and the Caribbean, sinking 121 ships in June. By July, this area too was included in the convoy system and provided with some air cover: sinkings dropped by one-third, while the number of U-boats lost increased to ten compared to three in June. Nevertheless, the first half of 1942 was something of a catastrophe for Allied shipping. Three million tons of shipping were lost in American waters. Allied resources, which had to wage war against the U-boat in the Mediterranean, the Arctic, the Atlantic and the Caribbean, were stretched to breaking point. The situation might have been worse. Japan's decision not to use submarines against merchant shipping at least kept losses in the Pacific within reasonable bounds.

As well as trying to starve Britain of supplies, U-boats also interfered with Allied aid to Russia via the northern port of Murmansk. U-boats were not the only threat. The remaining German battle fleet hiding in the Norwegian fiords, air assault by the *Luftwaffe*, and awful weather all made the Murmansk run a nightmare. In July 1942, only 11 of the 34 ships in British convoy PQ17 limped into Murmansk. For a short period, the Russian run was discontinued, resuming again in September. Convoy PQ18 with 40 merchant ships required an escort that included one carrier, two battleships, seven cruisers, 30 destroyers, two anti-aircraft ships, four corvettes and two submarines. Ten of the 40 merchant ships were still sunk. To a large extent, the Murmansk convoys represented a propaganda gesture – a sign that Britain and the USA were doing something to help Russia. In reality, only a quarter of Lend-Lease aid sent to support the Soviet effort went via Murmansk. Over half went via the northern Pacific to Vladivostok. The remaining quarter reached Russia via the Persian Gulf.

In the late summer of 1942, the U-boats switched to the 'Black Gap' area in the mid-Atlantic – an area where air escort was almost non-existent. Owing to Germany's accelerated U-boat-building programme, 30 new boats a month were reaching Donitz's command by late 1942. The cracking of a number of British codes meant that Donitz had intelligence on the timing and direction of major convoys. A change in the German code left the Allied navies without effective intelligence for most of 1942. With all these advantages, the U-boats kept up a devastating level of attack, sinking 101 ships in October and

134 in November. Donitz, who succeeded Raeder as head of the German navy in January 1943, looked forward to 1943 with optimism. He now had what he believed were enough U-boats to sever the Atlantic lifeline.

Allied victory in the Atlantic 1943–5

Atrocious weather conditions over the winter of 1942–3, which prevented the U-boats from operating, led to a reduction in the number of sinkings. The U-boats hit back in March, sinking 108 ships. Then suddenly, there was a total reversal of fortune. Forty-one U-boats were sunk in May 1943, forcing Donitz to withdraw them from the north to the south Atlantic. Between June and December 141 U-boats were lost and only 57 ships sunk. The hunters had become the hunted. Why?

Much that happened in 1943 was due to developments in 1942. In the second half of 1942, 65 U-boats were lost compared with only 21 in the first half. Although Donitz was still receiving more new boats than he was losing, the rising losses underlined the increased effectiveness of Allied countermeasures. The U-boats achieved little against the well-protected convoys supporting Operation Torch – the North African invasion in November 1942. Ultra intelligence helped the Allied cause. By 1943, British commanders again knew where the U-boats were concentrating. The fact that Britain also discovered that the Germans had been deciphering Royal Navy codes (which were consequently changed) was a double whammy. By May 1943, the convoys were protected by a variety of technical and tactical innovations: long-range Liberator aircraft with short-wave radar and powerful searchlights to pick out surfaced U-boats at night; a growing number of specialist escort vessels ready to go to the rescue of convoys; small aircraft carrier escorts to give the convoys protection from the air when the Liberators were out of range; escorts equipped with new radar systems capable of detecting submerged U-boats and armed with the multiple bomb projector, hedgehog; and the High Frequency Direction Finder which picked up radio messages between the U-boats. Often the first message a U-boat sent was its last. Amazingly, the Germans never caught on to this device. By contrast, the new U-boats had little new equipment. The Germans also found it difficult to man the new boats with experienced sailors. Without any real changes in their own technological and tactical effectiveness, the U-boats were quite literally sunk.

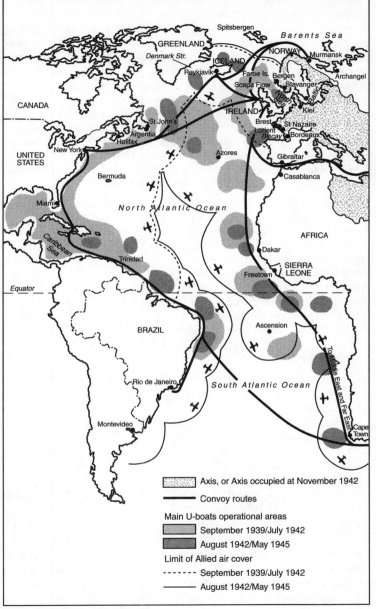

figure 15 the Battle of the Atlantic

The decisive factor in Allied victory in the Battle of the Atlantic, however, was the dramatic increase in US shipbuilding. Ironically, without the U-boat threat in 1941, US shipbuilding might not have reached sufficient levels early enough in the war to support the USA's diverse efforts. Some of the ships were warships. In April 1942, for example, the US embarked on a programme to produce 60 escort vessels in 60 days. When it achieved that goal, it announced another such programme. US mass production of merchant ships (including prefabricated assembly) helped to make good the shipping losses sustained in 1942. The defeat of the U-boats in 1943 resulted in an enormous expansion of the US merchant fleet during 1943–4. In 1943 alone, US production almost made up for the combined Allied losses of the first three years of the war.

After May 1943, Donitz placed his faith in technical innovation. The development of a schnorkel in 1944 enabled the U-boats to avoid surfacing. Acoustic torpedoes that homed in on the sounds made by propellers were introduced. The revolutionary type XXI U-boat, which was three times as fast underwater, would have given the Allies a real headache. Fortunately for the Allies, these developments came too late. (The XXI was not ready until 1945.) U-boats continued to operate and sink ships until the last days of the war, but they no longer posed a serious threat. The figures for tonnage lost to U-boats speak for themselves: 1942 – 6,266,215; 1943 – 804,277; 1944 – 358,609; January–May 1945 – 270,277.

Allied victory in the Battle of the Atlantic was won at a high cost: 32,952 out of the 185,000 men who served in the British merchant navy lost their lives – 17 per cent. This was a higher casualty rate than that suffered by any of the three British military services. Mistakes were made, not least the unwillingness of the Allied air forces to provide the planes needed to close the gap in the air cover over the central Atlantic. Nevertheless, the effort to thwart the U-boats was one of the high points of the war for Britain's armed forces. The mental flexibility of those responsible for the anti-submarine campaign, especially Admirals Percy Noble and Max Horton, ensured the integration of technology into effective tactical systems.

By contrast, Donitz's handling of the submarine campaign is open to criticism. The tight leash on which he held his U-boats robbed them of their flexibility; it also helped provide the vast set of messages needed to break the German codes. The U-boat command structure was too small and highly centralized. This resulted in the general exhaustion of those involved in running the U-boat campaign. Mistakes inevitably resulted. More importantly, U-boat command was unable to step back and take a longer look at the war, not least to implement technological improvement. It interested itself in technology only when the war turned against it, and by then it was too late. The German navy lost 696 out of 830 U-boats sent on operations: 75 per cent of the men who served in U-boats died in them. Some have questioned whether Hitler should have waged the Battle of the Atlantic, arguing that the resources expended on U-boats might have been better used on the air and ground campaigns. However, given its war-winning potential, the U-boat gamble was surely worthwhile. It nearly paid off. Had more U-boats been available during 1940–1, Germany would probably have won. Had the Germans managed to introduce the XXI pre-1944, partial strangulation might have become total.

The strategic bombing of Germany

On the night of 24 July 1943, hundreds of RAF bombers began a series of raids (aptly named Gomorrah after the Biblical city supposedly destroyed by God) on the German port of Hamburg. The first wave of bombers hit the north of the city. The second attack, which struck the city centre, was accurate and intense. A huge fire, fed by some of Germany's largest timber yards, soon engulfed the city and successive planes had no difficulty finding their target. The core temperature of the fire soon reached 1,500° Fahrenheit – a level where everything inflammable burns as if by spontaneous combustion. A firestorm resulted. The central conflagration devoured oxygen, causing winds which reached speeds of over 328 kilometres per hour (200 miles per hour). People in the streets were sucked into the flames. Those in air raid shelters often suffocated from lack of oxygen before the fire cremated them. The bombing continued, off and on, for a further ten days. In this period, a greater weight of bombs fell on Hamburg than fell on Britain during 1940–1. When the fire eventually burned itself out, only 20 per cent of Hamburg's buildings remained intact. Some 40,000 people were dead. Albert Speer, Nazi Armaments Minister, warned Hitler that six similar raids could halt the Reich's armament production. Hitler was less concerned – with due cause as it turned out. The RAF was unable to repeat this level of 'success' until Dresden in February 1945.

Before 1939, some pundits had predicted that strategic bombing by itself might win a future war. By 1943, the RAF and the US Army Air Forces (USAAF) had enough political and logistical support to put the theory into practice. Strategic bombing (as opposed to tactical bombing in support of the army or navy) covered a multitude of meanings from the bombing of specific targets (like oil refineries) to the blanket bombing of cities in order to kill and terrorize civilians. However, the distinction between 'precision' and 'mass' bombing was never totally clear-cut because of the proximity of factories and homes, and the lack of precision. The aim was the same – to destroy or limit the enemy's capability to wage war. Few aspects of the Second World War have proved as controversial as strategic bombing. How effective was it? Was it moral?

Strategic bombing 1939–42

Prior to 1939, there was an exaggerated fear of the bomber. Military experts were convinced that the bomber would always get through and that civilian casualties in any future war would be massive. The British government feared 600,000 dead in the first two months. (In reality, Britain lost 60,000 through bombing in the entire war.) The experience of the *Luftwaffe* over Britain during 1940–1 suggested that the pre-war assumptions were false. The Blitz had limited economic effect and may have stiffened civilian morale rather than undermining it. If German bombing of Britain was relatively ineffective, the RAF's bombing campaign over Germany during 1940–1 was a total failure. Only a third of the bombs dropped by British planes were within eight kilometres (five miles) of the target. RAF bomber losses, from German fighters and anti-aircraft guns, were considerable: 492 in 1940; and 1,034 in 1941. More British aircrews died than German civilian deaths from the bombing. They died because British bombers lacked speed, range and power as well as fighter escort. Yet the conclusion drawn by those in Britain who still advocated strategic bombing was that failure was the result of insufficient bombers. (Before 1939, Britain fortunately had concentrated on fighter production.) In the summer of 1941, the decision was taken to massively expand bomber command. The RAF hoped for 4,000 bombers by 1943. In the event, it never had more than 2,000.

The key advocate of the bombing campaign was Sir Arthur 'Bomber' Harris who was appointed Commander-in-Chief of

Bomber Command in early 1942. Churchill, FDR and senior officers of the USAAF like 'Hap' Arnold and Carl Spaatz were all similarly keen proponents of strategic bombing. From the British point of view, bombing was initially the only way to strike back at Germany. Night bombing was adopted to reduce the huge losses of planes which resulted from daylight bombing. The impossibility of precision bombing at night helped swing the aim of strategic bombing towards lowering enemy morale through mass bombing of urban areas which could (in theory but not always in practice) be located in the dark in a way that an individual factory could not. Few Britons had moral qualms about hitting civilian targets; most believed that the *Luftwaffe* had bombed British cities first. (In reality, the RAF had bombed Berlin prior to Hitler's order to bomb London.) Revenge bombing was a good way of maintaining British morale: it was the only way that Britain might conceivably bring Germany to its knees. Bombing was also a way of assisting Russia. When Churchill met Stalin in August 1942, he rebutted Soviet criticism about Britain not pulling its weight by maintaining that the British would 'pay our way by bombing Germany'. 'Bomber' Harris and Churchill's scientific adviser Professor Lindemann argued that success could be achieved through new navigation aids and massive production of four-engine heavy bombers. USAAF commanders argued likewise. Nonetheless, rather than mass bombing of cities, the Americans favoured precision bombing of key targets.

Germany had lost the air war by 1941. During 1939–40 it failed to put its aircraft industry on a wartime footing. The result was that Germany simply did not have enough planes. In June 1941, most of Germany's aircraft were needed in Russia. The *Luftwaffe*, therefore, had to suspend the Blitz. Although there were occasional attacks on British cities (for example, the Baedeker raids in 1942), they did not amount to much. Not until the summer of 1941, with the appointment of Milch to control aircraft production, did a major improvement begin. It was too late. By 1941, Britain and the USA were out-producing Germany in aircraft by a wide margin. In the last quarter of 1941, Anglo–American production of fighters was nearly four times greater than Germany's. In four-engine aircraft, it was 40 times greater. Given the potential of the US economy, Germany stood little chance of competing.

By 1942, Britain was producing long-range bombers, like the Lancaster and the Halifax, which were capable of carrying far larger bomb loads. This enabled Harris to considerably expand his attacks. In early 1942, major raids on Lubeck and Rostock destroyed half the cities. The success of these raids revived Bomber Command's prestige and ensured that the RAF would continue to receive a large share of Britain's industrial resources. During May 30–1, Harris sent 1,043 bombers for a night attack on Cologne, Germany's third largest city. Nearly 1,500 tons of bombs were dropped on the target: 600 acres of Cologne were devastated. Two more 1,000 bomber raids followed – on Essen and Bremen – in June. The damage, if considerable, was less than reported in Britain. At Casablanca in January 1943, Churchill and FDR reaffirmed their commitment to strategic bombing. It was also agreed that the RAF and the USAAF would conduct a combined bomber offensive. In fact, the operations would be separate: the USAAF would bomb industrial targets and communications by day, while the RAF would bomb cities by night.

The combined bomber offensive 1943–5

By 1943, the RAF and the USAAF had four-engine bombers available in increasing numbers and a host of new technological aids. In July, Harris introduced 'Window' – strips of aluminium which when dropped made German radar useless. A new Pathfinder force of elite crews, whose job it was to locate and mark the targets, ensured that 86 per cent of Bomber Command's planes dropped their loads within five kilometres (three miles) of the target by mid-1943. The RAF concentrated on bludgeoning the same targets over and over again: the Ruhr (March–July); Hamburg (July–August); north German cities (September–October) and Berlin (November 1943 – March 1944). Harris remained convinced that if he could destroy enough cities, Germany would crack. The raids on Berlin, while destroying large numbers of houses, killed relatively few Berliners (6,000), and resulted in a heavy loss of bombers. In late 1943, German night fighter defence improved significantly. German scientists developed a new airborne radar, enabling German night fighters to intercept RAF bombers. Between November 1943 and March 1944, Bomber Command lost 1,128 aircraft. Losses on the 1943 raids were often above the 'acceptable' maximum of five per cent. Since bomber crews had to fly 30 missions before qualifying for rest, in statistical terms the probability of being shot down was high.

The USAAF concentrated on daytime precision bombing. The main targets were German aircraft factories, U-boat yards, ball-bearing factories and oil refineries. The main problem, as the British knew, was that the US bombers, operating beyond the range of fighter escorts, were vulnerable to German fighters. Losses, in consequence, were high. On 17 August, for instance, the USAAF attacked the ball-bearing factories at Schweinfurt and Regensburg. Sixty B-17s were shot down – over 15 per cent of the attacking force. While the bombers did considerable damage, German production did not grind to a halt. Armaments Minister Speer was able to rebuild the lost facilities as well as increase ball-bearing imports from Sweden and Switzerland. In a second attack on Schweinfurt on 14 October, two-thirds of the US planes were destroyed or damaged. USAAF losses by the autumn had reached such a high level that daylight raids had to be postponed.

Harris's hopes that Germany would be brought to her knees by bombing were not fulfilled. In fact, German industrial production continued to rise into 1944, despite the destruction and disruption. Air raid precautions plus the tight grip exercised by the Nazi state meant that even after the worst raids, civilian morale did not break. However, the combined bomber offensive was far from a total failure. Germany survived the US air onslaught in 1943 by calling planes back from North Africa, Italy and Russia – with serious results for the *Wehrmacht*'s ground forces. While US bombers suffered heavy losses, they also inflicted serious losses on German fighters. In September, the *Luftwaffe* lost 276 fighters in the West (17.4 per cent of its total fighter force). A further 284 planes were lost in October. In November and December, close to ten per cent of German fighter pilots were killed or maimed each month. In statistical terms, a young German in 1942 had a much better chance of survival by joining the Waffen SS and fighting on the Eastern Front than by becoming a fighter pilot. A young American in 1942 had a better chance of survival by joining the marines and fighting in the Pacific war than by fighting with the 8th Air Force in 1943. While Germany increased aircraft production by 64 per cent in 1943, far more planes would have been built had it not been for the damaging effect of Allied bombing. There was such a heavy rate of attrition that German fighter units hardly grew in strength. Hitler, incensed by Allied attack, was more concerned with retaliation than defence. Rather than give priority to fighter production to meet the bomber offensive, he invested immense resources in the V-1 bomb and V-2 rocket programme.

The tide of aerial battle turned in the spring of 1944. In particular, the fortunes of the USAAF improved. The bombers of the 8th Air Force in Britain were now joined over Germany by the bombers of the 15th Air Force in Italy. More importantly, US fighters, principally the P-51 Mustang and P-47 Thunderbolt, were now able to escort B-17 Flying Fortress and B-24 Liberator bombers to their targets in Germany. The Mustang, an Anglo–American hybrid (it had a US airframe and a British engine) combined the speed, manoeuvrability and firepower of the fighter with the range of the bomber. Carl Spaatz and James Doolittle (hero of the 1942 Tokyo raid), the new commanders of the 8th Air Force, authorized US fighters, after accomplishing their main mission of escorting the bombers, to attack German aircraft anywhere in the Reich. Massive battles were fought over the skies of Germany in early 1944. The USAAF suffered attrition rates close to 20 per cent but inflicted huge casualties on the *Luftwaffe*. In February and March, the Germans lost nearly 1,000 fighters. Although plane production was maintained, Germany did not have sufficient pilots to replace those lost. Given the shortage of both pilots and oil, trainee *Luftwaffe* pilots spent less than 80 hours flying operational aircraft before being sent on their first mission. RAF and USAAF pilots received 225 hours. The result, not surprisingly, was that German pilots were more easily shot down. By May, the *Luftwaffe* was defeated. Forced to come up to protect Germany's industrial base, its fighters were shot down. The true nature of this victory was disguised by the fact that in the spring and summer of 1944, the Allied heavy bombers were redirected (despite Harris's opposition) to France to assist in the D-Day invasion.

The USAAF continued its bombing of synthetic oil plants even during the Normandy battle – to great effect. German oil production had been crippled by September. By the early autumn, the sheer weight of numbers brought on by Allied superiority in production and training capacity meant that air defences over the Reich began to disintegrate. The appearance of German jet fighters was a case of too few too late. By the winter of 1944–5 Allied planes attacked targets almost at will. RAF attacks on the Ruhr resulted in a fall in steel production of 80 per cent in the second half of 1944. Attacks on Germany's rail system meant that raw materials and the few finished goods that were produced could not be moved. Allied bombing in the last months of the war did undermine Germany's capacity to continue the war.

In the summer of 1944, the Germans tried to strike back with the pilot-less V-1 bomb and the V-2 rocket. Though technologically in advance of any comparable Allied device, the V weapons did not materially alter the course of the war. V-1s could be shot down by anti-aircraft fire or fast fighters. Thus, only about a third of the 2,452 launched in June reached London. The V-2, a far more sophisticated weapon, caused consternation when attacks on London began in September but production difficulties, created by bombing raids and the advance of Allied armies, meant that insufficient numbers were built. Between September 1944 and March 1945, an average of only three V-2s a day were launched – not enough to undermine British morale. A US survey estimated that the industrial effort and resources devoted to the V-1 and V-2 weapons equalled the production of 24,000 fighter aircraft. Measured against its return on investment, the V-2, while an engineering triumph, was the least cost-effective weapon of the war.

Conclusion

Those, like Harris, who thought that bombing would lead to the collapse of German civilian morale were proved wrong. Even with 600,000 fatal civilian casualties (a fifth of them children), the Germans continued fighting. Ironically, despite the bombing, German war production was at its height in 1944. However, without the effects of the bombing it would have reached far higher levels of productivity. An investigation by the US government concluded that bombing reduced German production by nine per cent in 1943 and 17 per cent in 1944. Albert Speer put the figure at more than 40 per cent. Whether or not devoting so much in the way of resources to strategic bombing was cost-effective is open to debate. Heavy bombers like the Lancaster were very sophisticated and therefore very expensive weapons, requiring a significant proportion of Allied resources, both material and human, to produce and maintain. The USA was rich enough to bear this burden. Britain's effort may well have been misdirected. It is also worth remembering that 140,000 Allied airmen died in the war.

Was strategic bombing morally correct? The destruction of Dresden on 14 February 1945 has been particularly criticized. Eight hundred RAF and 400 USAAF bombers reduced the beautiful city to a smoking ruin. Some 50,000 Germans probably died. The raid provoked criticism at the time and has been generally condemned since. However, Dresden was an important industrial base and a communications centre: its destruction helped the Russians by hampering German troop movement. Churchill quoted Moses 8:7, 'now those who sow the wind are reaping the whirlwind'. There is no doubt however, that many British politicians felt some guilt about strategic bombing after 1945. 'Bomber' Harris was denied the peerage given to all the other major British commanders, and the bomber aircrews were denied a distinctive medal of their own. This seemed to reflect the feeling that with mass strategic bombing the British had descended to the level of the enemy.

Strategic bombing failed to do what its architects claimed it could do: it did not, by itself, defeat Germany. Yet it did make a significant contribution to Allied victory, especially in the war's final stages. An ancillary result – the defeat of German air power – was to lead to a grave weakening of German military strength in 1944. Strategic bombing was not humane but it was effective. Perhaps the end did justify the means.

11 German defeat 1944–5

This chapter will cover:
- D-Day and the Normandy campaign
- the liberation of France
- the Battle of the Bulge
- Operation Bagration
- the defeat of Nazi Germany.

On 29 April 1945, Adolf Hitler married his long-term mistress Eva Braun. He had little to offer her. His empire had shrunk to a bunker 17 metres (55 feet) beneath the surface of the Reich Chancellery in Berlin. Russian forces were less than half a kilometre (quarter of a mile) away. During the night of 29–30 April, Hitler said farewells to the men and women who had attended him in the last few weeks – secretaries, cooks, adjutants and officials. After a brief sleep, he attended his last situation conference – progress of the fighting in Berlin – on 30 April. He then had lunch with his two favourite secretaries. They ate noodles and salad, and talked sporadically about dogs. Hitler had just had Blondi, his cherished Alsatian bitch, destroyed with the poison he intended to use himself. At about 3 p.m. Eva Hitler emerged from her quarters to join her husband. They shook hands with Bormann, Goebbels and the other senior Nazis who remained in the bunker, and then retired to their private quarters. Frau Goebbels made a brief and hysterical interruption to plead that they escape to Bavaria. Hitler was not persuaded. A few minutes later, Eva bit a cyanide capsule and Adolf shot himself with a pistol. Their bodies were incinerated, the remains buried in shell craters in the Chancellery garden. The next day, Goebbels and his wife poisoned their six children and committed suicide rather than fall into the hands of the Russians.

A year before, Hitler had still controlled much of Europe. Great swathes of conquered territory warded off Allied assault. Nevertheless, Germany could not compete with the Allies in terms of men and weapons. The imbalance of resources meant that German defeat was highly probable unless the Germans could come up with the secret weapons that Hitler was promising. He had some secret weapons – jet aircraft, long-range rockets – but not the crucial one: the atomic bomb. The main question in May 1944 was how long Germany could cling on. It still had certain advantages which, if they could be exploited, could postpone the day of reckoning and possibly even create the conditions for a negotiated armistice. What went wrong for Hitler? Why were the Allies so successful?

D-Day

By the summer of 1944, the conditions were finally right to open the Second Front in France (Operation Overlord). The U-boat threat had been defeated, the *Luftwaffe* largely eliminated and the necessary landing craft constructed. In spite of this, the success of Overlord was not guaranteed. Churchill was far from confident. Hitler, by contrast, was optimistic. He believed his forces would repulse a cross-Channel invasion, leaving him free to concentrate on the Eastern Front. He knew the invasion was coming and prepared accordingly. Rundstedt held overall command in the West but Hitler gave Rommel the task of energizing defensive preparations in France and the Low Countries. Rommel did his job well. By June 1944, the Atlantic Wall, a complex of shoreline obstacles, minefields, concrete bunkers and gun emplacements, was much stronger than it had been in January. There were 60 divisions – some of very high quality – to back up the coastal fortifications. Given the *Luftwaffe*'s terrible losses in the spring air battles over the skies of Germany, Rommel and Rundstedt knew their forces would have to fight while under massive air attack. Their main problem, however, was that they did not know when and where the Allied invasion would come. They thus had to spread their forces thinly. Moreover, much of Rommel's defensive work was wasted on beaches that would not be attacked.

Allied preparations for Overlord were a year in the making. Overall commander Dwight D. Eisenhower was appointed in December 1943. Air Chief Marshal Arthur Tedder, the air commander, and Admiral Sir Bertram Ramsey, the naval commander, were British. Montgomery, who was brought from Italy to command the initial landings, proved difficult. He did not conceal his opinion of US deficiencies: Americans, in turn, did not conceal their opinion of him. Eisenhower needed to use all his tact and charm to keep his team united. His plan envisaged the landing (ultimately) of two million men – the largest amphibious operation in history. Normandy was chosen as the destination since the most obvious invasion point with the shortest crossing (the Pas de Calais) was the most heavily defended. Although the Normandy beaches did not have a port, the Allies hoped to overcome this problem by transporting two floating harbours (mulberries), and they also laid oil pipelines under the ocean (PLUTO) to ensure fuel supplies. Preparations for the invasion were meticulous, the amphibious operations in North Africa, Sicily and Italy providing valuable lessons. Vast forces were assembled: 1,200 fighting ships (against 15 German destroyers); 12,000 aircraft (against 500 German); over 4,000 landing craft and 800 cargo ships. There were tanks with flails to clear minefields, amphibian tanks, tanks to destroy concrete and tanks for bridging dikes. By May 1944, the Allies had assembled the largest and best equipped invasion force ever seen. 'Only the great number of barrage balloons floating constantly in British skies,' said Eisenhower, 'kept the islands from sinking under the waves'.

The whole operation was made possible by complete control of both the sea and the air. French communications, especially railway lines on which the Germans were dependent for supply, were crippled by constant bombing. (Harris and Spaatz, the two bomber chiefs, were put under Tedder's command from April to September – much to their chagrin.) There was also an elaborate deception plan whereby the Germans were led to believe that the main attack was coming in the Pas de Calais area. To achieve this, more bombs were dropped on the Pas de Calais than in Normandy, and an entirely fictitious army was 'created' in south-east England, complete with a credible commander (Patton) and 'revealed' to the Germans by phoney radio messages and false information from double agents. The deception worked. Both Rommel and Rundstedt believed that the Pas de Calais was the most likely target for invasion. Consequently, the bulk of German forces were positioned in the north. This was not the only German problem. Rundstedt and Rommel disagreed about the best way to deal with the landings. Rundstedt favoured holding forces back and launching a counter-attack after the Allies had landed. Rommel, aware that mobility was not practicable without air cover, believed that the Allies had to be defeated quickly – on the beaches. Hitler's intervention pleased neither Rundstedt nor Rommel. He himself would decide when to use the mechanized reserves. Any chance of a prompt response to the invasion evaporated.

D-Day ('D' stands for deliverance) was planned for 5 June. Given the German beach defences, Eisenhower planned to land his forces at low rather than high tide so that they could spot and avoid obstacles. He also intended a dawn attack. There were thus few possible invasion times. Atrocious weather conditions on 5 June forced a postponement. Told by his weather forecasters that there was a brief improvement in the weather thereafter, Eisenhower decided to go for it. Early on 6 June, 23,000 Allied airborne troops landed in Normandy in anticipation of the 140,000 troops who attacked the beaches a few hours later. A brilliant glider operation by the British 6th Airborne succeeded in capturing Pegasus Bridge across the River Orne. Further west, a combination of clouds, heavy flak and inexperienced pilots spread US paratroopers across the length and breadth of Normandy. This dispersion had one advantage:

it totally mystified the Germans as to Allied intentions. The British and Canadians, who landed on the beaches designated Gold, Juno and Sword, met little resistance. The Americans landed further west on Utah and Omaha. On Omaha Beach, US troops were unfortunate enough to run into a German infantry division on exercises. The landing troops got little help from aerial bombardment, and the navy botched its job by dropping the amphibious tanks well beyond the drop-off point. Gradually, however, the attackers prevailed, helped by naval gunfire which took a heavy toll on German defenders. Two thousand and five hundred Americans died on Omaha Beach. Nevertheless, by the end of D-Day, 156,000 Allied soldiers were ashore, with much lighter casualties than anticipated.

The German high command was taken completely by surprise by both the timing and place of the invasion. Poor German weather forecasting had convinced Rommel and Rundstedt that there was little likelihood of an immediate Allied attack. Rommel was in Germany for his wife's birthday. Without his presence, the response to the invasion stalled. Rundstedt asked for release of the mobile reserves early on 6 June, to be told that Hitler was asleep and could not be awakened. Accordingly, the Germans failed to respond with their reserves until the early afternoon, and then only 21st Panzer Division launched a major counter-attack near Caen. It lost 70 of its 124 tanks. What really slowed the German response was the continuing belief that the Normandy landings were a ruse and that the real attack would come at the Pas de Calais. As Allied bombers had by now destroyed all the bridges over the River Seine, the Germans probably could not have moved their forces from the Calais region speedily. Allied air superiority made movement by day virtually impossible. The 2nd Waffen SS Division, which was supposed to take only two days to reach Normandy from Limoges, took nearly two weeks. Therefore, the Allies were able to link up the landing points, move inland 32 kilometres (20 miles) or so and reinforce. Even after one of the worst storms in Channel history, the Allies still managed to land over 500,000 troops by 14 June. By 17 July, that figure had grown to over a million.

Despite this, things did not go altogether according to plan. In the west, the Americans got bogged down in the bocage – a landscape of woods, small fields and orchards which provided the Germans with excellent defensive positions. Although US forces captured Cherbourg at the end of June, it was not usable as a port until September. Meanwhile, Montgomery got held up at Caen, a town he had hoped to take on D-Day. His critics, then and later, condemned his over-cautious approach. His supporters point out that he faced the bulk – and the best – of the German forces. Even so, British forces did miss opportunities to outflank Caen at Villers-Bocage in mid-June. The best that can be said (and Montgomery said it) is that the British provided a shield for the Americans in the west. For over a month, something of a stalemate developed. If Allied leaders were disappointed at the lack of progress, Rommel and Rundstedt had more reason for concern as Allied superiority wore down their forces. In late June, Rundstedt was replaced by Kluge, a tough soldier from the Eastern Front. Arriving full of optimism, his attitude soon changed. Rommel, badly injured when his car was attacked by Allied aircraft on 17 July, went home to convalesce.

In early July, Montgomery took northern Caen after a month of heavy fighting. On 18 July, helped by massive carpet-bombing of German front-line defences, he began an offensive south of Caen. British armoured divisions lost over 200 tanks and failed to breach the German positions. On 20 July, Montgomery called the attack off – it had been a clear failure. Yet British forces had held down most of the German troops. This enabled American General Bradley's 1st Army to break through west of St Lo on 25 July. Augmented by Patton's 3rd Army, US forces headed (somewhat futilely) into Brittany, before swinging south. Eastwards there were open roads and virtually no opposition.

Some German officers, aware that Hitler was leading Germany into the abyss, decided he must be replaced. The only way to replace him was to kill him. On 20 July, Colonel Stauffenberg placed a time bomb under the table in the conference room at the German leader's headquarters in East Prussia. The heavy table took much of the bomb's blast and it only succeeded in destroying Hitler's trousers. In the days that followed, scores of suspected conspirators were rounded up and tortured. Some were hanged with piano wire after a show trial before the People's Court. Others, like Stauffenberg himself, were simply shot. Rommel, suspected (wrongly) of implication in the plot, was given the choice between suicide, which would be presented as a hero's death, or a trial before the People's Court and the possible death of his family. He chose suicide.

In Normandy, Hitler ordered ten German panzer divisions to mount a counter-offensive at Avreches, hoping to cut the US lines of communication. German forces, battered by Allied fighter bombers and artillery, and massively out-tanked, reached Mortain and then stuck. The Allies now had a great opportunity to encircle and destroy the entire German army in Normandy. Montgomery and Bradley were too slow. Three hundred thousand Germans managed to escape before Allied pincers finally cut off the Falaise pocket on 20 August. Even so, the Germans lost 60,000 men and most of their armour. The Falaise engagement, albeit disappointing for the Allies, was an important victory. The battle for Normandy – indeed the battle for France – was won as German forces retreated back to the German border. Kluge, suspected of involvement in the bomb plot and of negotiating surrender, was ordered to return to Germany. On the way, he committed suicide. Model, assumed command in the West.

At the same time, Allied troops, who were mainly pulled from Italy, landed on the French Riviera on 15 August (Operation Dragoon). Churchill, who had wanted to step up the campaign in Italy, was overruled by the Americans who insisted that Italy was a sideshow compared with France. This new front was largely unopposed. Allied troops now advanced up the Rhone Valley. Operation Dragoon had little immediate significance. German forces in southern France would have had to withdraw once the north was lost. However, the capture of the great port of Marseilles proved a logistic godsend to the supply of Allied forces over the winter of 1944–5.

Eisenhower's original intention was to bypass Paris, leaving it under German control. In mid-August, nonetheless, French resistance forces went into action in the French capital. Soon in danger of being crushed, de Gaulle urged that a Free French armoured division should be sent to Paris. Eisenhower reluctantly consented. On 25 August, General Choltitz, the German commandant who ignored Hitler's order to destroy the city, surrendered Paris to de Gaulle. De Gaulle set about reasserting the authority of the French state. France re-emerged if not as a great power, at any rate as an independent country. During the rest of August, the Allied armies, nearly two million strong, rolled forward, liberating most of France. Eisenhower now assumed control of the ground battle from Montgomery. To assuage Montgomery's ego, as well as British public opinion, he was promoted to field marshal. By September, the Germans had suffered some 500,000 casualties in France. Allied casualties had also been heavy (225,000). The Normandy campaign, notwithstanding a number of mistakes, was a great Allied victory that set the stage for the final destruction of Nazi Germany.

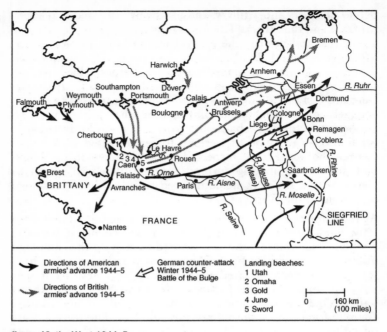

figure 16 the West 1944–5

The Western Front September 1944–January 1945

In early September 1944, as the Germans retreated back towards Germany, it seemed that the war might be over by Christmas. But Allied commanders disagreed about the best way to win it. Montgomery demanded that his British and Canadian forces should get the lion's share of supplies, enabling him to undertake a rapid drive upon Berlin on the northern flank of the Allied advance. The main US commanders – Eisenhower, Bradley and Patton – were determined that Montgomery should not get all the glory. Patton, on the Allied southern flank, was just as certain he could take the US 3rd Army all the way to Berlin. Not convinced that a deep thrust by either Montgomery or Patton could be adequately supplied, Eisenhower decided that Allied forces should advance simultaneously, on a broad front. His main objective was to capture the Ruhr, Germany's industrial heart.

In September, Montgomery advanced into Belgium, capturing the vital port of Antwerp in undamaged condition. Given that Antwerp lies up the Scheldt estuary, the Allies needed to capture both river banks in order to make use of the port. Montgomery failed to take control of the Scheldt, and so failed to trap the German 15th Army in the Low Countries. He had more ambitious plans – the taking of the Rhine bridges at Nijmegen, Eindhoven and Arnhem by airborne assault. His aim was to establish a bridgehead for an advance across the north German plain – Operation Market Garden. However, the operation (17 September) went badly wrong at Arnhem. The attack was poorly planned and poorly led. Moreover, German forces in the area were much stronger than expected and fought tenaciously and efficiently. Of the 9,000 Allied troops landed, fewer than 2,500 escaped. Arnhem proved that any assumptions about the *Wehrmacht*'s imminent defeat were premature. On the only occasion in his career when Montgomery threw caution to the wind, the outcome was tragic.

By the autumn, the Allied advance had stalled. There were three main reasons. First, the Allies were suffering from severe logistical difficulties. Montgomery's failure to capture key German positions on the Scheldt in September (they were not taken until November) meant that Antwerp was unusable as a port until 29 November. For most of the autumn, the Allies only had the port of Cherbourg in operation. German forces still held a dozen Channel ports. The destruction of the French railway system meant that supplies had to be carried across France by trucks. As well as supplying their troops, the Allies also had to feed substantial portions of the French and Belgian populations. Second, the Allied army was short of men. The British replacement pool had almost dried up. US manpower problems were precipitated by the decision to settle for an 89-division army. The result was that there was virtually no reserve. It was thus impossible to pull divisions off the front line for rest and refit. The US manpower shortage was exacerbated by the fact that its army had too many support troops – men who might easily have served in combat. Third, as German forces retreated to the West Wall (or Siegfried Line), their resistance stiffened. They were able to regroup and prepare to defend the Reich.

The Allied advance in Italy had also stalled. Kesselring held his Gothic Line through 1944. Given the Allies' concern with France, American and British forces were reduced rather than increased. The Allied armies in Italy, now hardly equal to the

Germans, continued a largely ineffective offensive. By December they had reached Ravenna but the valley of the River Po was still 80 kilometres (50 miles) away.

In France, the coming of winter put paid to any further Allied advance. Rather than attempt to cross the River Rhine, the Allies settled down to what they expected to be a quiet few months. The German collapse in France had been so complete that it was hard for Allied leaders to credit the notion of a revival of *Wehrmacht* forces. On 15 December, Montgomery told Eisenhower that he would like to go home for Christmas, and the next day he announced to his troops, 'The enemy is at present fighting a defensive campaign on all fronts; his situation is such that he cannot stage major offensive operations'. Montgomery was mistaken. Determined to regain the initiative, Hitler planned a daring counter-attack. Marshalling his dwindling resources, he planned a repeat performance of 1940. Two hundred thousand men and 600 tanks would attack through the Ardennes, recapture Antwerp, split the Allies in two, and roll them back to the sea. Hitler was clutching at straws. His panzers, with only enough fuel to get halfway to Antwerp, would have to capture Allied fuel dumps. Nevertheless, when the German attack came on 16 December, it took the Allies by surprise. It should not have done so. Ultra decrypts had revealed that something was going on but no one took the threat seriously. Eisenhower was playing golf when the attack – on the US sector – began. The foggy weather, which eliminated Allied air superiority, enabled the panzers to advance quickly. At the point of attack, the Germans had a three to one advantage in manpower, a two to one advantage in tanks, and general superiority in artillery. For the most part, US units resisted stubbornly and the German advance was soon behind its time schedule. Forced into a narrow corridor (or Bulge), the Germans failed to capture Bastogne, and were soon desperately short of oil. (Allied dumps were fired before the Germans could reach them.)

The weather cleared on 23 December, enabling the Allied air force to attack the Germans and to drop supplies to the besieged garrison in Bastogne. By Christmas the German offensive, which had only advanced 97 kilometres (60 miles), was halted. The Germans continued to batter Bastogne, even after Patton's 3rd Army had driven a relief column to the town on 26 December. In a ferocious series of battles, Patton steadily ground the Germans down. He realized the possibility of trapping large numbers of Germans in the Bulge. He was overruled.

Montgomery and Bradley were intent on pushing the Germans back rather than attempting to cut them off. By mid-January, they had achieved their objective. The defeat of the Germans in the Battle of the Bulge was a victory for the ordinary US soldier. It was not a victory for Montgomery: his false claim that he had saved the Americans did little to improve Anglo–American relations. Nor was it a victory for the US high command. Eisenhower had been taken by surprise, and for a few days was stunned and demoralized, demanding huge reinforcements which he did not really need. The Americans suffered 81,000 casualties (19,000 dead). The Germans had lost nearly 100,000 men and a great deal of equipment. German industry, devastated by Allied bombing, could not replace the losses. Hitler's last gamble had failed. The main consequence of the Battle of the Bulge was that by committing Germany's last reserves to the Western Front, it guaranteed the Red Army a rapid advance in its winter offensive.

Operation Bagration

Although there was not a great deal of military co-ordination between Russia and the Western Allies, Stalin did promise a summer offensive to coincide with the Normandy landings in 1944, and he was true to his word. Hitler, expecting the Russians to threaten the Romanian oilfields, sent most of his reinforcements south. Instead, the Russians planned to attack Army Group Centre. The operation – Bagration – was named after a Russian general who was mortally wounded resisting Napoleon in 1812. Prior to the attack, there was a preliminary campaign against the Finns in the north, which led to their surrender in September. The main Russian attack, when it came on 22 June (the third anniversary of Operation Barbarossa), was devastating. By concentrating their forces in one place, the Russians enjoyed overwhelming odds – 1.5 million men and 4,000 tanks against half a million Germans with only 600 tanks. By the end of the first week, the Germans, refused permission to retreat, had lost 200,000 men and hundreds of tanks. The Red Army drove deep into Poland. By the end of July, it was at the gates of Warsaw. There it stopped. It did nothing to help the Polish Home Army which rose against the Germans in Warsaw on 1 August. Perhaps Russian forces were exhausted: they suffered huge casualties in July. More likely, Stalin deliberately allowed the Germans to slaughter his Polish enemies: it fitted in with his plans to establish a communist regime in Poland once the war was won. The fighting in Warsaw lasted for some two months. Over 100,000 Poles were killed and the city left in ruins.

Hitler's static defence and reluctance to withdraw gave the initiative to the Russians who, after their success over Army Group Centre, now extended the offensive to the north and the south. In the north, the Red Army pushed into the Baltic States, cutting off German forces in Courland. In October, the Russians entered East Prussia and seemed poised for a full-scale invasion of the Reich itself. The Russian attack in the south, launched on 13 July, was even more successful. The invasion of Romania not only led to the loss of the oilfields but to the destabilization of Hitler's east European alliance system. In late August, the Romanians surrendered to Russia and switched sides. Bulgaria, overrun by the Red Army in September, did likewise. These developments forced Hitler to withdraw his forces from Greece, Albania and southern Yugoslavia. On 20 October, the Red Army entered Belgrade and joined hands with the Yugoslav partisans led by Tito. Hungarian defection was only prevented by German occupation in mid-October. That same month, the Russians entered Hungary and by December had Budapest surrounded. The Soviet offensive into the Balkans was an impressive achievement, destroying much of German Army Group South. Yet the campaign diverted significant Soviet military forces away from central Poland where a renewed offensive might have led to the defeat of Germany in 1944.

In December, there was a lull on the Eastern Front. This was partly because the Russians needed time to replenish their supplies. Furthermore, German resistance stiffened as the fighting approached the Fatherland. Skilful commanders managed to reorganize shattered units and inflict heavy casualties on the Russians through well-organized counter-attacks. These small victories could not hide the extent of the German defeat. German casualties in the summer and autumn of 1944 exceeded 1.5 million men. Innumerable tanks and aircraft had been lost. If the military situation looked grim, the diplomatic situation was even worse. Italy, France, Finland, Romania and Bulgaria had been lost. Many neutrals were now hurrying to join the Allied cause, while others like Sweden and Switzerland were scaling down their supplies to the Reich. By the end of 1944, most Germans knew that the end was nigh.

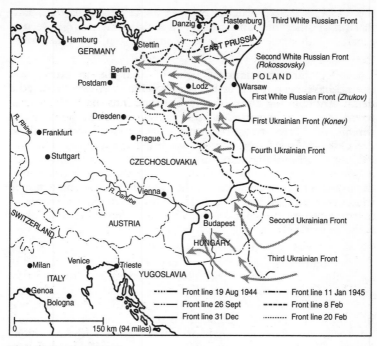

figure 17 the East 1944–5

The end of the Third Reich

On 12 January 1945, the Russian winter offensive began. The Red Army concentrated its forces in Poland. Hitler, unaware of where the Russians would strike, had denuded the centre by trying to hold on to parts of the Baltic and by sending his reserves to Hungary to protect his last remaining oil supplies. Thus, when the winter offensive began, 2.2 million Russians faced only 400,000 Germans. They had a 7.8:1 superiority in guns, 5.7:1 in tanks and 17.6:1 in aircraft. They also had vast fleets of Lend-Lease trucks which ensured reasonable logistical support. The Germans, deprived of most of their fuel by Allied bombing, were virtually immobile. In most places, German defences collapsed. The Red Army smashed through Poland, capturing Warsaw on 17 January. By early February it had advanced 483 kilometres (300 miles) and was on the banks of the Oder, only 72 kilometres (45 miles) from Berlin. East Prussia, Pomerania and much of Silesia (Germany's second greatest industrial zone) were occupied, while in the south Budapest was taken in February. Vienna fell in April.

Some Russian commanders believed that Berlin could and should have been taken in February. Stalin, however, ordered a delay. Anticipating considerable German resistance, he wanted to be sure that his forces were fully prepared. With Berlin threatened, Hitler struggled to assemble a credible defence along the Oder–Neisse River line. By stripping his western forces to the bone and mobilizing old men and boys in a people's militia, a force of nearly one million (poorly equipped) men was deployed on the approaches to the capital. The Germans hoped that the Russians could be held off long enough for most of Germany to be occupied by the Western Allies, who were likely to be less brutal.

By early 1945, the Western Allied forces had two million men (75 per cent of whom were American) ready for the invasion of Germany. Montgomery, predictably, wanted all efforts to be subordinated to a thrust to Berlin by his 21st Army Group in the north. Eisenhower, for military as well as political reasons, was not about to give Montgomery, an unlikely leader of lightning advance, command of the ground war. He stuck with his original strategy – a general advance to and across the Rhine, and then the envelopment of the Ruhr. In February and March, Allied forces, not least those under Patton, conducted an impressive campaign mopping up German forces west of the Rhine. Hitler's demand that his forces defend the Rhineland was disastrous. Model and Rundstedt lost over 250,000 men in defending the indefensible. The Allies were now poised to cross the Rhine. On 7 March, US troops found the railway bridge at Remagen intact. Blown up by the Germans, the explosion had lifted the bridge straight up in the air and it had come down on its pillars. A bridgehead was established. The main crossings came later. Patton crossed on 22 March and Montgomery on 23 March. Allied forces proceeded to surround the Ruhr. Three hundred thousand Germans in the Ruhr pocket surrendered on 18 April; Model shot himself. Montgomery, supported by Churchill, still wanted to push on to Berlin. Eisenhower resisted their entreaties. He knew that Berlin was going to be in the post-war Soviet zone and that its capture was likely to be a bloody affair. Not wishing to upset the Russians or suffer unnecessary losses, he assured Stalin that the Red Army could have the prize of Berlin.

On 12 April, FDR, who had been ailing for some time, died suddenly. His successor, Harry Truman, was inexperienced but determined to continue with what he thought FDR would have done. There was to be no reprieve for Hitler.

Eisenhower ordered British forces to press on to the Danish border and advance along the north German coast. Expecting the Nazis to mount a last stand in the Bavarian and Austrian Alps, he sent large US forces south. The Nazi redoubt here proved to be a fantasy. Other US troops pushed into Saxony where they met up with the Russians at Torgau on 25 April – a dramatic if short-lived demonstration of their comradeship in arms. German resistance in the west was an unpredictable mix of surrender and fanatical resistance. In April 1945, 10,677 Americans died in the European theatre, almost as many as had died in June 1944. The real German collapse did not come until the last week of April.

Meanwhile, the Allies opened an offensive on the Italian front on 9 April, crossing the River Po a fortnight later and pushing north. Brazilian troops took Turin. Japanese Americans, debarred from service in the Pacific, were the first Allied troops to reach the French frontier. Italian partisans took over Milan, Genoa and Venice. On 28 April, Mussolini and his mistress, Clara Petacci, were shot by partisans while attempting to escape to Switzerland. Their bodies were hanged upside down outside a garage in Milan.

Since mid-January, Hitler had confined himself to the bunker under the Chancellery in Berlin where his moods alternated between grim despair and hopes for a miracle. He continued to issue a series of unrealistic orders. By April, knowing that the end was near, he ordered Germany's total destruction – an order that Armaments Minister Speer disobeyed. Hitler was quite prepared to see Germany and the German people destroyed because he felt they had failed him. Yet many Germans fought and died for Hitler as long as they had guns and ammunition.

The Battle for Berlin finally began on 14 April. Stalin, having promised Zhukov that he could take Berlin, now turned it into a race between Zhukov, Konev and Rokossovsky. Stalin gave them two weeks to finish the job, and that turned out to be about right. The Russians had overwhelming force – some three million men, 6,250 tanks and 7,500 planes. The Germans, desperately short of fuel, had about 3,300 aircraft, 1,000 tanks, 320,000 soldiers and a million men in the people's militia. Atrocities by the avenging Russians elsewhere in conquered

Germany – looting, mass rapes and brutal murders – gave the defenders the strength of desperation. The Russians suffered over 350,000 casualties as they fought their way street by street into the rubble-strewn city. As the Russians neared Hitler's bunker, Hitler committed suicide on 30 April. The Berlin garrison surrendered on 2 May. Admiral Donitz, Hitler's appointed successor, tried to secure a surrender in the West while continuing the war in the East. Eisenhower refused. Donitz's delay in surrendering at least enabled some 1.8 million Germans to become Western POWs; 1.5 million became Russian POWs.

The end was ragged. The first large-scale German surrender came in Italy on 29 April. On 4 May, Montgomery accepted the surrender of German forces in Holland, Denmark and north-west Germany. The Germans in Bavaria surrendered to the Americans on 5 May. Full, unconditional surrender finally came on 7 May when General Jodl penned the document at Eisenhower's headquarters in Reims. This was repeated for the Russians in Berlin by Field Marshal Keitel at midnight on 8–9 May. On 8 May, President Truman and Prime Minister Churchill announced the victory in Europe (VE) to their people. The Russians celebrated victory on 9 May. Over the next few days, other pockets of resistance capitulated. Germany lay in ruins: it had suffered total defeat.

Conclusion

Many Germans, ideologically committed to Hitler, fought with fanaticism to the end. Fanaticism was not enough. By mid-1944, German forces were outnumbered and outgunned. It is a moot point whether they were also outfought. By the spring of 1945, US commanders, not least Patton, were ready and able to exploit every advantage. The encirclement of the Ruhr, the greatest US victory of the war, was evidence that the Americans had developed an excellent understanding of the art of twentieth-century war. Russian military leadership was even more impressive. From Bagration to the winter offensive of 1945, Russian commanders exhibited outstanding capabilities in deception, planning and the conduct of operations. Nevertheless, the Russians suffered huge casualties. The German army waged war professionally from first to last.

12

the defeat of Japan 1944–5

This chapter will cover:
- the war in Burma
- the battles for the Marianas, the Philippines, Iwo Jima and Okinawa
- Hiroshima and Nagasaki
- Japanese surrender.

On 16 July 1945, US scientists working on the Manhatten Project gathered in a remote spot in the New Mexican desert. They were about to test the outcome of their work – the production of the world's first atomic bomb. In a tense atmosphere, the plutonium device – nicknamed Fat Man – was detonated. A huge fireball enveloped the desert, sending out blinding waves of light. A column of cloud pushed upward forming the shape of a mushroom. The blast registered a force of 17,000 tons of TNT. Some of the observers felt jubilant: their project had succeeded. Others felt chastened by the destructive power that now rested in humankind's hands. Within the next month, two more atomic bombs were exploded – for real. These bombs brought an end to the war with Japan. How important was the atomic bomb in the defeat of Japan? Should it have been used?

Burma and China 1944–5

Although US forces were certain to bear the brunt of the fighting against Japan during 1944–5, Britain had a role in Burma. After inflicting a crushing defeat on Japanese forces at Kohima and Imphal, General Slim prepared to invade Burma. His 14th Army was a multicultural force: seven of its 12 infantry divisions were Indian; three were mainly African; and only two divisions were predominantly European. Slim, through careful training and painstaking logistical arrangements, had raised the morale of his men to the point where they had lost their fear of the Japanese. He was now in a strong position. The 100,000 Japanese troops in Burma were desperately short of supplies. Slim had a four to one superiority in aircraft and could count on US and Chinese forces for supporting operations in northern Burma. Meanwhile, General Wingate's Chindits wreaked havoc behind the Japanese lines. In late 1944, Slim crossed into Burma. His force, numbering 260,000, pushed southwards, crossing the Irrawaddy River in March 1945 in one of the most brilliant assault crossings of the war. By May, Slim had taken Rangoon. A Japanese counter-attack proved disastrous. Ambushed by Indian troops, they lost 11,000 men. The rout became a massacre as 10,000 more Japanese soldiers died along and in the Sitang River. The 14th Army lost only 435 dead. The Japanese, accepting defeat in Burma, withdrew most of their remaining troops to fight the Americans in the Pacific. They had lost more than 50,000 dead in the last year of the war in Burma.

Britain's war in the Far East was fought to recover an empire which it would soon abandon. While the humiliations visited upon British forces in Malaya and Singapore in 1942 are often highlighted, Slim's triumphs in India and Burma during 1944–5 have sometimes been forgotten. The British Empire had proved that it had the resilience to strike back. Australian success in mopping up stranded Japanese forces in New Guinea, the Solomons and Borneo during 1944–5 was another example of the Commonwealth doing its 'bit' for the Allied cause.

FDR's hopes that Chiang Kai-shek might be able to take on the huge Japanese forces in China proved illusory. Lend-Lease aid, sent in ever greater quantities after the Burma road was reopened, had little effect. By late 1944, it was clear that there would be no major challenge to the Japanese army by Chinese ground forces. Chiang's troops spent more time hounding the Chinese communists than fighting the Japanese. The stalemate in China forced US diplomats and military planners (against their better judgement) to look to Stalin for help. At Yalta in February 1945, Stalin agreed to join the war 90 days after Germany's defeat. His price for intervention was the restoration of Russia's losses after the Russo–Japanese war of 1904–5, a recognition that Mongolia was to be a Russian satellite, and the acquisition of the Kurile Islands.

The Marianas and the Philippines 1944–5

By 1944, the Joint Chiefs had reached a consensus on how best to defeat Japan. They saw no immediate value in liberating the southern Philippines or the Dutch East Indies. Instead, they were determined to go for the jugular – the home islands of Japan. They first needed to capture islands close to Japan. In the summer of 1944, Admiral King believed that the capture of the Marianas – Saipan, Guam and Tinian – was more important than MacArthur's move towards the Philippines. The Marianas had great potential as forward-operating bases for the new B-29 Superfortress bombers (which could fly 6,436 kilometres (4,000 miles) and carry a ten-ton bomb load) and US submarines. The latter, guided by navy code breakers, were already having a major impact, making it difficult for Japan to send troops to the Marianas and the Philippines. Submarines were also inflicting heavy losses on Japanese merchant shipping, especially oil

figure 18 the Far East 1944–5

tankers. King knew that Saipan, with some 32,000 Japanese troops, would be a hard nut to crack. US planes won control of the air before 8,000 marines went in on 15 June. The land battle soon became a murderous war of attrition.

Prime Minister Tojo, determined to hold the Marianas, ordered Admiral Ozawa, with several new carriers, to head to Saipan. US commanders knew the Japanese Mobile Fleet was coming. On 19 June, young Japanese Sea Eagles left the carriers to attack US forces. Known officially as the Battle of the Philippines Sea, US naval aviators of Task Force 58 called the engagement 'the Marianas Turkey Shoot'. US veterans, fully exploiting the radar intercept systems in their Hellcat fighters, shot down 300 enemy planes. The Americans lost less than 30. That afternoon, US submarines sank the *Taiho* and another Japanese carrier. The *Taiho* had been at the cutting edge of technology: its crew, however, had not mastered the technology. US Admiral Spruance mistakenly called off the action and ordered Task Force 58 to sail east to protect the amphibious force from a possible surface attack. Ozawa, with very little air protection, turned for home. On 20 June, 200 US aircraft went after him. They scored hits on six warships and sank a light carrier for the loss of 20 planes in action. Eighty planes were lost, however, as they returned to their carriers in the dark and with empty oil tanks. This loss took away some of the lustre from the victory of 19 June. Nevertheless, the two-day battle had broken Japanese naval air power.

Ozawa's defeat meant that the Japanese could not hold Saipan. Even so, the fighting raged for almost a month. US ground forces suffered over 14,000 casualties. Virtually the entire enemy force was annihilated. Hundreds of Japanese defiantly shot, beheaded, drowned and blew up one another rather than surrender. In July, the Americans attacked Guam. Eighteen thousand and five hundred Japanese again put up ferocious resistance. The island finally fell into US hands on 10 August. Some Japanese soldiers, unaware that the war had ended, remained in the hills until 1972. The Americans suffered 7,800 casualties. Tinian was captured by the start of August. The marines destroyed the 8,000-strong garrison with methodical daylight advances and stubborn night defences against predictable *banzai* (suicidal) charges. Tinian soon became the main base for the B-29s assigned to bomb the home islands of Japan.

General MacArthur was determined to recover the Philippines, especially Luzon. By contrast, Admirals King and Nimitz wanted to bypass the Philippines and attack Formosa. King believed the proposed Philippines campaign was essentially about salvaging MacArthur's reputation, and he thought that liberating Luzon would result in the killing of thousands of Japanese, Americans and Filipinos without any important impact on Japanese power. FDR travelled to Honolulu in July 1944 to hear the arguments from Nimitz and MacArthur. MacArthur claimed that retaking the Philippines would cut the Japanese off from the oil and other essential resources of the East Indies. He also took the high moral ground that the US owed the Filipinos their freedom having abandoned them in 1942. MacArthur got his way. His assault on the Philippines would be supported by the navy. While Nimitz took the key islands of the western Carolines, Admiral Halsey roamed the western Pacific, attacking airfields and harbours on Yap, Mindanao, the Palaus and Formosa. Halsey urged MacArthur and Nimitz to abandon Mindanao as an objective and go straight for Leyte, a recommendation approved by the Joint Chiefs in September. Concurrently, US marines waged a bitter four-week battle to take Peleliu in the Palaus.

The way was now clear for a landing in the Philippines. MacArthur landed at Leyte on 20 October. Wading ashore, he announced to the Filipinos that he had 'returned'. The Japanese, hoping to destroy MacArthur's transports, brought in fleets from three directions. The Americans, with radio intelligence, submarine sightings and air patrols, had excellent intelligence. On 24 October, Halsey ordered Task Force 38 to attack the Japanese Centre Force, led by Admiral Kurita, inside the San Bernardino Strait. Seriously damaged by submarine and air attack, the Japanese ships retreated from the Strait. Soon after midnight, the Japanese Southern Force made contact with Admiral Kinkaid's fleet in the Surigao Straits. Kinkaid took decisive action and won a dramatic victory in an old-fashioned naval battle.

The Japanese Northern Carrier Force aimed to decoy the US fleet from Leyte. The plan worked. Once the carriers were spotted sailing south, Halsey immediately ordered his fleet north, leaving no task force to cover San Bernardino Strait. Kurita, far from beaten, now turned his Centre Force around. After dawn, his fleet, comprising four battleships and eight heavy cruisers, threaded through the Strait and bore down on the US transports with nothing to impede it except six small escort carriers and seven destroyers. In a desperate fight against far superior firepower, two US destroyers and one escort carrier were sunk. The losses were not in vain. US ships and planes disabled three enemy cruisers. A confused Kurita – within sight of the US transports – broke off and ordered his force back through the Strait where it had to endure more submarine and air attacks. He later claimed that an intercepted message persuaded him that massive US reinforcements were on the way.

The last major engagement took place off Luzon. This was carrier versus carrier action. Although Japanese planes had greater ranges than their US counterparts, most Japanese pilots had little training or experience: the best pilots had already been killed. US planes sank four carriers and three destroyers before the fleet broke off to (unsuccessfully) chase Kurita. The three encounters on 25 October are known collectively as the Battle of Leyte Gulf. The battle, which saw 282 warships involved, remains the greatest naval engagement in history. The Japanese lost most of their remaining sea power – three battleships, four carriers, ten cruisers, nine destroyers – and the ability to protect the Philippines.

US ships now had to face a new threat – suicide attacks. Virtually all the men who made up the 'kamikaze' units were volunteers. (They were named kamikaze after the 'Divine Wind' which had saved Japan from Mongol invasion in the thirteenth century.) The first kamikaze crash-dived into US carriers on 30 October. In November, four more carriers suffered substantial damage. The Americans set about refitting their carriers so they were better able to deal with kamikaze attack. This meant that MacArthur's ground forces lacked crucial air support.

MacArthur underestimated the scale of Japanese resistance on Leyte. General Yamashita, the Japanese army commander in the Philippines, increased the Leyte garrison from 23,000 to 70,000 during the course of the campaign. While the US 6th Army's initial landings went deceptively well, the landing beaches, anchorages and air bases were soon the target for Japanese planes, thrown into the battle in both conventional and suicide attack. US losses were severe. The 6th Army's embattled divisions pushed forward, struggling over the mountain roads towards the ports that were used to bring in enemy reinforcements. For more than a month the battle was a dogged war of attrition. Not until late December did US forces finally surround the Japanese and bring the campaign to a successful conclusion. The Japanese lost nearly 70,000 dead, inflicting over 15,000 casualties on the Americans.

On 9 January 1945, after a massive naval bombardment, the US 6th Army landed in Luzon. Manila, the Philippines' capital, was

MacArthur's main goal. Yamashita, with 267,000 men, waged a ruthless and brilliant defensive campaign. (It was one for which MacArthur eventually hanged the Japanese general.) The battle for Manila raged for almost a month. The combined effect of house-to-house fighting and massacres by the Japanese resulted in the deaths of 100,000 Filipino citizens. The US suffered some 7,000 casualties. The US press showed relatively little interest in the Philippines after Manila's capture. This was fortunate for MacArthur who fought a lacklustre campaign. The Japanese continued to fight to the death, not just against US forces but also against ruthless Filipino guerrillas. Yamashita did not surrender until September 1945.

Iwo Jima and Okinawa

Iwo Jima, a speck of volcanic rock, was the next US marine target in February 1945. The island, some 1,207 kilometres (750 miles) from Tokyo, was needed to provide fighter escort for bombers and as a landing strip for disabled B-29s. Defended by 21,000 well-entrenched Japanese, six weeks of ferocious fighting were required to conquer an island just 13 kilometres (eight miles) square. Nearly 7,000 Americans were killed. (Twenty-seven marines and US sailors received Medals of Honor – a wartime record.) Only 216 Japanese soldiers were taken alive.

On 1 April, 50,000 US troops (their numbers subsequently increased to 250,000) landed on the island of Okinawa in the largest amphibious operation of the Pacific war. General Ushijima, with 100,000 men, did not try to fight the Americans on the beaches. Instead, he established strong defensive positions inland, where naval guns could not assist the invaders. The struggle for Okinawa itself consisted of a slow and bloody advance by US troops. Kamikaze bombers did their best to destroy US supply ships. Although they posed a serious threat, only three per cent of the kamikaze planes actually hit their targets. Suicide submarines and small boats were no more successful in stopping the US advance. Finally, the giant battleship *Yamato* and nine other ships – the remnant of the once-great Imperial Navy – headed for Okinawa. The small fleet, with no air cover and fuel for only a one-way trip, was intercepted by US planes and largely destroyed (*Yamato* was sunk). On Okinawa, fighting continued until late June. The Japanese lost an estimated 90,000 dead. (Virtually all their senior officers committed ritual suicide). Tens of thousands of Japanese civilians also died. Okinawa cost the USA 7,000 dead, 32,000 wounded and a further 26,000 non-battle casualties, largely consisting of troops suffering from breakdown under the stress of battle.

By mid-1945, Japan was nearing collapse. Two-thirds of its merchant shipping had been sunk. Industrial production was at a near standstill. US ships roamed the coastline of Japan, shelling targets ashore. Hundreds of B-29s attacked Japan almost at will, inflicting terrible destruction. In a single raid on Tokyo on 8 March, 83,000 people were killed – 20,000 more than all the British deaths from air attack throughout the war. By July 60 per cent of the ground area of Japan's 60 largest towns had been destroyed. As the Allied blockade grew ever more effective and internal communications were disrupted by air raids, many Japanese were close to starvation.

In April 1945, Admiral Suzuki, aged 78, became Japanese premier. Although more disposed to peace than his army predecessor, he was not prepared to accept unconditional surrender, which meant there was no guarantee that the semi-divine Hirohito would remain as Emperor. The Japanese government, riven with conflict, tried to enlist Stalin as intermediary. Stalin, now resolved on intervention in the Far East, showed no interest. The war, therefore, continued. There was no question that Japan would be defeated. The question was how many Allied lives would be lost in the process. By June, the Allies were planning three massive invasions – Olympic, Coronet and Zipper – to capture the Japanese homelands. Given what had happened on Okinawa, it was feared that all three operations would result in huge – perhaps a million – Allied casualties. President Truman was aware that he could soon expect Russian assistance. By the summer of 1945, however, many Americans viewed Russian intrusion in the Far East war with some misgivings. Stalin was far from trustworthy. Not unnaturally, the Americans were keen to end the war as quickly as possible and win it themselves.

Hiroshima, Nagasaki and Japanese surrender

By July 1945, a new force had come into being which changed all strategic calculations. For three years FDR had supported the

Manhattan Project – the development of an atomic bomb. The strands of scientific development that produced the bomb ran back to Germany. Had Nazi bigotry not driven Jewish scientists into exile, Germany might well have developed the atomic bomb first. In 1939, FDR, fearful of German intent, set up a committee to co-ordinate information in the nuclear fusion field. After August 1942, millions of dollars were secretly poured into the Manhattan Project. In December 1942, Dr Enrico Fermi and other scientists achieved the first atomic chain reaction in a squash court at the University of Chicago's Stagg Field, removing any doubts of the bomb's feasibility. Gigantic plants sprang up at Oak Ridge, Tennessee and Hanford, Washington, to make plutonium, while a group of physicists under Dr Robert Oppenheimer worked out the scientific and technical problems of bomb construction at Los Alamos, New Mexico. The Manhattan Project, very much the brainchild of FDR, employed 120,000 people and cost US$2 billion. The secrecy surrounding the project was demonstrated by the fact that Vice President Truman knew nothing about it until he became President on FDR's death in April 1945. By the summer, the US had three bombs ready. (One of these was successfully tested in New Mexico on 16 July.) It fell to Truman to make the decision to use the weapon.

Truman went to Potsdam in July to meet Stalin and Churchill. The latter was soon replaced by Clement Attlee, the Labour leader who defeated Churchill in the July 1945 election. Stalin did not react when Truman hinted that the USA had a 'super bomb'. He probably knew as much about US nuclear weapons as Truman: he had his own nuclear programme and had access to espionage reports from Los Alamos. On 26 July, Truman approved the Potsdam Declaration demanding that Japan surrender immediately or face 'prompt and utter destruction'. The Declaration, which did not mention the Emperor or his future, was rejected by Japan.

On 27 July, Truman confirmed an earlier order that the 20th Air Force should drop an atomic bomb on one of four target cities if Japan did not surrender before 3 August. The target choice and timing was to depend on the weather and other local considerations. US navy warships had already brought two devices to Tinian: one a second plutonium Fat Man; the other a uranium Little Boy. Hiroshima was selected as the target because it had some military value; its T-shaped bridge made a perfect aiming point, and it was not thought to contain Allied

POW camps. (This was a wrong assumption.) On 6 August, the *Enola Gay*, a B-29 bomber, set out from Tinian with a crew commanded by Colonel Paul Tibbets. At 8.15 a.m. Little Boy was dropped above Hiroshima. Some 60,000 people were killed instantly. Thousands more died from wounds, burns and the effects of radiation in the weeks that followed. On 8 August, Russia declared war on Japan and 1.6 million Soviet troops launched a massive invasion of Manchuria. The following day, another B-29 dropped Fat Man on Nagasaki, with slightly less horrific results – 40,000 people died.

Some Americans at the time (for example, Eisenhower) were convinced that Japan was close to surrender and that the use of the atomic bomb was unnecessary. Since 1945, many more have questioned Truman's decision. He had few qualms. There is no doubt that his main concern was to bring a speedy end to the war and save Allied lives. Truman believed if he had not used the bomb, he would not have been able to look in the eyes of the parents of US military personnel who died because he lacked the moral courage to use it. For him, it was one of the easier decisions of his presidency. It was a bonus that the bomb would reveal US power to Stalin and, assuming it brought a quick end to the war, forestall Russian advances into China. Public opinion in the USA and Britain showed support for using the bombs. There was little sympathy for Japan, particularly as the horrifying evidence of the treatment by the Japanese of POWs and captured civilians had already come to light.

The atomic bombs did hasten the war's end. While some Japanese leaders wanted to surrender well before 6 August, others still wished to continue the fight, even after Hiroshima and Nagasaki. On 9 August, Suzuki's cabinet remained deadlocked on the issue. That night, Emperor Hirohito attended the cabinet meeting and listened to the debate. Sometime in the early morning he spoke, urging the cabinet to accept the inevitable and surrender, the sole condition being that he remained as sovereign. His message was communicated to Washington, London and Moscow. Truman decided to accept the deal. Attlee agreed: Britain had for some time favoured the preservation of the Japanese emperor system. Only Stalin, who wanted a major victory, felt cheated. On 12 August, the Allies accepted the Japanese terms with the caveats that the Emperor would be held responsible for a co-operative surrender and that the 'ultimate form' of a future Japanese government would depend on 'the freely expressed will of the Japanese people'.

Inside the Japanese army, a group of junior officers planned to assassinate the peace faction and force the Emperor to fight on. Suzuki, aware of the threat of a military coup, wavered. Hirohito acted decisively. Gathering his main cabinet officers and advisers on 14 August, he demanded that they all accept his decision to surrender: 'The unendurable,' he said, 'must be endured'. There was a last alarm. Hirohito had recorded a radio address which would tell the Japanese people of his decision. Junior officers broke into his palace, hoping to destroy the recording and force the Emperor to fight to the last man. They failed to find the recording and hesitated to lay hands on the Emperor's sacred person. Troops loyal to the Emperor quickly squashed the attempted coup. On the morning of 15 August, the recording, the first ever made by a Japanese sovereign, was broadcast. The Emperor ordered his troops to lay down their arms and to co-operate with Allied forces to preserve order and discipline. Given that Hirohito spoke the flowery language of the court, many Japanese did not understand what he was saying.

In Washington, Truman announced that Japan had accepted unconditional surrender. After preliminary arrangements by Japanese emissaries in Manila, US troops landed in Japan on 28 August without incident. On 2 September, MacArthur accepted Japan's formal surrender on the deck of the battleship *Missouri* in Tokyo Bay. By Truman's decree, this marked V-J day (Victory over Japan).

Conclusion

The USA, with a smidgen of assistance from Britain, China, Australia, India and Russia, had defeated Japan. It had done so at a reasonably low cost. It devoted only 15 per cent of its war effort to Japan; the other 85 per cent had been devoted to Germany. Once Germany was defeated, Japan stood no chance. The USA was determined to smash Japanese militarism, and prepared to kill as many of the enemy as was necessary to win the war. Japanese suicidal courage proved no match for superior US technology and resources.

13

why did the Allies win?

This chapter will cover:
- morale
- resources
- technology and intelligence
- leadership and co-operation.

In his excellent book, *Why the Allies Won*, Richard Overy makes the point that explanations of Allied victory contain a strong element of determinism – the Allies had superior resources and god on their side, and so were bound to win and did. In reality, there was nothing predetermined about Allied success. The margin between victory and defeat was slender. For instance, what would have happened if the *Luftwaffe* had kept bombing RAF airfields in September 1940; if Japan had attacked Russia in 1941; and if Hitler had not sent forces into Stalingrad? It is worth remembering that by 1942 almost the entire resources of continental Europe were in German hands, and Japan had carved out a huge empire in Asia. Overy stresses the need to consider not just the economic resources of the two sides but the use made of those resources, the will to fight, the unity of the two sides and leadership. If the outcome was not inevitable, did the Allies win or did the Axis lose the Second World War?

National morale

The lesson of the First World War, it was widely believed, was that failure to maintain civilian morale could lead to internal collapse, revolution and defeat. Civilians were involved in the Second World War to a far greater extent than in the First, and suffered even greater casualties than the armed forces. All the belligerent states were aware of the importance of maintaining national morale. All made strenuous efforts to control and persuade their populations to stand firm. All maintained ministries of propaganda or information, using the widest possible range of means available – films, radio, press and posters. The autocratic states had coercive and propaganda systems in place well before the outbreak of war. Wartime governments in Britain and the USA proved equally adept at manipulating opinion.

Britain

The image of Britain at war, a Britain 'that could take it', a people united and defiant, cheerful and confident, is virtually indestructible. Cultivated by a skilful media (which preferred the selective telling of the truth to blatant propaganda), the image was believed by many at the time probably because it was largely true. Despite strikes and a lack of commitment in some quarters, the war effort did generate a real sense of unity.

Civilians and the armed forces alike proved willing to meet Churchill's call for 'blood, toil, sweat and tears'. While the Emergency Powers Act (May 1940) gave the government virtually unlimited powers, the authorities did not adopt the kind of draconian coercive measures common in Germany and Russia.

Germany

Most Germans remained loyal to Hitler's regime from first to last. Passive loyalty to the regime was due in part to the degree of control exercised at home by the Nazi Party and the security organs of the state (such as the Gestapo). Nasty penalties awaited those who opposed the regime or spread defeatism. However, German tenacity cannot be explained simply by oppression. The fact that the German civilian population was handled with kid gloves by the Nazi government for much of the war possibly helped morale. More importantly, most Germans, both in and out of uniform, believed that Germany was fighting the good fight against international capitalism and Jewish Bolshevism. Victory and limited calls for sacrifice sustained German morale in the early years of the war. By the time the going got tough in 1943, Hitler's regime had built up such a reservoir of goodwill that most Germans remained loyal – even though Hitler almost disappeared from view after 1942. After Stalingrad, Propaganda Minister Joseph Goebbels was highly successful in inspiring Germans to wage 'Total War' – a war for racial survival against barbaric Slavic hordes. In contrast to 1918, German society did not fracture under the strains of looming defeat. Workers continued to produce and soldiers to fight to the bitter end.

The Soviet Union

The peoples of the Soviet Union endured more hardship than anyone else. Some 25 million probably died during the war. The feared security apparatus, even more pervasive than in Germany, was partly responsible for maintaining commitment to Stalin's regime. A huge network of labour camps operated through the war, as it had in peace, for suspect citizens. The wretched nature of the communist regime made some non-Russians potentially disloyal. Yet the barbarity of German occupation policies made Stalin seem the lesser of two evils. All-pervasive state propaganda also helped to maintain public support. The conflict was portrayed more in terms of the 'great patriotic war' rather than as a great class struggle. Russian heroes of the past, like Peter the Great, were rehabilitated, and even the Orthodox Church was enlisted to preach the crusade against the invaders.

The USA

The experience of US citizens was very different to that of civilians in other combatant states. The war effort meant full employment, rising living standards and no air raids. (Even in the US armed forces, pay and conditions were significantly better than in the services of other countries.) This helped morale, which was also sustained by a vast Hollywood public relations machine. Most Americans felt – in many ways rightly – that they were the good guys, fighting against evil.

Japan

Japan was at war from 1937. From early on there were food shortages and rationing. In 1945, air raid attacks caused horrendous casualties. Nevertheless, the Japanese tenaciously supported a cause they believed to be their Emperor's.

The belief that bombing raids would destroy civilian morale proved false. British morale survived the Blitz; German and Japanese morale survived much more intensive bombing. It may be that bombing improved morale because it made people hate the enemy and made them more determined to fight. The exception was Italy, where bombing seems to have made Mussolini rather than the bombers unpopular. Mussolini's fall in 1943 is the only instance of internal discontent bringing down a major combatant government. From start to finish, the Italians showed little stomach for the war. By contrast, the Germans and Japanese remained defiant to the end. Importantly, they did not have a monopoly of staying power. The Russians withstood incredible hardship. The average Briton grumbled but put up with things, while the average American did not have much to grumble about. Allied will remained strong if only because the war then – as now – seemed just. Axis triumph threatened to herald a new dark age of barbarism. There was also the simple morality of self-defence.

Resources

Victory in war, thought Napoleon Bonaparte, usually goes to the 'big battalions' – the side with most men and most resources. The Allies had far greater resources than the Axis powers. Britain's imperial possessions amounted to a fifth of the world's land surface. The population of Russia (170 million) was approximately the same as that of Germany, Italy and Japan combined. The USA easily out-produced the combined Axis powers in terms of aircraft, guns and tanks.

Perhaps the most important natural resource was oil. The Allies had access to 90 per cent of the world's oil. (The USA produced two-thirds of it.) The Axis powers needed to acquire oilfields in order to continue to fight – thus the importance of Romania, the Dutch East Indies and the Caucasus. Allied air attack in Europe and submarine action in the Pacific reduced the flow of oil imports to Germany and Japan to such a degree that by mid-1944, petrol shortages crippled parts of their industrial base and did serious damage to their armed forces. As well as oil, the Western Allies had access to almost every strategic raw material. Russia, largely self-sufficient before and during the war, had what it needed to maintain a massive arms industry – coal, iron ore, chrome, phosphates and manganese. Allied farmers did their part to win the war, especially US farmers who fed their fellow countrymen and virtually every ally except China. US and British workers, even with rationing, received the food they needed to function, (generously) estimated at a minimum of 3,500 calories a day. While Britain did its best to grow more food, it was still dependent on imported foodstuffs for 30 per cent of what it ate. The Germans depended on confiscating the foodstuffs of occupied nations. These flowed back into Germany until 1944 when territorial losses and the effects of Allied bombing disrupted food distribution. The fact that Russia lost almost half its arable land during 1941–2 resulted in near-famine conditions for much of the war. Japan, reliant upon imported foodstuffs, was on the verge of mass starvation in 1945.

Germany

Germany's war economy generally underperformed. Hitler had not planned or prepared for a lengthy war. Even when it was clear that the war would be long, the country did not fully mobilize its population or resources. Germany produced far fewer weapons than her raw materials, manpower, scientific skill and factory infrastructure should have made possible. The first problem was her lack of key resources, not least rubber and oil. Conquest, trade and efforts to manufacture substitutes only partially filled the gap. Nazi ideology, especially the failure to use German women efficiently, was the second problem. Despite Hitler's belief that women should stick to their roles as wives and mothers, there had actually been more employed females in Germany in 1939 than in Britain. However, no great effort was made to increase the female work force after 1939 or direct more of it to the armaments industries. A third problem was Hitler's reluctance to impose heavy burdens on the civilian population. This, he believed, had led to German collapse in 1918. A fourth problem was the inefficiency of the Nazi state. Run by competing authorities, there was massive in-fighting between those in positions of responsibility. Chaos at the centre prevented rational direction of people and resources. From 1939 to 1941, the German economy was not significantly different from that of peacetime. The material needs of the armed forces were sustained but not significantly increased. A fifth problem was the failure to standardize and mass produce. German manufacturers produced small quantities of very good weapons; her enemies simply produced much more. In 1943, for example, Russia turned eight million tons of steel and 90 million tons of coal into 48,000 heavy guns and 24,000 tanks. Germany turned 30 million tons of steel and 340 million tons of coal into 27,000 heavy guns and 17,000 tanks.

Not until Albert Speer became Minister for Munitions in 1942 did Germany begin to streamline her war production. Competition for resources between services and industries was reduced and production tailored to available resources. Older men (aged 60–5), as well as women (aged 17–45), were partially mobilized for war work. In 1944, full wage and price controls and more stringent rationing scales were introduced. Speer's work paid dividends as war production increased dramatically. By 1944, Germany was producing four times as many tanks and military aircraft as in 1940. Despite heavy Allied bombing, German production levels actually peaked in the last six months of 1944 – by which time it was too late. The problem was that the Allies were even more successful in organizing war production. Despite all Speer's efforts, Germany in 1944 was still massively out-produced.

Increase in output was partly the result of the intensified exploitation of Germany's occupied territories. Germany's population base – 76 million in 1939 – was much smaller than that of its combined adversaries, with knock-on effects on available military and civilian manpower. Fortunately for Speer, the Third Reich could draw on vast foreign labour reserves. By 1944, eight million foreigners were employed in the greater Reich. Voluntary and conscripted skilled and semi-skilled labour was imported from western Europe. The bulk of unskilled labour was forcibly brought in from the East. Yet the quantity and quality of food provided to those conscripted from the East was so poor that their capacity to work was far below potential. Labour apart, Germany was not particularly successful at exploiting the resources of the conquered territories.

Italy

Italy's economic war effort was as lamentable as its battlefield effort. Its industrial production actually fell after 1940. This was largely due to lack of natural resources. Failure to rationalize production and engage in development was also a factor. Inferior weaponry put Italian forces at a huge disadvantage. The same was true of the forces of Germany's other European partners – Finland, Romania and Hungary. These states did not have the industrial capacity to produce modern weapons on any scale.

The Soviet Union

The move to a war economy required no essential change in Soviet economic practice. Russia's main problem was that during 1941–2 she lost land where 40 per cent of her grain and 60 per cent of her coal and steel had been produced. Despite this, the strength of Russia's armed forces steadily grew, as did her armament production. A new war economy was created in Siberia, the Ural Mountains and beyond the River Volga. Factories about to be overrun by the Germans were 'packed up' and transferred to the east. Over 1,500 factories – and ten million workers – were relocated. Coal and steel industries had been developed in the east before the war, and these provided the basic resources for renewed armament production. Central planning dictated targets: attaining the targets at factory level depended on the initiative of managers and workers who squeezed production from improvised machines. The fact that

Russia had only a small number of different types of weapon –
two main types of tank and five types of aircraft – helped to
maximize output. In 1942, arms production exceeded 1941
levels and, more importantly, exceeded those of Germany.
During 1943–4, Russia turned out 6,000 more tanks and self-
propelled guns and over 10,000 more combat aircraft than
Germany. US Lend-Lease aid, not least with regard to trucks,
food and high quality steel, greatly assisted the Russian war
effort. By 1943, the Red Army advanced in US jeeps, trucks and
boots. Nevertheless, it was the Soviet economy that bore the
brunt of war production demands. The cost was high. Human
resources were ruthlessly exploited by the state to meet the
needs of war. All labour was directed which, among other
things, meant a high proportion of women in industry and the
armed forces (including – uniquely – the combat arms). Working
conditions were harsh and hours long. In December 1941, all
war industry workers were placed under military law and could
be shot if they failed to turn up for work.

Britain

Britain's record in armaments production was reasonably
impressive, especially for a cash-stripped democracy, dependent
on an inefficient industrial structure. By 1940, Britain's economy
was more geared to war than that of Germany, and actually
produced more tanks and planes. Though tank production
thereafter lagged behind Germany's, the lead in aircraft
production was retained until 1944. British productive
performance was close to a realistic optimum, given the
maintenance of reasonable living standards. Civilian
consumption was regulated through rationing, and virtually all
labour progressively mobilized, women included (though as
elsewhere traditional assumptions concerning gender roles set
limits to female participation). Coal mines, shipping and the
railways came under government control. However, the
relatively small size of the British population (47 million) meant
there were limits to the size of the war economy. In 1944, with
the army at its maximum strength of over 2.7 million, British
industry produced 5,000 tanks and 26,461 planes; in the same
year, Germany produced 17,800 tanks and 39,807 aircraft. Even
with US aid, Britain could not compete with a German economy
moving belatedly into top gear. Moreover, certain war items (like
planes) were more costly to produce than their German
equivalents, while others (like tanks) were inferior in quality.

The USA

The US war economy was by far the most successful of all the belligerents. This was largely because of the latent pre-war strength of the US in terms of workers, raw materials, modern industries and mass production techniques. When FDR's administration, working through the War Production Board and other new agencies, began to pour huge amounts into the war effort, the productive potential of the USA was realized. Huge new assembly-line factories, employing tens of thousands of workers, were quickly built for everything from heavy bombers to synthetic rubber. The USA harnessed capitalism for war. The government and the military gave out orders and left private enterprise, especially the USA giant corporations, to get on with the job. Almost overnight, General Motors and Ford came to be amongst the biggest arms manufacturers in the world: automobile production stopped and planes and tanks rolled off production lines. The output was phenomenal across the board. In 1943, when production had not yet reached its peak, US firms produced over 29,000 tanks and over 86,000 combat aircraft (enough to give the Allies an overall advantage of 3.5:1 over the Axis), not to mention vast quantities of everything else needed to fight a modern war. There was enough to equip not only US armed forces but also, through Lend-Lease, to give substantial help to Britain and Russia. By 1945, the USA had manufactured 40 per cent of all the weapons produced by all the belligerents. The war impacted negatively on some aspects of US civilian life: there were fewer consumer goods on the market; fuel was rationed; and working hours were lengthened. Yet the wages of war industry workers increased and the demand for labour was great enough to bring four million women into the workforce, more commonly as office workers than riveters.

Japan

Japan's shortage of raw materials and the inadequacy of her industrial base made it impossible to produce enough modern weapons to fight the USA on equal terms.

Technology

The capacity to produce high quality weapons and detection systems was just as important as the ability to produce large quantities of war material. Many German land-based weapons,

	1939	1940	1941	1942	1943	1944	1945
Aircraft							
Britain	7,940	15,049	20,094	23,672	26,263	26,461	12,070
USA	5,856	12,804	26,277	47,826	85,998	96,318	49,761
Soviet Union	10,382	10,565	15,735	25,436	34,900	40,300	20,900
Germany	8,295	10,247	11,776	15,409	24,807	39,807	7,540
Japan	4,467	4,768	5,088	8,861	16,693	28,180	11,066
Major vessels							
Britain	57	148	236	239	224	188	64
USA	–	–	544	1,845	2,654	2,247	1,513
Soviet Union	–	33	62	19	13	23	11
Germany (U-boats only)	15	40	196	244	270	189	0
Japan	21	30	49	68	122	248	51
Tanks[1]							
Britain	969	1,399	4,841	8,611	7,476	5,000	2,100
USA	–	c.400	4,052	24,997	29,497	17,565	11,968
Soviet Union	2,950	2,794	6,590	24,446	24,089	28,963	15,400
Germany	c.1,300	2,200	5,200	9,200	17,300	22,100	4,400
Japan	c.200	1,023	1,024	1,191	790	401	142
Artillery pieces[2]							
Britain	1,400	1,900	5,300	6,600	12,200	12,400	–
USA	–	c.1,800	29,615	72,658	67,544	33,558	19,699
Soviet Union	17,348	15,300	42,300	127,000	130,300	122,400	31,000
Germany	c.2,000	5,000	7,000	12,000	27,000	41,000	–

Dashes indicate reliable figures unavailable.

[1] Includes self-propelled guns for Germany and the Soviet Union.

[2] Medium and heavy calibre only for Germany, USA and Britain; all artillery pieces for the Soviet Union. Soviet heavy artillery production in 1942 was 49,100, in 1943 48,400 and in 1944 56,100.

table 1 weapons production of the major powers, 1939–45

especially machine-guns and anti-tank weapons, were superior to those of their foes. The newer German tanks, the Panther and the Tiger, were a match for the best Soviet tanks and outclassed British and US medium tanks such as the Cromwell and Sherman. Thus, while Germany was borne down by weight of numbers, in individual engagements the technological superiority of German arms (combined with considerable tactical skill) impeded Allied advance. Nevertheless, the *Wehrmacht* in 1944 was still essentially what it had been in 1940 – a horse-drawn army with specialized panzer and mechanized units. British and US armies, by contrast, were fully mechanized.

In the air, the Allies had a qualitative technological – as well as a very great numerical – advantage in the second half of the war. Germany failed to maintain its early superiority in aircraft development largely because too many ambitious and competing projects were started between 1939 and 1942: most were dropped after much investment of time, money and materials. Germany thus lost the opportunity to create a second generation of aircraft. Once lost, air superiority could not be regained. The Russians, British and Americans drew ahead in 1944. The US P-51 Mustang was the best all-round piston-engine fighter of the entire war. Hitler's personal interventions in the war production process did not help matters. He insisted, for example, on trying to convert the Messerschmitt 262 – the world's first jet fighter and a plane that might have turned the air war in Germany's favour – into a fighter bomber. This delayed its introduction into front-line service by at least a year. His constant desire to strike back funnelled precious resources into the rocket programme, the end result being the V-1 and V-2. These inordinately expensive weapons came to fruition in too small a quantity during 1944–5 to seriously threaten Britain.

The war at sea was in part a struggle to deploy or counter more advanced detection devices and weaponry. Mines were one focus of attention. The Germans developed first magnetic and then acoustic mines. British countermeasures included degaussing (which eliminated the magnetic field of a ship's hull) and sound magnification (which caused acoustic mines to explode prematurely). Late in the war, the Germans deployed a new device, the pressure mine, triggered by changing water pressure as a ship's hull passed over it. There was no obvious countermeasure but by 1944 Allied material superiority was so great that ship losses caused by the pressure mine could easily be made good. Devising means of defeating U-boat attack occupied even more Allied attention. This involved, among other things, developing more effective sonar and radar sets to pinpoint the location of U-boats, and new weapons systems such as the 'hedgehog', designed to throw depth-charge bombs ahead of a ship. By the time the Germans had developed a new generation of U-boats, the war was all but over.

The fact that the Allies could put much greater scientific and material resources into research and development gave them a huge advantage. Significantly, the most sophisticated weapon of all, the atomic bomb, was developed in the USA (with aid from Britain and Canada). Germany had led the way in nuclear technology in 1940 but Hitler showed little interest in the German atomic project which ran out of steam in 1942. The Allies continued to regard the bomb as a practical enterprise and were inspired – ironically – by the belief that Germany was well on the way to producing it. The Germans were ahead in chemical and biological weapons that fortunately, perhaps surprisingly, were never used.

Intelligence and deception

The Allies had advantages on the intelligence and deception front. Aerial observation was important and all air forces devoted some of their resources to it. Success depended to a great degree on the extent of air superiority. The Germans consequently had the advantage early in the war and the Allies had all the advantages later. Captured equipment could be invaluable in revealing the enemy's technology. Spies played a role in intelligence gathering. Resistance groups passed on useful information to the Allies. Germany suffered from a lack of co-ordination between its various intelligence agencies. In addition, unbeknown to Germany, most of its agents in Britain were quickly neutralized or turned into double agents, enabling Britain to feed Germany false information. Having nurtured extensive spy rings long before 1939, Russia probably had the best agents. One of its most effective spies was Tokyo-based Richard Sorge. His warnings of Barbarossa went unheeded but his assurance that Japan had no plans to attack Russia in the autumn of 1941 enabled Stalin to move vital reinforcements to the West. Ironically, the most successful espionage was conducted by Russia at the expense of its Allies. 'Fellow travellers' within the US and British intelligence and scientific establishments provided a steady flow of secrets to their ideological homeland, not least on atomic research.

Signals intelligence and the work of cryptographers were more important than the work of spies. Intercepting enemy radio transmissions was relatively simple; deciphering them was much more problematic. Careless use of ciphering equipment by diplomatic or military personnel, combined with a good deal of luck and guesswork, allowed both sides to eavesdrop on certain types of messages before systems were routinely modified or changed. The Germans believed their Enigma encrypting machine was foolproof. However, thanks to pre-war Polish intelligence and some brilliant mathematical minds (plus the world's first digital computer), it was possible for British code breakers, based at Bletchley Park in England, to decipher German radio messages. The resulting intelligence was called Ultra. The need to keep Ultra a secret (so that the Germans would continue to use Enigma), combined with slow translation, meant that it was of limited use initially on a day-to-day basis. Nonetheless, it did help predict general trends and, after 1942, provided crucial specific information. For instance, it helped Allied leaders assess the strength and intentions of German forces in North Africa and Normandy. Though Ultra gave the Allies a singular advantage, it did not mean that Britain and the USA could always anticipate German moves. Radio messages could be misinterpreted or ignored at Bletchley Park or by senior generals. The Western Allies, for example, failed to 'spot' Hitler's 1944 Ardennes Offensive. In the Far East, both the British and the Americans (who used their Magic system) were able to read Japanese signals from early in the war.

The Allied advantage in signals intelligence made it easier to run deception operations since the enemy's response could be gauged. Both sides, at various times, tried with some success to deceive enemy aerial reconnaissance through building and deploying dummy tanks, aircraft and even ships. Both sides also used false radio traffic to try to mislead the enemy about the timing and strength of major operations. The Allies were more successful than the Axis powers in large-scale deception operations. Operation Fortitude, for example, convinced the Germans that Normandy was only a diversion and that a much larger force would attack the Pas-de-Calais in 1944.

Leadership

The Allied powers

Leadership – appointing the best people, making the right decisions, inspiring the nation – is crucial in war. Of the 'Big Three' Allied leaders, Churchill was the only one who was technically not Commander-in-Chief, but that did not stop him from acting as though he were. Churchill has long been regarded as one of Britain's greatest prime ministers. Recently his 'greatness' has been questioned. Certainly the Churchill of myth was not always the Churchill of history. FDR said of him, 'he has a hundred [ideas] a day and about four of them are good'. Erratic, impulsive, intuitive, Churchill made a number of strategic errors, and it was fortunate that some of his wilder schemes were thwarted by his military advisers. In Sir Alan Brooke he had an outstanding Chief of the Imperial Staff. Yet Churchill continues to have more defenders than critics. His constant probing, suggestions and demands imparted a sense of urgency to all who came under his scrutiny. His oratory inspired the British and the Americans. Furthermore, he worked tirelessly to maintain (what he called) the Grand Alliance, despite his suspicions of Stalin. The eldest Allied leader, Churchill travelled far more than FDR and Stalin to conduct his own brand of personal diplomacy. Stalin made some terrible errors during 1941–2. Subsequently, he learned to place some trust in the judgement of proven commanders (like Zhukov), thereby increasing the effectiveness of Soviet military operations. FDR proved to be a brilliant war leader. Exuding confidence, but aware of his own weaknesses, he delegated well, interfered far less than Churchill, and had an excellent grasp of the overall direction of the war. Aided by his brilliant Chief of Staff Marshall, he made virtually all the right main strategic decisions. Humane, idealistic, always in command, FDR was, in Churchill's view, 'the greatest man I have ever known'.

The Axis powers

Axis leaders were less effective. Mussolini did little right from the moment he took Italy into the war. It is impossible to say who was in charge in Japan. Ministers came and went. The country was run by more or less anonymous committees. Emperor Hirohito's only real involvement in the war came in August 1945 when he agreed to Japan's surrender. Hitler's role continues to generate controversy. In the first years of the war, while determining general strategy, he was prepared to modify his designs to meet the practical objections raised by his military leaders. He nevertheless took strategic risks – risks that his generals would not have taken. The risks paid off – until Barbarossa. Barbarossa's failure led to a crisis which changed Hitler's role. Stunned by the Soviet counter-attack in December 1941, most German generals counselled retreat. Hitler would have none of it, insisting that all captured territory be held. The front did stabilize, confirming Hitler's belief that he was a better soldier than his generals. Thereafter, he made all major operational decisions as well as many minor ones. If he had been right in the winter of 1941–2, his subsequent decisions were often wrong. Fixated on offensive action and holding ground at all costs, he refused to listen to contrary advice concerning the merits of strategic defence or the possibility of a separate peace with Russia. He bears prime responsibility for the disasters that befell the *Wehrmacht* on the Eastern Front during 1942–3 and in Normandy in 1944. His intuitive decisions, often based on false racial and social assumptions (for instance, the Americans were decadent, the Russians inferior), cost Germany dear. The shock of continuous defeats, his unhealthy lifestyle, and the drugs administered by the quack Dr Morrell, turned him into a physical wreck by 1944.

Co-operation

The Axis powers

Relations between the European Axis powers and Japan were virtually impossible because of the distances involved. However, neither Italy nor Germany developed effective mechanisms for strategic consultation or operational co-ordination. The underlying problem was the fact that both Mussolini and Hitler wanted to pursue their own goals, while paying as little heed to their nominal ally as possible. Only Hitler possessed the material means to do so. In 1940, Mussolini, angry at Hitler's previous lack of consultation, attacked Greece and Albania as well as the British in North Africa without informing the führer of his intentions. Italian setbacks forced German intervention in the Balkans and North Africa. Hitler did not warn Mussolini of Barbarossa before the event. The Italian troops sent to serve in Russia were even more subordinate to the German high command than those serving in Libya. The enforced nature of Italian–German co-operation only exacerbated suspicion and mutual antipathy at all levels. To the Germans, the Italians were incompetents who had to be propped up. To the Italians, the Germans were arrogant overlords.

The Allied powers

The Grand Alliance that defeated the Axis was a remarkable thing. Capitalist USA, Imperial Britain and Communist Russia were strange bedfellows. They came together out of necessity rather than love. To Stalin, the importance of the Western Allies lay partly in Lend-Lease but mostly in their ability to draw off pressure on the Eastern Front by mounting an offensive in the

West. The repeated postponing of the Second Front generated a great deal of friction, while both distance and mutual suspicion militated against much co-ordination of Soviet and Anglo–American military action. Indeed, in many respects Russia and the Western Allies waged two parallel but separate wars against Germany. Distrust in the alliance became serious in April 1943 when the Germans revealed that the Russians had massacred over 10,000 Poles at Katyn in 1940. The ill-will generated a real fear that Stalin might negotiate a separate peace with Hitler. During 1944–5, political differences over the shape of post-war Europe caused a further deterioration in relations. The need to defeat the common enemy, nonetheless, allowed for competing political visions to be put aside long enough to bring the war to a successful end.

Joint Anglo–American co-operation predated formal US involvement in the war, starting with secret staff meetings in early 1941. These talks were followed by a meeting between FDR and Churchill aboard ships at Placentia Bay, Newfoundland in August 1941. Issuing a joint public statement of liberal internationalist principles (the Atlantic Charter), the two men set out Allied war aims, even though the US was not at war! In December 1941, Churchill crossed the Atlantic and spent several weeks with FDR planning future strategy. This visit helped to cement the partnership between the two countries – a partnership closer than had ever previously existed between major allies in wartime. By early 1942, important mechanisms for consultation were established, particularly the creation of the Combined Chiefs of Staff (CCS) made up of the Chiefs of Staff of the services of the two powers. The CCS operated strategies laid down for them by Churchill and FDR. The Anglo–American alliance, to a large extent, rested simply on the two leaders' personal relations. 'My whole system,' said Churchill in November 1942, 'is based upon partnership with Roosevelt'. While FDR and Churchill did not agree on everything (not least about the British Empire), they got on well together. The good relations at the top were replicated at lower levels where various joint boards and committees worked efficiently under the auspices of the CCS. Although individuals clashed – Montgomery, for example, was never popular with the Americans – there was considerable mutual trust, respect and friendship.

There was much Allied consensus about strategy – about strategic bombing, about unconditional surrender and about 'Europe first'. Yet there was considerable disagreement about the direction of the ground war, particularly about whether to adopt an immediate Second Front strategy (invading northern France) or whether to engage in an indirect approach via the Mediterranean. US generals led by Chief of Staff Marshall were strongly in favour of the former, while Churchill and his leading generals preferred the latter. The relative weakness of US forces, combined with FDR's willingness to be led by Churchill, meant that a cross-Channel attack was put on hold. In the summer of 1942, Marshall reluctantly acceded to a plan for an Anglo-American landing in North Africa. Success in North Africa by May 1943 allowed for the possibility of opening up a major front in the Mediterranean. Churchill strongly supported the idea. Marshall still favoured an immediate Second Front. Which option to pursue was the main item of debate at the three 1943 summits held at Casablanca (January), Washington (May) and Quebec (August). Once again, Marshall was pressured into accepting first an invasion of Sicily and then a landing in Italy.

In November, Stalin met FDR and Churchill at Teheran. FDR was now set upon agreement with Stalin, even if this meant the exclusion of Churchill. FDR wanted a Second Front in the spring of 1944. So did Stalin. Churchill, whose influence was much diminished, agreed. The most difficult issue was Poland. While the Polish government-in-exile in London refused to contemplate the loss of any of its pre-war territory, Stalin was determined to retain the land he had annexed in September 1939. At Teheran it was agreed that Poland would lose land to Russia and be compensated by taking parts of eastern Germany. Stalin signed up to the United Nations (UN), an international organization planned as a successor to the League of Nations. He also promised that Russia would enter the war against Japan when Germany was defeated.

Poland remained a major area of British concern. The Polish government-in-exile was still unwilling to work with the Russians or the Russian-backed Polish 'Committee of National Liberation'. Events in Warsaw in August 1944 aggravated the situation. Expecting Russian aid, Poles in the capital rose up against the Germans. Stalin gave no help and the rising was crushed. By 1944, Churchill was seriously worried about Russian aims and apparent US aimlessness with regard to eastern Europe. He tried to salvage the situation by forging an old-fashioned balance of power agreement with Stalin in October. Essentially, Churchill recognized Soviet dominance in Poland, Hungary, Romania and Bulgaria while Stalin recognized British dominance in Greece. In February 1945,

Churchill, FDR and Stalin met at Yalta. After 1945 many politicians, echoing Churchill, claimed that a dying FDR was misled into making too many concessions to Russia at Yalta. However, it is hard to see how the Western Allies could have won better terms. Stalin held most of the cards because he held most of the territory in eastern Europe. FDR, who quite sensibly hoped to remain on good terms with Stalin after the war, had not really been duped. While he spoke in public of Yalta as a triumph, in private he was far more doubtful about Stalin's intentions. Despite growing suspicions about future intentions, the Grand Alliance held – just.

Conclusion

There is no doubt that greater material preponderance was a key factor in Allied victory. Given the speed and scale of US rearmament and the amazing performance of the Soviet economy, it does look as though the Axis could not win. Nevertheless, Davids do sometimes defeat Goliaths. Resources by themselves do not explain the Second World War's outcome. Human factors, not least in ensuring effective exploitation of the resources, were equally significant. German and Japanese tenaciousness, combined with greater tactical skill in land warfare, could conceivably have negated the resource differential if the Allied populations had not proven willing to make the necessary sacrifices. They did prove willing. The British never looked like giving up. The Americans belied Hitler's view that they could not stomach high casualties. The Russians showed a colossal capacity for sacrifice. If the Allies had been divided or badly led, they might well have lost. In the event, they were reasonably united and pretty well led. They proved to be better at planning, better at logistics and better at mobilizing their people than the Axis powers. Eventually, despite the immense fighting capacity of the Germans and the suicidal courage of the Japanese, they were also better at fighting.

It is sometimes asked which power contributed most to Allied victory. It is obvious that Britain could not have won without US aid and equally obvious that the Western Allies could not have won without the enormous sacrifices of Russia. Stalin suggested that in the cause of victory, Britain had provided the time, the USA the money and Russia the blood. There is still much truth in this.

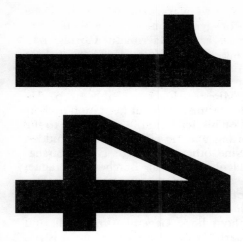

14

consequences

This chapter will cover:
- the cost of the war
- peacemaking
- the results of the war.

On 16 October 1946, ten Nazi war criminals mounted the gallows erected in the prison gymnasium at Nuremberg. One was missing: a few hours earlier Hermann Göring had committed suicide by taking a cyanide pill. There were three scaffolds painted black. Two were used alternately; the third was kept in reserve. First to enter the execution chamber at 1.11 a.m. was Foreign Minister Joachim Ribbentrop. He climbed the 13 steps to the platform without hesitation and, as the black hood was placed on his head, said, 'I wish peace to the world'. The trap was sprung and he fell from view, hidden behind a dark curtain. Nine others followed: Field Marshal Wilhelm Keitel; Ernst Kalenbrunner, the Butcher of Prague; Alfred Rosenberg, chief exponent of the master race theory; Hans Frank, Governor of occupied Poland; Wilhelm Frick, Protector of Bohemia; Julius Streicher, an infamous anti-Semite; Fritz Sauckel, the slave labour boss; General Alfred Jodl; and finally Arthur Seyss-Inquart, Hitler's Governor in Austria. Seyss-Inquart called for peace and understanding between peoples before he met his death. These men were among the last victims of the Second World War – a war in which millions of peoples died. What were the main costs and consequences of the conflict?

The cost of the war

Seventy million men were engaged as combatants at one time or another. Seventeen million of them were killed: 1:22 Russians, 1:25 Germans, 1:46 Japanese, 1:150 Italians, 1:150 British, 1:200 French and 1:500 Americans. Civilian casualties far exceeded military casualties. Some died as a result of bombing; others were killed as partisans or hostages. Many more were murdered in execution of Nazi racial doctrine, and millions died as result of brutal treatment or harsh wartime conditions. Russia suffered the most deaths – possibly in excess of 25 million. China may have lost 15 million. Poland suffered most in proportion to her population – six million deaths – over 15 per cent of her pre-war population (about half the victims were Jews). Yugoslavia suffered between 1.5 and two million deaths. The number of casualties, military and civilian, was far higher in eastern than in western Europe. Over 13 million Soviet and over three million German soldiers (as well as over a million Finnish, Italian, Hungarian and Romanian servicemen) died fighting on the Eastern Front. The British armed forces lost 244,000 men. Their Commonwealth and imperial brothers-in-arms suffered another 100,000 deaths: Australia, 23,000; Canada, 37,000; India 24,000; New Zealand 10,000; and South Africa 6,000. Sixty thousand British civilians were killed by bombing, and 35,000 members of the merchant marine died. British casualties were about half those the country sustained in the (shorter) First World War. The USA lost 300,000 servicemen. Germany lost some six million people and Japan over two million. France lost 600,000 and Italy 800,000. In total, some 60 million people may have died – over three times the figure for the First World War.

In late 1945, western Europe swarmed with refugees. Millions of displaced people found it difficult or impossible to go home. In some instances, political conditions in their home areas had so changed as to make return inadvisable. In other cases, the people who did try to go home found themselves so unwelcome upon return that they had to flee once again. Surviving Jews, for example, encountered great hostility when they tried to return to Poland. Many Jews headed for Palestine. Fearful of damaging relations with the native Arabs, Britain (which still controlled Palestine) attempted – unsuccessfully – to limit the number of Jewish immigrants to 75,000.

Populations had been on the move in much of Europe since 1939. The Nazis had tried to change the ethnic map of Europe, expelling Poles from land incorporated into Germany, and encouraging Germans living outside the Reich to move into it. During 1944–5, many of these Germans were forced to move again. Millions of Germans fled westwards to avoid Russian vengeance. Others were deliberately expelled from regions, like the Sudetenland, where Germans had lived for generations. Over ten million Germans fled or were expelled – the largest single migration of people in such a short period in world history. Tens of thousands died in the process. The Germans were not the only people forced to move. Millions of Poles, from territory now assigned to Russia, found new homes in the land acquired from Germany. There were other such movements, though on a smaller scale, elsewhere in Europe. In this brutal way – moving people to fit boundaries, as opposed to the 1919 effort to adjust boundaries to people – the national minorities problem was largely solved, except in Yugoslavia and Russia. The forced movement of minority nationalities which had taken place within Russia during the war continued afterwards: for example, Volga Germans, Baltic peoples and Chechens, all suspected of potential disloyalty, were uprooted from their homelands and moved east.

The mass transfers were not limited to Europe. Some seven million Japanese were repatriated from the former Japanese empire to the home islands, while tens of thousands of Koreans, many of whom had been forced labourers, were returned to Korea. The Allies, fearing a retributive bloodbath in parts of the Japanese Empire, made great efforts to ship Japanese troops back home.

The Western Allies had a moral dilemma in dealing with Soviet soldiers who had enlisted in the German military, willingly or under pressure. As a result of agreements with Stalin, tens of thousands were forcibly repatriated to Russia, despite the fact that Western leaders knew they were being sent to almost certain death. Even Soviet POWs who had survived in German camps were usually treated as traitors on their return home. German soldiers fell into Allied hands in huge numbers, especially in the last weeks of the war. The Western Allies used them as forced labourers for several months. Russia used German prisoners for ten years, in some cases, to assist in the reconstruction of the Soviet economy. The Western powers released the few Japanese prisoners they had captured during hostilities and the vast numbers who surrendered at the end of the fighting fairly quickly. Russia moved much more slowly in repatriating the thousands of Japanese soldiers captured during the campaign in Manchuria in August 1945.

The physical destruction caused by the war had been tremendous. In eastern Europe, practically every town and city from the River Vistula to the River Volga had been bombed, shelled and laid waste. In addition, bombing had caused immense damage in numerous cities in Britain, western Europe, Germany and Japan. There had also been extensive damage in China and the Philippines. Millions of tons of shipping had been sunk, factories destroyed or damaged, and bridges and dams blown up by one side or the other. Lack of fuel and equipment meant that across Europe transportation and communication networks had broken down. All the participants had poured enormous financial resources into the conflict. Only the USA emerged from the war with its economy strengthened rather than weakened.

In 1945, Europe was prostrate. Its first requirement was food, which had fallen to half the pre-war production level. Starving civilians did menial work for Allied occupation armies to get basic rations. Others bartered sexual favours, war souvenirs and family heirlooms. One hundred and fifty million people were dependent on some sort of relief food distribution during 1945–6. The USA and the UN played crucial roles in providing food, fuel and clothing. (The USA provided most of the money for the UN.) Troubled by the rise of communism in France and Italy, President Truman's administration created the European Recovery Programme in 1947, usually known as the Marshall Plan (in honour of its sponsor General Marshall). Sixteen nations and Allied-occupied Germany eventually received US$13 billion between 1947 and 1951.

Peace (and war)

Unlike most wars, the Second World War did not end with a major peace treaty. The Allies had insisted on unconditional surrender, and in 1945 there was no German or Japanese government to negotiate with. While the USA took over control of Japan, Germany (and Berlin) was divided into four occupation zones – British, US, French and Russian. These zones, agreed in 1944 and confirmed at Yalta, more or less mirrored the extent of Anglo-American and Soviet military advances in the last months of the war. Most envisaged that once Germany had been de-Nazified it would be reunited. This did not happen. In the years after 1945, neither the USA nor Russia was prepared to see the other dominate a united Germany. Two separate Germanies thus emerged: the German Democratic Republic controlled by Russia; and the German Federal State closely linked with the West. In this unplanned way, Germany was partitioned – and remained so for 45 years.

Peace was concluded with the lesser European enemies, Bulgaria, Finland, Hungary, Italy and Romania in 1947. A peace treaty was signed with Japan in 1951. Russia refused to sign and made its own settlement with Japan later. Austria, like Germany, was partitioned between the four powers. They remained in occupation until 1955. Austria then became independent, accepting permanent neutrality as its condition.

There were fewer changes to the map of Europe after 1945 than after 1918. Alsace-Lorraine was returned to France and the Sudetenland to Czechoslovakia. Russia regained her 1941 frontiers rather than those of 1939, taking part of pre-war Poland, the Baltic States, and half of East Prussia. Poland was moved 161 kilometres (100 miles) westwards at Germany's expense.

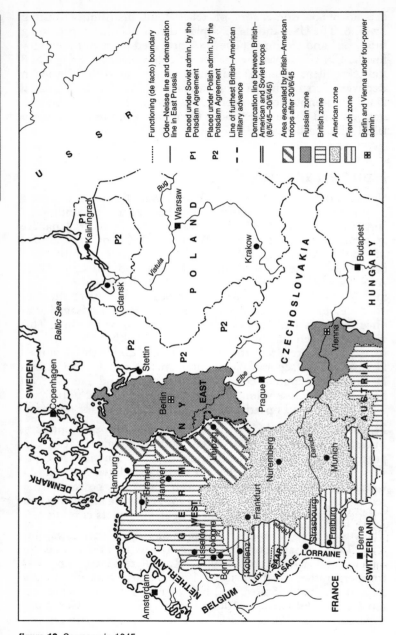

figure 19 Germany in 1945

The Allies did agree to set up a tribunal to punish Germany's main war criminals. The Nuremberg Tribunal sat between November 1945 and October 1946. Twenty-one leading Germans, headed by Göring, were charged with war crimes and crimes against humanity. Eleven were sentenced to death, eight to various terms of imprisonment. (Rudolf Hess, who had fled to Britain in 1941, remained imprisoned until his death in 1987 aged 93.) Two were acquitted. The victims hardly got a fair trial. The victors provided the judges, prosecutors and hangmen. Nevertheless, the trial did at least put on record the appalling story of Nazi inhumanity, and many of those condemned probably deserved to die. A few were unfortunate to be executed. One or two of those who escaped the death sentence, like Albert Speer, were perhaps fortunate.

The victors were determined to punish the crimes of the Third Reich and dismantle every remnant of Nazism at a lower level. In the Soviet zone, Russian authorities simply executed lesser war criminals/Nazis or sent them to Siberia. The Western Allies were less brutal. Some 600,000 Germans stood trial for war crimes after 1945. Thirty-one thousand were imprisoned. (Few served their full sentences.) Most of the rest were fined or lost their jobs. Perhaps as many as 20,000 German war criminals escaped in the chaos of 1945, eventually ending up in Latin America, the Middle East or the French Foreign Legion with new identities. Elsewhere, Europeans settled their own accounts, sometimes by legal process, sometimes not. In France, some 200,000 people were convicted for war crimes or collaboration. Two thousand were executed, including Vichy Premier Pierre Laval. (Immediately after liberation, French communists had murdered thousands of suspected collaborators.) Norway took legal action against 18,000 people. In Holland, 66,000 people were convicted of collaboration. Jewish groups hounded down Holocaust perpetrators, German and non-German, for the rest of the twentieth century.

General MacArthur pursued Japan's major war criminals. The desire for revenge and the need to impress other Asians – not least the Japanese themselves – may have been more important than legal considerations. Twenty-eight of Japan's leaders were tried before an International Tribunal in Tokyo in the autumn of 1945. Two defendants died during the proceedings, while another became too insane to try. (Several other potential defendants had already committed suicide.) Seven defendants (including Tojo) were condemned to death, while 16 were given life imprisonment. At a show trial in Manila in December 1945,

Generals Yamashita and Homma were sentenced to death – Yamashita for atrocities in the Philippines, and Homma for his association with the Bataan Death March. Over a six-year period, Allied tribunals tried 5,700 Japanese war criminals who had committed atrocities against POWs and civilians. Half were convicted and about 1,000 executed. These trials at least had roots in international law. Some Japanese escaped retribution, not least General Ishii Shiro, a medical doctor and the evil genius behind Unit 731, an organization devoted to bacteriological warfare research and other medical 'challenges'. Human 'guinea pigs' (including POWs) were used during his 'research'. Some experiments involved vivisection; others studied the effect of hypothermia and extreme gravitational pressure. Ishii and his team bargained all their 'scientific' findings in return for not being prosecuted by US war crimes investigators.

Fighting did not cease everywhere in 1945. Tito's communists, who continued to wage a bitter war against Chetniks and Slovenian and Croatian irregular forces, did not establish full control in Yugoslavia until 1946. His success encouraged the Greek communists to resume fighting. The Greek civil war dragged on until 1949. In Palestine, Zionist terrorists were soon up in arms against British rule – upheld in early 1946 by 80,000 British troops. In 1948, Britain pulled out of Palestine, part of which became the independent state of Israel. In the Dutch East Indies, the Javanese fought for independence. French troops waged a brutal war with communist guerrillas, led by Ho Chi Minh, for control of Indo-China. In China, the war between the communists, led by Mao Zedung, and the nationalists, led by Chiang Kai-shek, first begun in the 1920s, continued despite the best efforts of US mediators. The communists finally triumphed in 1949.

Some results of the war

The Cold War

In order to deny Germany's and Japan's bids for world power, the USA and Russia had become world powers themselves. Capitalist, democratic USA and communist, authoritarian Russia had been forced together by the common threat of Germany. During the war, the Western Allies had tended to gloss over the vile nature of Stalin's regime. That was no longer the case after 1945. President Truman was committed to free elections and universal suffrage everywhere. Stalin had

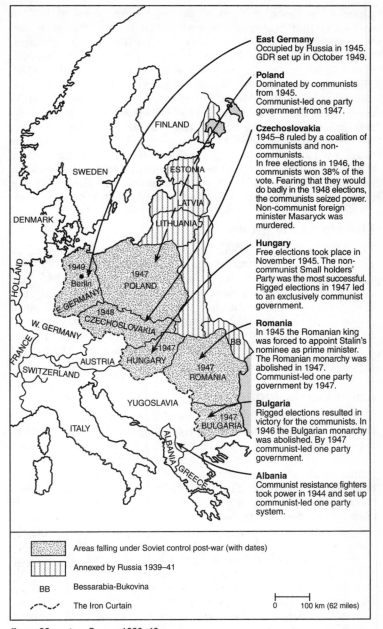

East Germany
Occupied by Russia in 1945.
GDR set up in October 1949.

Poland
Dominated by communists from 1945.
Communist-led one party government from 1947.

Czechoslovakia
1945–8 ruled by a coalition of communists and non-communists.
In free elections in 1946, the communists won 38% of the vote. Fearing that they would do badly in the 1948 elections, the communists seized power. Non-communist foreign minister Masaryck was murdered.

Hungary
Free elections took place in November 1945. The non-communist Small holders' Party was the most successful. Rigged elections in 1947 led to an exclusively communist government.

Romania
In 1945 the Romanian king was forced to appoint Stalin's nominee as prime minister. The Romanian monarchy was abolished in 1947.
Communist-led one party government by 1947.

Bulgaria
Rigged elections resulted in victory for the communists. In 1946 the Bulgarian monarchy was abolished. By 1947 communist-led one party government.

Albania
Communist resistance fighters took power in 1944 and set up communist-led one party system.

Areas falling under Soviet control post-war (with dates)

Annexed by Russia 1939–41

BB   Bessarabia-Bukovina

The Iron Curtain

0   100 km (62 miles)

figure 20 eastern Europe 1939–49

promised as much at Yalta. However, by the spring of 1945 it was clear that Stalin was not about to honour his promises. Wherever the Red Army was – Czechoslovakia, Poland, Bulgaria, Hungary or Romania – one-party regimes emerged. Communist opponents were liquidated and elections rigged. There was nothing the Western leaders could do about it – except protest. In 1946, Churchill spoke of an Iron Curtain descending across Europe. In 1947, Truman, urged on by Britain, committed the USA to the Truman Doctrine. The USA would stand firm against communism wherever it reared its head. By 1950, Europe was sharply divided. On either side of the Iron Curtain, states were organised into hostile blocs dominated by the USA on the one hand, and Russia on the other. The Cold War was to last for nearly half a century.

The United Nations

The UN, which the USA, Britain and Russia had agreed to establish as a more effective successor to the League of Nations, and which came into being at San Francisco in April 1945, was intended to be an instrument of international peacekeeping. The UN assumed the continuing unity of the Security Council Powers – Britain, the USA, Russia, France and China. Once that assumption was proved wrong, its authority was quickly emasculated. The UN became essentially a forum for US–Russian confrontation.

European colonies

The war transformed the relations of European states with their colonies. Japanese victories in Asia destroyed the mystique of white supremacy. After 1945, there was a wave of decolonization in Asia and the Middle East. Most European states could no longer easily afford, or were committed to, the upkeep of their empires, particularly if this meant fighting imperial wars. French forces left Syria and the Lebanon in 1946. Britain gave up control of the Indian sub-continent in 1947, and granted independence to Burma and Ceylon (Sri Lanka) in 1948, the same year that Holland granted independence to Indonesia. France finally pulled out of Indo-China in 1954. The tide of colonial nationalism spread to Africa. In 1945, the only independent countries in Africa were Liberia and South Africa. By 1961, 24 African states were already in existence. In 1939, 500 million people in Asia and Africa were ruled by Europeans. By 1970, the number had fallen to 21 million.

Japan

In Japan, MacArthur presided over a set of dramatic reforms, using the Emperor to endorse a process designed to turn Japan into a democratic state. The Imperial armed forces were dissolved; some 200,000 'undesirables' left government ministries and industrial conglomerates were broken up – only to re-emerge in the 1950s.

The USA

In 1945 the USA was the most powerful nation in the world. The only nuclear power, she was able to out-produce all the other powers put together. The USA gained the most and lost the least from the war. Between 1939 and 1945, the US annual Gross National Product (GNP) rose from US$91 billion to US$166 billion. Industrial production doubled. US workers enjoyed rising wages and a higher standard of living. After 1945, most Americans had 'grand expectations' about the future; some of these expectations were realized, others were not. Generally, however, the USA retained its economic prosperity and its superpower status. For the USA, the war meant the end of isolationism and the beginning of a continuous and demanding world role.

Communism

The Second World War gave communism a huge boost. It was sustained by Soviet military power. However, communism did not work. After 1945, the Soviet system was unable to provide a decent standard of living for its people. The unfortunate Russians won neither freedom nor prosperity for their tremendous wartime efforts – efforts that enabled many other warring states to enjoy both.

Women's roles

Did the war change women's place in society and the workplace? Women undoubtedly played a major role in the war. All the combatants had been dependent on female labour at home to maintain production and essential services. Yet there was no major immediate change in women's positions after 1945. Most women returned to their traditional pre-war roles – and did so gladly. War work was not always all it was cracked up to be. As the servicemen returned home, the majority of women married and had children, contributing to the 'baby boomer' generation in the USA and across Europe. Economic and technological developments were far more important than women's experience of war in bringing about female emancipation in the late twentieth century.

European economics

Given the colossal destruction of material assets, Europe seemed destined to endure poverty and stagnation after 1945. Until 1948, most western European states did experience some economic hardship. Nonetheless, in the 1950s and 1960s, western Europe enjoyed two decades of sustained expansion. There were a variety of reasons for this 'golden age': scientific and technical progress, in some cases sparked by the war, continued apace after 1945; many governments acted positively to promote economic growth; and Marshall Aid played a vital role in helping recovery.

European unity

The situation in 1945 encouraged and gave opportunities to those who sought a new way of organizing Europe. Many European politicians blamed nationalism for causing both world wars. Some politicians dreamed of creating a United States of Europe – a new superpower to rival the USA and Russia. Supporters of European union believed that economic unification was the first step to political unification. In 1950, six countries – France, West Germany, Belgium, Holland, Luxemburg and Italy – established the European Coal and Steel Community (ECSC). Its success led to formation of the European Economic Community (EEC) in 1957. The hope of creating 'an ever closer union among the peoples of Europe' was to become a reality over the next half century as the EEC (now the European Union) expanded.

Britain

Despite popular myth, the war was hardly a glorious success for Britain. If it was fought to save Poland, it failed. If it was fought to keep totalitarianism out of Europe, it failed. If it was fought to preserve Britain's great power status, it failed. By 1945, Britain was bankrupted by its 'victory', and had ceded its world power to the USA. It is thus possible to claim that Britain's finest hour was its gravest error.

The Axis powers

Perhaps the great paradox of the war is that the Axis powers lost but throve in the next five decades. Germany and Japan became, next to the USA, the leading economies of the late twentieth century. This led cynics to pose the question of who won the war. This is an easy question to answer. Essentially the war was fought to defend and liberate peoples from Nazi and Japanese tyranny. In this it succeeded. As a result of their defeat, both Germany and Japan renounced militarism and for the remainder of the twentieth century posed no threat to their neighbours. It is likely that people were freer, happier and more prosperous than if Nazi Germany or Imperial Japan had won. 'Despite all the killing and destruction that accompanied it, the Second World War was a good war,' thought A. J. P. Taylor. His conclusion still seems correct.

Conclusion

For those who lived through the Second World War, the conflict defined their lives and shaped their world for decades to come. Above all, the war brought an end to the great power rivalries of Europe, to European imperialism and to European dominance of the world's economic, political and cultural developments. Europe lost its dominance to the USA and Russia. This was not a bad thing. After 1945 most Europeans enjoyed decades of peace and prosperity. The USA and Russia, though bitter ideological rivals, did not blunder into war against each other as Europe's great powers had done in 1914 and 1939. The invention of nuclear weapons made the consequences of another war so horrifying that they have so far been an effective deterrent. The Second World War may hopefully have been the war to end all world wars – if not all wars.

glossary

Allies   The countries that opposed the Axis powers during the Second World War. The main Allied powers were Britain (and its Commonwealth and colonies), France, Russia and the USA.

Anschluss   The union of Austria and Germany, which was proclaimed in March 1938.

Anti-Comintern Pact   The agreement between Germany and Japan, signed in November 1936, which stated both countries' hostility to international communism. (Italy signed in 1937.)

anti-Semitism   The term used to describe animosity towards the Jews, either on a religious or a racial basis – or both.

Axis   A term first used by Mussolini in November 1936 to describe Italy's relationship with Germany. In September 1940 Germany, Italy and Japan signed a tripartite agreement that led to the term 'Axis Powers' being used to describe all three (as well as their East European allies).

Barbarossa   The code name for the German invasion of Russia in June 1941.

Big Three   The leaders of the major Allied powers during the Second World War: Churchill, Stalin and Roosevelt.

Blitz   A shortened form of the German word *blitzkrieg*. The term was used to describe the bombing of British cities by the German air force in 1940–1.

Blitzkrieg   This translates from German as 'lightning war'. The word was used to describe German military operations, particularly the use of aircraft and highly mobile armoured forces, in 1939–40.

Bolshevik   A term used to describe Russian communists who came to power in Russia in November 1917.

Chetniks Serbia guerrillas who opposed German occupation in the Second World War. Some Chetnik leaders collaborated with the Germans and Italians against Tito's Partisans.

collaboration Support by (part of) the population for an enemy occupier of a country.

Comintern The abbreviated title of the Third International established in 1919 to promote world communist revolution.

concentration camp A camp for the detention of political and other opponents. Millions of people – Jews, gypsies, political opponents – died in Nazi concentration camps (like Auschwitz and Belsen).

co-prosperity sphere The term used by Japan to describe the area of Asia that it controlled during the Second World War.

D-Day Code name for 6 June 1944 – the first day of Operation Overlord, the Allied landings in Normandy.

Eastern Front The term used in both World Wars to describe the battle-front between Germany and Russia.

Enigma The machine used by the Germans to encrypt their radio messages.

Fascism An Italian nationalist, authoritarian, anti-communist movement developed by Mussolini after 1919. The word is often applied to authoritarian and National Socialist movements in Europe and elsewhere.

Free French The French servicemen who continued the fight against Nazi Germany after the fall of France in 1940.

Isolationism The policy of avoiding alliances and having minimal involvement in international affairs.

Kamikaze Bomb-carrying Japanese aircraft that made suicidal attacks on Allied warships. The word, which also described the pilots, is derived from the Japanese 'divine wind'.

Lebensraum This German word translates as 'living space'. The Nazis hoped to expand Germany's 'living space' in the east, at Russia's expense.

Lend-Lease The act passed by the US Congress in March 1941, allowing President Roosevelt to lend or lease arms and equipment to states 'whose defence the President deems vital to the defence of the United States'. American aid went to Britain, China and Russia.

Luftwaffe The German air force.

Maginot Line   French defensive fortifications stretching along the German frontier.

Manhattan project   The code name for the development of the atomic bomb.

Maquis   French guerrilla resistance fighters.

Nazi   Popular contraction of National Socialist and used to describe both the National Socialist German Workers Party and its individual members. The party, led by Adolf Hitler, came to power in Germany in 1933.

Overlord   The code name for the Allied landings in Normandy in June 1944.

Plebiscite   A popular vote (like a referendum) by the people of a district on a special point.

Salient   An outward-pointing angle of a line of defences. Salients were usually weak points that could be attacked from several sides.

Second Front   The term used to describe the Allied invasion of northern France. Stalin appealed to the Western Allies to launch a Second Front to ease German pressure on Russia since 1941.

Soviet Union (or USSR)   The name of Russia from 1922.

SS   Abbrevation of German *Schutzstaffel* or Guard Detachment. Led by Heinrich Himmler, it was the main Nazi paramilitary organization before 1939. In the Second World War the SS had its own elite regiments, separate from army control. Other sections of the SS provided concentration camp guards and police squads in occupied territory.

Third Reich   The term used to describe the Nazi dictatorship in Germany, 1933–45.

U-boats   German submarines.

Ultra   The single most important British source of secret intelligence about Nazi Germany. Code-breakers at Bletchley Park, 60 miles north-west of London, succeeded in breaking German military radio codes, enciphered on the Enigma machine.

V-1s   Flying bombs used by the Germans to bomb London in 1944–5.

V-2s   German rockets, first used against London in September 1944.

Vichy   French provincial spa town where the interim French government was set up between July 1940 and July 1944. The Vichy regime, led by Marshal Petain, collaborated extensively with Nazi Germany.

Waffen SS   An elite military force, part of the Nazi SS (*Schutzstaffeln*) composed of Germans and anti-communist volunteers from most European states.

taking it further

There are an enormous number of books on the Second World War. What follows is only a portal to the information available, and the books listed here are a limited, personal selection of those which should prove useful as a follow-up to issues and topics touched on in this book.

General texts

Calvocoressi, P., Wint, G. and Pritchard, J., *The Penguin History of the Second World War*, Penguin, 1995.
This book has appeared in several forms over the years, sometimes as one and sometimes as two volumes. It was extensively revised in 1989 and runs to over 1,300 pages.

Churchill, W. S. *The Second World War*, Houghton Mifflin, six volumes, 1948–1953.
I can't leave this out but it's not the easiest (or best) thing to read.

Dear, I. C. B. and Foot, M. R. D. eds *The Oxford Companion to the Second World War*, Oxford University Press, 1995.
This contains over 1,750 alphabetically arranged entries, written by nearly 150 contributors.

Gilbert, M. *The Second World War*, Weidenfeld and Nicholson, 1989.
This adopts an unusual but effective almost day-by-day approach.

Keegan, J. *The Second World War*, Arrow Books, 1990.
An excellent read by an excellent writer.

Keegan, J. ed. *The Times Atlas to the Second World War*, Harper & Row, 1989.
This provides a very useful service.

Liddell-Hart, Captain Sir Basil (editor-in-chief) *History of the Second World War*, Purnell and Sons, 1966.
This monumentous collection of well-illustrated articles is well worth dipping into.

Murray, W. and Millett, A. R. *A War to be Won: Fighting the Second World War*, The Belknap Press, 2000.
This is a powerful military history of the war, comprehensive and highly readable.

Parker, R. A. C. *The Second World War*, Oxford University Press, 1997.
This provides good detail and analysis – in just over 300 pages.

Taylor, A. J. P. *The Second World War: An Illustrated History*, Penguin, 1975.
This remains a classic – succinct, controversial and very well illustrated.

Weinberg, G. L. *A World at Arms, A Global History of World War II*, Cambridge University Press, 1994.
Over 1,000 pages long, this book is still perhaps the finest one-volume history of the war.

Wright, G. *The Ordeal of Total War, 1939–1945*, Harper & Row, 1968.
This book, old though it is, still provides an excellent general survey of the European War.

Readable books on various aspects of the war

Rather than just give you a long list of 'other' books, I have decided to suggest one book for each chapter. The list is totally eclectic. All I can say in mitigation is that I enjoyed – and was informed by – all the books. They provide some kind of guide to deeper reading.

Chapter 1

Taylor, A. J. P. *The Origins of the Second World War*, Penguin, 1961.

This book caused a storm of protest in the 1960s. Read what Taylor has to say but keep your critical wits about you and don't accept everything he says as gospel truth.

Chapter 2
Horne, A. *To Lose a Battle, France, 1940*, Macmillan, 1968.

This book, part of a mini-series on France in the late nineteenth and early twentieth centuries, is an excellent read.

Chapter 3
Calder, A. *The People's War: Britain 1939–1945*, Jonathan Cape, 1969.

This is a brilliant evocation of life in Britain during the struggle against Nazi Germany. The first half of the book deals with 'Britain Alone' but do read the whole book.

Chapter 4
Overy, R. *Russia's War: Blood upon the Snow*, Penguin, 1997.

Read the first chapters on Barbarossa and just keep going!

Chapter 5
Prange, G. W. *At Dawn We Slept: The Untold Story of Pearl Harbor*, Penguin, 1982.

An exhaustive account.

Chapter 6
Beevor, A. *Stalingrad*, Viking, 1998.

A wonderfully readable book which tells of the real horror of war.

Chapter 7
Barnett, C. *The Desert Generals*, (revised ed.) Indiana UP, 1986.

Much has been written upon the fighting in the Western desert but nothing better than this.

Chapter 8
Rings, W. *Life with the Enemy: Collaboration and Resistance in Hitler's Europe, 1939–1945*, Doubleday, 1982.

This is a highly original account.

Chapter 9
Goldhagen, D. J. *Hitler's Willing Executioners: Ordinary Germans and the Holocaust*, Knopf, 1996.

Highly controversial: it sets out to excite passion and succeeds.

Chapter 10

Hastings, M. *Bomber Command*, Dial, 1987.

An excellent study of the effects of the bombing campaign both on the Germans and the aircrews.

Chapter 11

Ambrose, S. E. *Band of Brothers*, Simon & Schuster, 1992.

Turned into an excellent television series, this tells the story of E Company, 506th Regiment, 101st Airborne from Normandy to Hitler's Eagle's Nest.

Chapter 12

Spector, R. *Eagle Against the Sun: The American War with Japan*, Free Press, 1985.

Enthrallingly written, this remains the best general history of the Pacific war.

Chapter 13

Overy, R. *Why the Allies Won*, Jonathan Cape, 1995.

An outstanding book, posing and answering one of the great questions of the twentieth century.

Chapter 14

Thomas, H. *Armed Truce: The Beginnings of the Cold War, 1945–1946*, Atheneum, 1987.

An essential guide to the war's immediate aftermath.

Access to History

The Hodder & Stoughton Access to History series is aimed primarily at the A level student, but is suitable for the general reader:

Brett, P. *The USA and the World, 1917–45*, Hodder & Stoughton, 1997.

Darby, G. *Europe at War 1939–45*, Hodder & Stoughton, 2003.

Farmer, A. *Anti-Semitism and the Holocaust*, Hodder & Stoughton, 1998.

Farmer, A. *Britain: Foreign and Imperial Affairs 1939–64*, Hodder & Stoughton, 1994.

Films

There are thousands! You really must see *Schindler's List* and *Saving Private Ryan*.

Fiction

There are tens of thousands of novels set during the Second World War. My favourites are *The Cruel Sea* by Nicholas Monserrat (Cassell & Co, 1951), and *Schindler's Ark* by Thomas Keneally (Hodder & Stoughton, 1982).

index

the cold war
0340 884940 £8.99

nazi germany
0340 884908 £8.99

the middle east
0340 884916 £8.99

the second world war
0340 884932 £8.99

special forces
0340 884924 £8.99

the first world war
0340 884894 £8.99

teach
yourself

the first world war
david evans

- Gain a better understanding of key events during the First World War
- Discover the reasons behind the conflict
- Gain an insight into the experiences of those involved

teach yourself the first world war is a compelling introduction to a conflict on a scale never experienced in the world before. When war broke out in 1914 some predicted that it would be 'over by Christmas', yet four years later, following the slaughter of over nine million men, still no peace had been made. This book considers the roles of the leading politicians and explores the impact on the civilians and societies involved.

David Evans is an established writer and lecturer. He has written over twenty books covering aspects of modern European history and is a contributor on both television and radio.

nazi germany
michael lynch

- Discover this extraordinary period
- Understand the motives of the individuals who created and led the Nazi movement
- Gain an insight into the experiences of those involved

teach yourself nazi germany is an accessible introduction to one of the most controversial periods in modern history. The years 1933–45 witnessed the take-over of Germany by a man and a movement whose racial and political policies are now regarded with universal abhorrence. Yet in all of European history there has never been a more genuinely popular regime than that of the Nazis. This book immerses you in the remarkable Third Reich story and the controversies that still surround it.

Michael Lynch is a tutor at the University of Leicester and is also a writer, specializing in modern European and Asian history.

teach
yourself

the cold war
c. b. jones

- Understand the period that gave us the Cuban crisis, the Berlin wall, nuclear weapons and James Bond
- Discover more about this hidden conflict
- Read a compelling guide to this 45-year-long war

teach yourself the cold war is an accessible introduction to a war that shaped the latter half of the twentieth century. It covers all aspects, from questioning whether the tension really ended with the fall of the Berlin wall, to examining what JFK and his assassin had in common. Understand the global reach of this hidden conflict and its effects on the world in recent history and today.

C. B. Jones is an experienced teacher and Head of Faculty. She is also an A Level examiner with a specialist knowledge of twentieth century history.

teach
yourself

special forces
anthony kemp

- Gain an overview of the history of Special Forces
- Understand how anti-terrorist units function
- Find out how Special Forces began and evolved

teach yourself special forces is a concise introduction to the secret world of Special Forces units, giving you a fascinating insight into how they are recruited, trained and armed, what they can and cannot achieve, and their role in controlling modern-day terrorism. Read a compelling history of Special Forces, from the birth of small-scale raiding forces during the Second World War, to the Iranian Embassy siege.

Anthony Kemp is an established military historian, writer and film producer who specializes in the Special Air Service Regiment.

teach yourself

the middle east since 1945
stewart ross

- Read an accessible guide to today's political hotspot
- Understand the development of the region
- Discover more about a major world issue

teach yourself the middle east since 1945 tells the story of the modern world's most troubled region. It is lively yet authoritative, examining the origin and developments of issues that have made the headlines over the last half century. This book addresses many questions about the region, including why the Israeli–Palestinian conflict has lasted so long and the background to the two Gulf Wars and presents each aspect with engaging objectivity.

Stewart Ross taught in a variety of institutions worldwide before becoming a writer, lecturer and broadcaster. He has written over 175 books, including widely acclaimed historical works.

teach® yourself

the A-Z of teach yourself

Afrikaans
Access 2002
Accounting, Basic
Alexander Technique
Algebra
Arabic
Arabic Script, Beginner's
Aromatherapy
Astronomy
Bach Flower Remedies
Bengali
Better Chess
Better Handwriting
Biology
Body Language
Book Keeping
Book Keeping & Accounting
Brazilian Portuguese
Bridge
Buddhism
Buddhism, 101 Key Ideas
Bulgarian
Business Studies
Business Studies, 101 Key Ideas
C++
Calculus
Calligraphy
Cantonese
Card Games
Catalan
Chemistry, 101 Key Ideas
Chess
Chi Kung
Chinese
Chinese, Beginner's

Chinese Script, Beginner's
Christianity
Classical Music
Copywriting
Counselling
Creative Writing
Crime Fiction
Croatian
Crystal Healing
Czech
Danish
Desktop Publishing
Digital Photography
Digital Video & PC Editing
Drawing
Dream Interpretation
Dutch
Dutch, Beginner's
Dutch Dictionary
Dutch Grammar
Eastern Philosophy
ECDL
E-Commerce
Economics, 101 Key Ideas
Electronics
English, American (EFL)
English as a Foreign Language
English, Correct
English Grammar
English Grammar (EFL)
English for International Business
English Vocabulary
Ethics
Excel 2002
Feng Shui

Film Making
Film Studies
Finance for non-Financial Managers
Finnish
Flexible Working
Flower Arranging
French
French, Beginner's
French Grammar
French Grammar, Quick Fix
French, Instant
French, Improve your
French Starter Kit
French Verbs
French Vocabulary
Gaelic
Gaelic Dictionary
Gardening
Genetics
Geology
German
German, Beginner's
German Grammar
German Grammar, Quick Fix
German, Instant
German, Improve your
German Verbs
German Vocabulary
Go
Golf
Greek
Greek, Ancient
Greek, Beginner's
Greek, Instant
Greek, New Testament
Greek Script, Beginner's
Guitar
Gulf Arabic
Hand Reflexology
Hebrew, Biblical
Herbal Medicine
Hieroglyphics
Hindi
Hindi, Beginner's
Hindi Script, Beginner's
Hinduism
History, 101 Key Ideas
How to Win at Horse Racing
How to Win at Poker
HTML Publishing on the WWW
Human Anatomy & Physiology
Hungarian
Icelandic
Indian Head Massage

Indonesian
Information Technology, 101 Key Ideas
Internet, The
Irish
Islam
Italian
Italian, Beginner's
Italian Grammar
Italian Grammar, Quick Fix
Italian, Instant
Italian, Improve your
Italian Verbs
Italian Vocabulary
Japanese
Japanese, Beginner's
Japanese, Instant
Japanese Script, Beginner's
Java
Jewellery Making
Judaism
Korean
Latin
Latin American Spanish
Latin, Beginner's
Latin Dictionary
Latin Grammar
Letter Writing Skills
Linguistics
Linguistics, 101 Key Ideas
Literature, 101 Key Ideas
Mahjong
Managing Stress
Marketing
Massage
Mathematics
Mathematics, Basic
Media Studies
Meditation
Mosaics
Music Theory
Needlecraft
Negotiating
Nepali
Norwegian
Origami
Panjabi
Persian, Modern
Philosophy
Philosophy of Mind
Philosophy of Religion
Philosophy of Science
Philosophy, 101 Key Ideas
Photography
Photoshop

Physics
Piano
Planets
Planning Your Wedding
Polish
Politics
Portuguese
Portuguese, Beginner's
Portuguese Grammar
Portuguese, Instant
Postmodernism
Pottery
Powerpoint 2002
Presenting for Professionals
Project Management
Psychology
Psychology, 101 Key Ideas
Psychology, Applied
Quark Xpress
Quilting
Recruitment
Reflexology
Reiki
Relaxation
Retaining Staff
Romanian
Russian
Russian, Beginner's
Russian Grammar
Russian, Instant
Russian Script, Beginner's
Sanskrit
Screenwriting
Serbian
Setting up a Small Business
Shorthand, Pitman 2000
Sikhism
Spanish
Spanish, Beginner's
Spanish Grammar
Spanish Grammar, Quick Fix
Spanish, Instant
Spanish, Improve your
Spanish Starter Kit
Spanish Verbs
Spanish Vocabulary
Speaking on Special Occasions
Speed Reading
Statistical Research
Statistics
Swahili
Swahili Dictionary
Swedish
Tagalog

Tai Chi
Tantric Sex
Teaching English as a Foreign Language
Teaching English One to One
Teams and Team-Working
Thai
Time Management
Tracing your Family History
Travel Writing
Trigonometry
Turkish
Turkish, Beginner's
Typing
Ukrainian
Urdu
Urdu Script, Beginner's
Vietnamese
Volcanoes
Watercolour Painting
Weight Control through Diet and
    Exercise
Welsh
Welsh Dictionary
Wills and Probate
Wine Tasting
Winning at Job Interviews
Word 2002
World Faiths
Writing a Novel
Writing for Children
Writing Poetry
World Cultures:
    China
    England
    France
    Germany
    Italy
    Japan
    Portugal
    Russia
    Spain
    Wales
    Xhosa
Yoga
Zen
Zulu